Sixth Edition

The Helping Relationship

Process and Skills

Lawrence
The Un

Ginge
Se

Boston • London • Toronto •

Senior Editor: Ray Short
Editorial Assistant: Christine M. Shaw
Senior Marketing Manager: Kathy Hunter
Editorial-Production Service: Holly Crawford
Composition Buyer: Linda Cox
Manufacturing Buyer: Aloka Rathnam
Cover Administrator: Linda Knowles
Cover Designer: Susan Paradise

Library of Congress Cataloging-in-Publication Data

Brammer, Lawrence M.
    The helping relationship : process and skills / Lawrence M.
Brammer, Ginger MacDonald. — 6th ed.
        p.   cm.
    Includes bibliographical references and index.
    ISBN 0-205-17439-6
    1. Helping behavior. 2. Professions—Psychological aspects.
3. Interpersonal relations. I. MacDonald, Ginger II. Title.
BF637.H4B7   1995
158'.3—dc20   95-20311
                                                            CIP

Printed in the United States of America
10 9 8 7 6 5 4 3 2 1   00 99 98 97 96 95

Contents

Preface   **vii**

1   Helping: What Does It Mean?   **1**
What Is Your View of Helping?   *1*
The Helping Process   *3*
Facilitating Helpee Growth   *4*
Helping by Agreement   *7*
Meeting Helpee Needs   *8*
Seeking Wellness   *10*
To Be or Not to Be a Helper   *12*
Science and Art of Helping   *14*
Structured and Unstructured Helping   *14*
Professionals and Paraprofessionals   *15*
Community, Peer, and Cross-Age Helping   *18*
Self-Help Groups   *21*
Helpers Gain, Too   *22*
Helping Is Learning Self-Help Coping Skills   *22*
Helping Skills Model for Understanding, Support, and Action   *23*
Suggestions for Further Study   *25*

2   Characteristics of Helpers   **27**
Why Is Helping Effective in Assisting People to Grow?   *27*
Levels and Styles of Functioning   *28*
The Helper Personality   *30*
A Concluding Statement   *47*
Suggestions for Further Study   *49*

3   The Helping Process   51
Relationship   52
The Helping Process as Experienced   56
Stages in the Helping Process   56
A Process Dilemma   73
Suggestions for Further Study   74

4   Helping Skills for Understanding   76
Rationale for Skills Training   77
Skill Cluster 1: Listening   77
Skill Cluster 2: Leading   83
Skill Cluster 3: Reflecting   87
Skill Cluster 4: Confronting   90
Skill Cluster 5: Interpreting   98
Skill Cluster 6: Informing   102
Skill Cluster 7: Summarizing   105
Suggestions for Further Study   106

5   Helping Skills for Loss and Crisis   108
Human Conditions of Concern   109
Definitions of Terms   112
Strategies for Helping in Crises   119
Skills for Support and Crisis Management   127
Suggestions for Further Study   136

**6   Helping Skills for Positive Action and
Behavior Change   138**
The Action Approach to Helping   140
Problems and Goals   141
Problem Solving, Decision Making, and Planning   145
Behavior Changing   152
Suggestions for Further Study   168

7   Ethical Issues in Helping Relationships   169
What Are Ethics?   169
Helper Self-Care   170
Ethics and Interpersonal Relationships   172
Helper Competence and Limitations   175
Emergency/Crisis Response   177
Suggestions for Further Study   178

8   Thinking about the Helping Process   179
Theory as a Guide   179
A Personal Theory of Helpfulness   180
General Theories of the Helping Process   186
Social Issues Awareness   193
Tying Theory to the Practice of Helping Skills   194
When Helpees Do Not Change   196
Helping through Groups   198
Personal Epilogue   199
Suggestions for Further Study of Helping Theory   199

Bibliography   201

Index   209

Preface

The basic purposes of *The Helping Relationship: Process and Skills* are to describe in nontechnical language the human helping process and to provide a road map through the complex concepts and research on helping. The organizing idea of this book is that all help is aimed at self-help. The focus is on empowering the person to solve his or her own problems. This state is reached through encouraging the development of inner strength. We are confident that, with support, people can create their own futures. Thus, self-responsibility is encouraged and rewarded in the helping process.

There is a great social need for people skilled in the art of helping others. Although great progress has been made in material technology, we are still in the dark ages of human relations and exploration of human potentiality. Now that we humans have substantial mastery over nature, we are searching for better ways to manage ourselves. We want improvements in our relationships so that we can be better neighbors, parents, workers, spouses, and friends. The popularity of self-help psychology books, growth centers, parent education, peer helper groups, and voluntary services are ripples on the surface of our strong desire to serve others and improve ourselves. Once basic survival needs are satisfied, people search for deeper meanings in their lives through service to others.

Our basic problem is how to apply the vast resources for helping to the acute human problems plaguing our society. The rapidity of change and the accelerating rate of social change are putting a great strain on our coping skills and traditional beliefs. This condition makes helping relationships essential to our psychological survival. We cannot depend solely on helping specialists and human relations experts to close this large gap. Helping communities must be encouraged and helping skills must be widely dispersed in the population until human satisfactions and better social organization make formal helping, as we know it, unnecessary. One scenario is the possibility that we all become helpers, facilitating one another's development and search for happiness. The other extreme would be to leave helping services to specially trained and committed professionals.

Even though we are at a primitive stage of research and development in our human relating skills, a keen interest in human problems is present in all of our institutions. Helping attitudes and skills have penetrated schools, with counseling at last achieving more central attention than previously. Severe problems associated with suicide, violence, drug abuse, pregnancy, AIDS, and dropouts have accelerated this development. Business and industry have given much attention to human factors in light of the evidence that humane environments, employee assistance programs, career ladders, and managerial training in human relationships, for example, increase performance and profits as well as employee satisfaction. Government and military organizations have developed similar helping and human relations programs. Developments like these have created many opportunities for formal and informal acts of helping in spite of reduced governmental funding for human services in the public sector. These reductions in sponsored helping programs make even more imperative the development of a helping society in which all of us are responsible helpers of one another in need.

While there is a need for specialists trained to cope with the complexities of human problems, most human needs can be met by nonspecialist helpers. This book is written mainly for such nonspecialists who want a framework in which to view their helping functions, and for those who wish to join classes studying helping functions and skills in a systematic manner. Thus, people who work as generalists in counseling, group leadership, child care, youth work, teaching, nursing, rehabilitation, business, police work, community relations, mental health, parent education, crisis centers, or church work will, it is hoped, apply these principles and techniques to their work settings. In addition to these special helpers it appears that about half of all jobs involve some human contact service, and this proportion is likely to increase. Therefore, all people with personal contact positions will find this book useful.

Persons in consulting and instructional roles in community agencies and educational institutions will be able to use this book for in-service education on helping skills and human relations. Those persons following a programmed learning approach to human relations, communication skills, or counseling will find this text a useful framework for their skills training.

This book focuses on helping normal individuals to function at a higher level. It emphasizes self-help and improved coping skills. It is not a book on psychotherapy and the pathology of human interaction. We emphasize basic communication skill improvement, since a fundamental problem in all human relations is our difficulty in reaching one another successfully.

The two keys to the helping process are the helper as a person and his or her skills. This book concentrates on the helper's task of becoming a more aware and effective person. He or she is first of all a human being, and secondly, a helping instrument in the form of parent, teacher, counselor, adviser, interviewer, or friend. The second key the helper needs is precise skills to realize the outcomes people desire. These skills are presented in the categories of understanding, support, and action.

We have attempted to present in simple form many principles and skills gleaned from over fifty years of combined experience as teachers, counselors, and behavioral science researchers in the people-helping realm. Yet we recognize that the helping function can be complex and controversial. We possess no neat body of valid knowledge about the helping process, but we have a good start. *The Helping Relationship* is an effort to describe this evolving process and to consider the helping process in light of changing social needs and diverse definitions of helpfulness.

We have minimized citations, quotations, and technical terms in our quest for clarity and simplicity and have included, reluctantly, only a sampling of the extensive literature from the helping professions. Activities to apply the helping principles and skills, along with suggestions for further readings, are included with each chapter. An Instructor's Manual available on request from the publisher contains further exercises, films, and study aids.

The sixth edition includes a few significant changes. In order to respond to a more heterogeneous world, we have included more examples from diverse populations. We have also expanded our examples of helping children and families. Similarly, we have increased our examples from the business workplace. In addition, we have written an entirely new chapter on the ethics of helping.

We wish to acknowledge Noreen T. Chapman, Quinebaug Valley Community College, and Thomas L. Millard, Montclair State College, who reviewed the manuscript for Allyn & Bacon. We especially wish to acknowledge with thanks the patience of our families during the development of this book. We also wish to express our gratitude to Karen Kuhn and Julie Ellis for their assistance with manuscript preparation.

1

Helping: What Does It Mean?

This is a book about people helping other people to grow toward their personal goals and to strengthen their capacities for coping with life. Few of us achieve our growth goals or solve our personal problems alone. We need other people in some kind of helping relationship to us, but what does this need imply for helpers and the helped?

What Is Your View of Helping?

Think about your own view of what helping means and examine your motives for helping people. Our principal goal in this chapter is to assist you in thinking through and in extending your views of the helping process, because you must develop a style of help that is comfortable and effective for you. Take some time for the following activities. First, lean back, relax, and picture yourself helping another person. Imagine a specific setting.

1. What are you doing? What are you saying? What are you feeling? How is the other person responding? What does it mean to be a helper? Make a list of the behaviors you regard as helpful.
2. Try to recall people who have helped you. What were their behaviors and personal qualities that made them helpful people? How did you feel about their actions and being the recipient of help? What did you infer about their attitudes? List their helpful behaviors.
3. Ask close friends or relatives to describe incidents when your behavior was helpful to them. List their descriptive words and phrases.

4. Compare your three lists of your concept of a helper, your perceptions of others as helpers, and other people's views of you as a helper. Keep them for later comparison with lists in the following chapters.

5. Spend time thinking of all the phrases and feelings that occur to you when you consider the questions: Why do I want to be a helper? Is my helping motivated by healthy or pathological needs? Whom do I want to help? What do I get out of the helping process? How am I, the helper, changed by this process? How do I want to be perceived by those I intend to help? How do I feel about what comes to my awareness during this activity? Write a descriptive paragraph about yourself as a helper before these thoughts and feelings disappear.

If possible, share these ideas and lists with others doing the same activities. Sharing and receiving reactions helps to clarify and amplify one's ideas and feelings about such a personal topic. It is difficult to be honest about motives for helping others. Compare your lists with the discussion of illustrative motives in later paragraphs and in Chapter 2.

No doubt you found that *helping* is a difficult process to describe because it has such individualized meanings. It is necessary to understand these numerous meanings of help, however, because all of us have work, community, or family responsibilities that demand helping relationships. In some contexts helping is direct assistance or giving information. Other situations require facilitating or consulting kinds of help.

A further complication in definition is that *help* means different things to people in various subcultures. The idea of helping, in the formal sense of counseling, is largely an American white middle-class phenomenon. In most other cultures, helping functions are unobtrusive acts performed in informal settings, such as families. *La familia* brings up immediate meanings of loyalty and service, for example, when mentioned in Spanish-speaking groups. One's concept of helpfulness must be placed in a cultural framework and must take into account the special meanings and unique language associated with it by various racial, ethnic, and sex groupings.

This chapter explores these meanings further, and the following chapter examines the characteristics of effective helpers. A detailed presentation of helping skills and action principles is made in the remaining chapters.

For purposes of this book the helping person will be designated as the *helper,* and the helped as the *helpee.* While awkward terms, they serve as more generalized designations for counselor-counselee, worker-client, therapist-patient, parent-child, teacher-pupil, and interviewer-interviewee commonly used in public agency and private practice settings. Our underlying assumption is that the basic interpersonal communication processes implied by these specialized helping relationships are similar.

Outcomes You Can Expect from This Chapter

By studying this chapter you should be able to (1) state your own view of helping and why you want to help; (2) list three sources of personal gain to the helper from engaging in the helping process; (3) identify the basic points of view of this book; (4) describe the essential nature of the helping process in terms of need fulfillment and responsible independence; (5) list three arguments that support, and three that refute, the professional and nonprofessional approaches to helping; (6) describe and illustrate self-help, peer, cross-age, and community helper projects; and (7) list thirteen basic helping skills and six key coping skills.

The Helping Process

Figure 1-1 shows that the main elements of the helping process, the helper's personality combined with specific skills, produce growth conditions that lead to definite outcomes important to the person, the helper, and society in general. Whereas helper personality and skills constitute the basic ingredients of the process, specialists add a third element that broadens helpers' awareness and realizes their helping potential. Specialists investigate the recorded experience of other helpers as well as the contributions of the behavioral sciences, and they formulate helping theories of their own. Helping specialists also commit themselves to strict ethical standards and legal requirements. The more specialized helpers also ask questions about the usefulness of their helping services and learn research skills with which to answer those questions.

Considerable emphasis is placed on outcomes of the helping process. Issues around cost effectiveness, accountability, and efficacy of different helping methods add to the importance of outcomes. The goals of helping have been stated many ways, but generally they reduce to changes in behavior and life-style, awareness or insight and understanding, relief from suffering, and changes in thoughts and self-perceptions.

Another view of *process* is described in Chapter 3, where process is defined as the sequence of events and their meaning to the helpee. It has two simple phases—*building a relationship* and *facilitating positive action*. Initially, the helper uses understanding and support skills to develop the relationship. In the second phase of the process, decision and action skills become important.

One purpose of this book is to make some of the learnings of helping specialists more available to persons not having specialist responsibilities, and to encourage more widespread volunteer helping behaviors. Specialist helpers

Personality of Helper	+	Helping Skills	→	Growth-Facilitating Condition	→	Specific Outcomes
Traits		For understanding		Trust		For the person
Attitudes		For comfort		Respect		For society
Values		For action		Freedom		For the helper

FIGURE 1–1   The Helping Process

are far too few to make a strong impact, and it is a social tragedy to restrict basic helping functions to a few specialists. This effort is not designed to minimize the contribution of specialists nor to disparage the skill and knowledge acquired in years of research, study, and practice. Meeting the health, psychological, and spiritual needs of dysfunctional people in our increasingly dehumanized society is so complicated and demanding that specialists will continue to be needed. But these specialists should be employed only when their unique knowledge can be used effectively. Overreliance on a specialized approach to helping often ignores and fragments the needs of the whole person.

Facilitating Helpee Growth

Helping another human being is basically a process of enabling that person to grow in the directions that person chooses, to solve problems, and to face crises. Facilitating growth is the central idea of this book. The helping process assumes the helpee is aware of alternatives and is willing to take responsibility for acting on an alternative. Helping involves facilitating awareness of such alternatives and assessing readiness to act. Help, however, should be defined mainly by the helpees, who select the goals of their own growth, and who also determine whether they want help at all. To avoid feeling patronized, helpees define desired help on their own terms and to fulfill their own needs. They may, for example, ask for information, or for assistance in making a decision, solving a problem, or expressing their feelings. We need to be aware, though, that people seldom admit directly that they want help, because it is difficult to admit having a problem one cannot solve on one's own. Even when helpees admit to themselves that they have problems, the degree of trust they feel will determine the extent of their sharing with a helping person. In any case, this view of helping assumes that people know their needs.

This voluntary quality of the helping process is a crucial point since many persons wanting to help others have their own helping agenda and seek to meet their own unrecognized needs. Some helpers, for example, *need* "victims," meaning that the helpers may maintain relationships to satisfy their own affiliative or dominance needs and may even continue their relationship longer than necessary in order to feel needed. Doing anything for other people without their initiative and consent frequently is manipulative and often is destructive. Even when the help is solicited and given with the best of human motives, it may have an unplanned detrimental effect on the helpee. The reason is partly that persons being helped experience a loss of self-esteem. Although appearing outwardly grateful, they may interpret the gift or act of help as a message that they are incompetent. This interpretation is accompanied by feelings of dependency, helplessness, inferiority, or inadequacy. They say to themselves, for example, "Receiving this help makes me feel as if I can't take care of myself; I don't like leaning on somebody else." On the other hand, some people accept the help with dependent eagerness and relief. They say, in effect, "Good, now I do not need to be responsible for carrying this burden alone anymore." Such feelings often turn quickly to resentment or guilt, especially for informal help. This common self-protective reaction is one reason the helping process has such unpredictable outcomes and why helping actions are often resented or rejected.

The underlying issue of this section is the extent to which one should or can take responsibility for another person. Helpers vary over the full spectrum of responsibility, from feeling a deep sense of human obligation to meet the needs of others to a view that others are totally responsible for their own experience and need fulfillment. The former group believes strongly that "I am my brother's keeper." The latter group claims that giving help perpetuates dependency and immaturity in the helpee. Help may vary over the entire range depending on the circumstances. Generally the aim is to make the helpee self-sufficient; thus, bids for help and our inclinations to be helpful need to be scrutinized with this goal in the foreground. There are times, though, when the human thing to do is to give total support to another without regard to dependency problems.

Important questions for helpers to ask themselves are: What is this person's capacity for responsible independence and self-support at this time? How can I be supportive without reinforcing this person's dependency? What needs and rationalization prompt my own desires to be helpful at this time? To what extent should I attempt to be helpful when the person does not seem to want help or appears to be on a self-destructive path (e.g., taking illegal drugs, driving recklessly, jeopardizing health)? Do people have the right to self-neglect or even self-destruction? If so, how does this view affect their families and the society that bears the social and financial costs of this individual freedom? What are your views on these issues of personal responsibilities and choice? What is your responsibility to those seeking your help and to the broader society?

A dilemma facing helpers is, help for whom—the person, the agency, or society? If helpers indicate by behavior or attitude to their helpees that they are looking after the agency's interests only, they incur wrath and rejection. On the other hand, helpers cannot always support their helpees with the attitude that society or the agency is the enemy. The most helpful stance is to assist helpees to see how their present behavior is shaped by their environment. The aim is understanding, not blame.

The act of helping people with the presumed goal of doing something for them, or changing them in some way, has an arrogant quality also. This implication of superiority raises hostile feelings in the helpee because the act presumes that the helper is wiser, more competent, and more powerful than the helpee. Although these conditions may be true, as judged by external observers, the motive for help and the nature of the helping task as perceived by the helper must be made clear to the receiver.

Sometimes helpers set conditions on their help, often without an awareness that they are placing the helpee in an awkward position. An example is a mother who says verbally to her daughter, "I will help you," but communicates nonverbally that the help will be forthcoming as long as the daughter shows that she needs and appreciates her mother's help. Sometimes this conditional help is extended to control the helpee and to extract promises of love, obedience, or submission from a defiant and sullen helpee.

The principle that helpees must initiate the help request is confusing in another way. Must they always ask for help in words? A hurting child, for example, often cannot state clearly what he or she wants verbally, but facial expressions and body tension may be crying out "Help me!" Our inferences from reading these behaviors could be wrong, but the only way we can know is to respond and then be alert to the reactions. A similar and unusual situation is the attempted suicide, which may be interpreted as a desperate call for help. The idea that help must always be requested in verbal terms certainly can be carried to extremes, particularly in situations that present danger to the person.

The aim of all help is *self-help* and eventual self-sufficiency. We have emphasized that much of our growth is the result of self-help and self-searching rather than something done to or for us. Needs for autonomy and self-actualization are strong, yet sometimes they are subdued temporarily by life experiences. These needs must be respected and strengthened for psychological survival, at least, and self-actualization at best.

A further assumption we wish to include here is that each of us behaves in a competent and trustworthy manner if given the freedom and encouragement to do so. Sometimes this confidence is shaken when working with people who have been hurt deeply by life and who behave consequently in an irresponsible and untrustworthy manner. We must communicate to helpees our confidence and trust in their ability to move toward goals best for them and for society. In this discussion of helping we have stressed the significance of helpee *responsibility* for such goals and self-determined growth because, in our view, this is the main purpose of helping. To assist helpees in carrying out their responsibilities we provide them with life management skills whereby they can help themselves. Improving interpersonal communication skills alone can have a dramatic positive effect on other areas of living also (Authier, Gustafson, Guerney, & Kasdorf, 1975; Myers, Finnerty-Fried, & Graves, 1981; Ivey, Ivey, & Simek-Downing, 1994; Ivey, 1991).

We, as helpers, also must assume some responsibility for creating conditions of trust whereby helpees can respond in a trusting manner and help themselves. Helpers do this through the *process,* a term that refers largely to their methods for reaching helpee goals. These outcomes are realized through managing the environment, providing conditions for understanding and comfort, and modeling trusting behaviors. A trusting approach means that helpers view their task as facilitating and supporting rather than teaching or persuading. Helpers who are open and honest about their own ideas and feelings tend to be perceived as trustworthy by their helpees. Consistent behaviors that show caring and are clearly in the helpees' best interests also inspire trust.

While we are concerned with the helpee's feelings, values, and goals, we must be alert also to the impact on the helpee of other people and of the physical environment. One implication of this view is that the helper needs to understand the special life circumstances of helpees and to "get out of the office and into the street." Another implication is that a helpee is anyone who brings a matter to the helper's attention—a teacher or parent concerned about a child or a supervisor about an employee, as well as people who ask for help directly for themselves.

Finally, helping takes place over the life span. Each developmental period and the transitions between usually require some form of outside help to make life more effective and satisfying. Professional counselors usually think of their help as time-limited and problem-focused, whereas informal helpers tend to view their help as more intermittent, sustained, and broadly based support concentrated on the changing needs of the person. For example, extended family members, pastoral workers, and health care providers often see such persons over long developmental periods. Even mobile helpees need different forms of help at different periods in their lives. They often think of helpers as someone available when they need them and not in terms of an office visit for a one-shot "cure."

Helping by Agreement

As a helping relationship develops, an important consideration is the nature of the agreement or "contract" between the helper and helpee. When help is requested outside of a friendship setting, it is important that the terms and conditions of the help be agreed on early. Helpers get themselves into difficult situations in which they try more than they can capably or ethically deliver when the expectations of both parties are not explored and agreed on. How this is done formally and informally will be described in Chapters 3, 6, and 7 under "structuring," "contracting," and "informed consent." An example of a working agreement in *formal* helping settings is to tell helpees, "I agree to meet with you for an hour a week for about three weeks to work on this concern; you will come here to work with me and will do some work outside our interviews. We will decide in three weeks how we will proceed." Sometimes this simple agreement is formalized into a more detailed contract with written terms about what each will do.

The nature of the *informal* agreement should imply a growth contract—that helpees will try to change under their own initiative, with minimal helper assistance. If helpers become preoccupied with the notion that *they* must help other people, that *they* must produce some change, then helpees have a demanding hold on them which could be very manipulative and destructive for all. One pitfall of a growth contract, for example, would be lack of resolution so that the relationship continues interminably. All of us have had acquaintances who have made endless demands on us, and they do not appear to have changed. Disturbed people with persistent adjustment problems often seek out such helping types, but they only frustrate their helpers' efforts. Helpees in this instance are looking for something very idealistic or are demanding that something specific and unrealistic be given to them. Helpers who fall into this trap reinforce the "helpless" or "sick" games of helpees, thus preventing them from taking responsibility for helping themselves. This topic will be expanded in later sections, but it is important for our introductory purposes here to realize the serious and complex nature of the commitment one makes as a helper.

Meeting Helpee Needs

Help consists of providing conditions for helpees to meet their needs. Help varies (across a spectrum) from strong physical intervention, such as averting a suicide, to subtle emotional support, such as counseling for finding a new job. The kind and amount of help given depend on the helpee's needs at the time. These human needs can be classified in various ways. A scheme that makes the most sense to us was developed by Maslow (1962), and we offer it here as an example of a need system to understand the nature of help. Maslow arranged needs in a complex interrelated hierarchy of five levels according to their primacy in human existence as indicated in Figure 1-2. These five levels are *physiological, safety, love and belonging, self-esteem,* and *self-actualization.* Frankl (1965) described a higher-level need for meaning. People want to experience their existence as meaningful and purposeful. So, we would place Frankl's meaning needs at a sixth level.

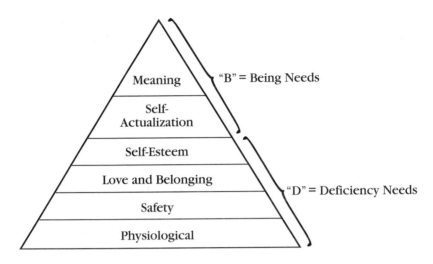

FIGURE 1–2   The Hierarchy of Human Needs

Physiological needs for sustaining life are so primary that until people have enough to eat, for example, any other form of helping is irrelevant. These physical needs are self-preservative and reproductive. Thus, helping means meeting a basic physical need such as food or clothing. While sometimes, such as in cases of domestic violence, helpers provide physical safety needs, usually the focus is on psychological safety. For purposes of this book, however, helping processes will be restricted largely to acts of counseling, consulting, teaching, or facilitating the satisfaction of psychosocial needs to be described below.

A second level of needs is for psychological safety. We want to feel secure. We want to know that our future is predictable. We are suspicious of change, and we want to reduce the tension from conflict, cruelty, injustice, and uncertainty.

The third level is love and belonging. We want to feel part of some enduring group where we are accepted, wanted, loved, and respected. When these conditions are reasonably satisfied, we can give love and respect to others. We then are able to show others we care and are interested in being helpful. If these love and belonging needs are not fulfilled in ourselves, we tend to resort to numerous self-defeating or attention-getting behaviors, such as control, suspicion and aggression. It is at this level that many Americans express their deepest needs.

The fourth need level in Maslow's system is for achievement of self-esteem. To feel good about ourselves we need to be liked and regarded as valuable and competent by others. As we grow in awareness of our self-worth and get more in touch with our deeper needs, feelings, and values, we depend less on others' judgments of our worth. The key implication here for the helping process is to find ways for people to think well of themselves, to believe in their competence and worth, through relationships with us.

It is difficult to define or describe the fifth need level, which functions best when the four lower levels of need are in the process of being satisfied. This self-actualizing level is a striving for self-development, integration, autonomy, stimulation, and challenge. It involves reaching out, often in risky ways, to move to higher levels of satisfaction and growth. It also involves the need for appreciation of aesthetic beauty.

The first four levels Maslow calls "D," or deficiency, needs. This person strives for fulfillment of a felt deficit, such as hunger, desire for love, or need for social response. Gratification brings a kind of calm and satisfaction for a time; satisfaction averts the usual physical and emotional problems that deficits bring about. Yet what most people feel quickly after gratification is a vague craving for "something more." Maslow classified these needs for becoming more integrated, challenged, and individualized "B," or being, needs, to maintain a sense of high-level humanness and self-actualization (the fifth level). People must do what they feel they can—paint, write, love, or serve—for example. Teachers can help children move through these developmental processes. Shrunk (1991) clearly describes an educational perspective using Maslow's hierarchy.

Seeking Wellness

The significance of need theory for understanding the helping process is that many requests for help come in the form of meeting deficiencies in needs for love, security, self-respect, or social stimulation. We must help people fulfill their basic physical and psychological needs before they can achieve higher levels of being, achievement, and meaning. If their basic needs are met, people will be less inclined to satisfy their deficiencies through crime, violence, and emotional distress. This level of well-being is often called a state of *wellness*. It is more than the absence of physical or emotional distress. It is a process rather than a state where people make choices that make them aware of a high level of health and well-being in all modalities of life—physical, mental, spiritual, occupational, and social (National Wellness Institute, 1989). Thus, helping people to fulfill their basic needs is a form of *prevention* of later problems.

It is paradoxical, however, that this self-actualization need is achieved largely through help from other people. Yet Maslow's model of self-actualized persons was characterized by the independence and self-sufficiency to accomplish these states with their own initiative and resources. In other words, it is possible that helping relationships beyond a certain point might retard the helpee's independence and self-esteem. This paradox translates into the assertion that the most helpful thing we can do for other people is to "help them help themselves" by creating conditions that release their powerful growth tendencies and abilities to use their own resources. These growth conditions are the cumulative effect of the helper exhibiting many of the traits described in Chapter 2. Helper values such as prizing and encouraging the freedom and individuality of others as well as having positive regard for helpees are especially potent.

It is difficult for the helper to determine when helpees are concerned about some basic need satisfaction and when they are asking for help with their dimly perceived strivings for more creativity, autonomy, integration, or achievement. Helpees often have difficulty expressing their wants, since all they experience are feelings of dissatisfaction with themselves, their status, or their behavior. They are aware only that they want something more than satisfaction of their appetites.

In the process of exploring possibilities for their becoming more self-actualized, "becoming" persons discover that their moment-to-moment satisfactions are occasionally punctuated with "peak experiences." These are feelings described by Maslow as transient states of being characterized by joy, delight, or even ecstasy. Thus, helping can be construed as a process of assisting helpees toward higher levels of self-actualization and the joyful realization of their unused possibilities. This joyful state can be prolonged by setting a goal of optimal performance, which means using all of one's ability and time to the maximum. Optimally functioning people look after their physical and psychological health. They also take some risks, take time out for reflection and refreshment, manage their time effectively, build networks, image high performance, and focus on building competencies necessary for excellence (Garfield, 1986). Sports psychologists also promote these basic principles when priming their athletes to perform their best.

Helping can be a process also of achieving awareness of the conflict between the attractions of safety and comfort, on the one hand, and the risks and magnetism of growth on the other. Growth means change and risk. The helping relationship can provide a temporary safe haven while one is exploring and experimenting with new behaviors as well as achieving new goals.

Helpees also have needs for life skills to survive and add to their quality of life. Helping, therefore, is also conceived to be the process of aiding people in acquiring these life skills (Gazda, Childers, & Brooks, 1987). There are many ways to classify life skills, but Gazda and his co-workers found in their research that these skills could be classified as human relating, maintaining fitness, problem solving, and acquiring a purpose in life.

People also report that they want help to feel better—to be happy. Psychologists describe this search for happiness as the quest for "subjective well-being" (Diener, 1984). This idea includes personal definitions for quality of life, satisfactions from achievements, and fulfilling personal relationships. Helping, in this frame of reference, is largely a matter of assisting people in arranging their lives in such a way that happiness results from choosing satisfying activities. One approach is the building block method. This is the act of helping the person find the next level of satisfaction—the homeless person's next meal, for example. This may be the first link in a chain leading to a sense of well-being, and ultimately to an awareness of happiness. Happiness as a goal in itself is very elusive.

Subjective well-being by definition is a very personal perception of one's status. People can look on their lives (which from objective conventional indices may be very miserable) as happy. The homeless person just mentioned may experience the sense of freedom, autonomy, and apparent aimlessness of living as happiness. Thus, it is very important that helpers strive to apprehend the helpee's own idea of well-being and happiness and not project his or her subjective standards on another individual. It would be equally problematic if the helper were to compare, as Aristotle advised, the helpee's lifestyle to an external standard of virtue.

To Be or Not to Be a Helper

In the previous discussion on the nature of helping and human needs, the focus was on the receiver of help. The helper has needs too. The following partial list of needs and reasons for being a helper can be used as a template for assessing yourself. These needs become problems only when they are expressed without awareness of their presence or how they might adversely affect the other person. When properly expressed, they serve as powerful motivators for being helpful in the ways described in this chapter. By thinking about your motives for being helpful, you can make clear distinctions about those Maslowian needs that must be fulfilled in your personal life and those that can be appropriately fulfilled in your helping relationships.

Needing to Be Helpful

Most of us have a strong altruistic urge to be of service to others. It makes us feel worthwhile—more human. It is only when this need becomes excessively strong and we become possessive, or fanatically controlling and protective, that it tends to become a negative motive. An example is the so-called rescuer in families with disabilities or alcoholism where the person wanting to be helpful covers for and excessively protects the other, thus reinforcing denial of the problem. This need when understood and properly focused, however, can be a positive motive for wanting to be a helper.

The need to be helpful must be understood in another way as a possible compulsive need for love and attention from other people. While helping is often done in a context of loving concern for others, the important factor is awareness of this need to be needed. One possible consequence of this need is to focus so exclusively on the needs of others that one's own needs as a helper are ignored. This is a fast road to helper burnout and lessened ability to be helpful. On the other hand, it is important to face the fact that helpers receive much personal satisfaction in seeing helpees grow and feel better. For example, one helper said, "I just feel good about myself when I see other people like Jane grow in social skills." Just as some people experience pleasure creating a poem, so helpers experience a glow of satisfaction in witnessing human growth and realizing their creative part in that growth.

Helping to Solve Helper Problems

In meeting one's own needs, it is important to be aware of when the helping relationship is used to solve one's own problems. Helpers often see their problems in the people they are helping. For example, you may be having problems receiving enough love and attention in your own life and might tend to use the other person to help yourself. It is true that many effective helpers evolve from their working through a tough personal problem so they can help people with similar problems. The key difference is that they have become aware of their needs and have taken steps to resolve these problems *before* they try to help others with similar problems. Examples are former alcoholics becoming alcohol counselors, divorcees leading marriage encounters, or former abused children becoming child protective workers.

Desiring to Make a Social Contribution

Much helping is motivated by people's strong desire to leave this world a better place than they found it. They want to make a significant mark. They want to feel that their lives are worthwhile, and they see that people relationships are the vehicle. While this motive may express itself in grandiose ideas about saving the world, obviously it must be reduced to tangible and manageable pieces. Helping one person, such as a child who is disabled, have a better life is a start in this direction. Volunteering at a nursing home or working with the Big Brothers and Big Sisters movements are additional examples.

Some helpers perceive their helping efforts as manifestations of their spiritual commitment. Helping others is their way of expressing love and commitment to service. Some see their helping activities as a personal ministry to create a better society. Others might see this powerful motivation as a tool to proselytize and recruit for cults, for example. In any case, strong spiritual motivation for helping needs to be balanced with equally strong awareness of the consequences of using the helping relationship to fulfill other agendas.

Becoming an Expert

Helping relationships often convey considerable power to the helper because of his or her presumed knowledge. The need to influence others, to give advice, and to be admired for special expertise is strong. Again, awareness of our own needs for power, control, prestige, and praise is the key to correcting any exaggerations of this need. We are then able to accept the gratitude of those we help with the proper perspective.

Science and Art of Helping

Helping is both science and art. The science portion involves elaborate research and theory on helping, mainly from the behavioral sciences, whereas the artistic aspects of helping refer more to the intuitive and feeling elements of interpersonal relationships that are based largely in the humanities and creative arts. The scientific aspect is concerned with descriptive data, predictions, and generalizations about behavior. Nonprofessional helpers, although lacking this sophisticated behavioral science background and skill training, often can apply helping principles in their intuitive artistic fashion. One implication of the research to be cited below is to select persons as helpers who already possess these artful qualities, and then quickly and systematically give them basic helping skills and behavior concepts. Throughout this book we will emphasize this dual behavioral science and artistic approach to the helping function.

Structured and Unstructured Helping

Helping affiliations can be classified into various levels, from formal and structured to informal and unstructured, as illustrated below.

Structured

Professional helpers. (Examples: social workers, ministers, psychologists, teachers, mental health counselors, school counselors, physicians, nurses, psychiatrists, marriage and family therapists, and legal counselors with specialized training and legal responsibility)

Paraprofessional helpers. (Examples: trained interviewers, receptionists, aides in mental health and rehabilitation, and persons in correctional, educational, employment, and social agency settings)

Volunteers. (Nonpaid persons with short-term training in basic helping skills and agency orientation)

Unstructured

Friendships. (Informal, mutual, and unstructured helping relationships over time)

Family. (Informal mutual helping system, interdependent in variable degrees)

Community and general human concern. (Informal, unstructured, ad hoc helping acts to alleviate danger, suffering, or deprivation)

The focus of this book is on the more structured forms of helping. Yet, it is striking to realize that formalized helping relationships in the form of counseling, treatment, ministering, or psychotherapy have characteristics in common with all effective human relating.

Professionals and Paraprofessionals

One of the main reasons for the increased employment of mental health helpers outside of traditional professions is that data from some earlier investigators (Rioch, 1966; Carkhuff, 1968) suggested that the effectiveness of professional helpers is much less than claimed or believed. These findings, coupled with the data on the speed with which productive helping skills can be learned by nonprofessionals, suggest the desirability and feasibility of involving more such persons in the formal helping process.

We would like to point out, as an editorial aside, that we have learned to depend heavily on experts in the helping professions, and society has allowed them to appropriate normal growth-producing processes into the mystical and sometimes exclusive domain of a professional guild. Too often elaborate professional entrance rituals are associated with a "divine right" to practice. This attitude leads frequently to interprofessional rivalries and jurisdictional disputes, such as those between psychiatrists and psychologists or between counselors and social workers. Such helping professionals often look disdainfully at helpers without formal credentials. Paraprofessional or volunteer helpers should be prepared for criticism and rejection by professional groups. These attitudes and conditions often put guild welfare ahead of personal service. Laws have been passed, for example, that define psychotherapy and counseling and that designate who can perform these functions as a service to the public. Although designed to protect the public from unscrupulous fee-charging helpers, such laws also tend to constrict helping services to the more knowing and *affluent* people. This is a social dilemma that we must resolve soon so that helping services can be more available.

Helpers without the usual credentials sometimes are regarded as a threat to those with certificates and degrees in a helping specialty. Yet, it is social folly not to utilize the untapped resources of helping talent in the nonprofessional population. Guerney (1969) made one of the first persuasive cases for the use of nonspecialist helpers to meet personnel needs, particularly in services to children. Such nonspecialists, often called paraprofessionals or "indigenous nonprofessionals," are widely used in service delivery in all kinds of helping agencies (Steenland, 1973; Lewis & Lewis, 1989; Lewis, Hayes, & Lewis, 1986). While there has been a continuing debate on the relative effectiveness of professional and paraprofessional helpers, the evidence at present is that paraprofessional helpers are effective additions to helping services. They are especially effective with groups, such as widowed and divorced people or drug abusers, where the helper has experienced the specific problem and has overcome it (Hattie, Sharpley, & Rogers, 1984). Furthermore, there are abundant roles in training, research, and consultation for those helpers with more extensive and specialized skills and knowledge. The important consideration is who can be the best helper to the person with emotional-social problems, and who can supplement parents and teachers with close sustained relationships to children. Many professional helpers, for example, depend on verbal means of treatment and thus limit their effectiveness to verbally facile, educated middle- and upper-class people. Numerous persons needing help find direct nonverbal communication means more helpful.

Length of contact affects the helping process. Usually the professional spends little time with a helpee compared to others significant in his or her life. If these others received training in basic helping skills to supplement whatever natural helping attitudes they had acquired in normal development, they might make an even greater impact on the helpee than a whole clinic of professionals. The key question is, Who can serve the helpee most effectively? We must define effectiveness more precisely, however, before we can answer.

There is a consensus among helping professionals that our society needs another mental health "revolution," focused on prevention and coupled with an expanded human potential movement (Albee, 1982; Freiberg, 1991). To facilitate this revolution we will need masses of helping persons who are easily available and political specialists who can change our culture from one that exploits to one that serves its people. Prevention means focusing on conditions that generate human problems rather than only helping people in trouble.

To bring about this transformation a massive educational effort aimed toward teaching skills in human relations, interpersonal communications, and self-care is needed. Futurists such as Cornish (1990), Ferguson (1980), Naisbitt and Aburdene (1990), and Simmons (1990) cite evidence that we are well along toward these goals. "Psychological education" of the 1970s (Ivey & Weinstein, 1970) was an effort to make the specialized skills and knowledge of helping specialists more widely known and used by the general population. The self-help movement of the 1980s, emphasizing self-care, support networks, wellness, stress management, and coping skills, is an extension of psychological education. Prevention rather than treatment continues to be the key emphasis through the 1990s and will be essential in the twenty-first century.

Many people have natural capacities to be helpful because of their fortunate life experiences. They have the intellectual capacity to understand and nurture such natural helping characteristics so that they can be even more helpful to others. We believe that many of these persons, furthermore, have the capacity for insight into the destructive potential of these natural helping processes if they are not used for the benefit of the helpee. It is necessary, for example, that helpers become aware of their power over others when they are intending to help, and of how easy it is to abuse that power unknowingly.

In spite of their many advantages, nonprofessional helpers are subject to the same tendencies as professionals to distort their views of helpees or to project their own problems on the helpees. Furthermore, nonprofessionals are less likely to be aware of these possible distortions than professionals, who go through extensive supervision and training. The nonprofessional helper also is likely to pick up "contagious" feelings from the helpee, whereas the professional has learned a kind of professional "distance" to counter this tendency. Both of these limitations can be greatly reduced if the helper seeks or is assigned a supervising person skilled in promoting self-awareness.

Although this tendency toward emotional overinvolvement can be a limitation, it has the potential for being a strength as well. For example, the tendency for nonprofessionals to immerse themselves deeply in the emotional life of the helpee may facilitate helpee growth more than professionals' relative detachment. This complicated issue will be explored further in Chapter 7.

In this era of accountability for outcomes, supervision from a professional can transmit an awareness of responsibility for what happens to helpees. This ethical commitment to helpees and a sense of social responsibility are significant aspects of formal helper training.

We have been comparing the specialist professional with the generalist nonprofessional helper, but classifying helpers into these two categories is artificial and limiting. Professional helpers earn their hard-won credentials through completing a prescribed program of training, meeting competency examination and licensing requirements, adhering to prescribed ethical standards, and being accountable for the outcomes of their help. *Paraprofessional,* on the other hand, is a term applied to persons with some of the skills and natural helping talents of the professional. They usually work directly with helpees under the professional's supervision for training and accountability. A more descriptive term without the lower-status connotations of paraprofessional is needed, but this is the designation being used for the present time.

In agencies that use both professional and paraprofessional staff, issues soon arise over distinctive roles, client responsibility, essential qualifications, pay scales, and evaluation of helping effectiveness. Arguments and research around these issues could go on endlessly, but effective solutions can come about only with honest staff discussions of their respective strengths, limitations, and contributions. Each may be effective in meeting certain helpee needs and expectations, yet both helper groups are handicapped by helpee expectations that exceed current knowledge about the helping process. The basic problem, then, is matching helper self-perceptions of qualifications with helpee and agency expectations.

A second problem is determining and evaluating the complex variables that are assumed to be related to helping effectiveness. These variables are basic empathic qualities, knowledge of research and theory, skill performance, legal and ethical accountability to helpees and agencies, special knowledge from training or experience, and evaluation of competence by peers and professional associations.

Research during the last decade has given strong evidence of the benefits of paraprofessional helping. For example, students with eating disorders have been helped by the Paraprofessionals as Companion-Therapist (PACT) program (Lenihan & Kirk, 1990). The Compeer Program matches mentally ill patients with a volunteer friend for weekly helpful visits (Meer, 1985). In yet another arena, Byrne and Overline (1992) suggested that properly trained paraprofessional workers within a structured format can be effective in facilitating divorce adjustment through marathon experiential weekends.

Opinions in psychology and social work literature are divided between those who feel that paraprofessional helpers should function under close supervision as support and administrative personnel, on the one hand, or as independent helping persons, on the other. By now it should be clear that our opinions support the latter view, provided that due attention is given to supervision and accountability for performance.

Community, Peer, and Cross-Age Helping

Additional applications of the informal helping principle are peer and cross-age helpers, people of similar ages, or persons with similar problems, who help others of comparable age or condition. An example is Alcoholics Anonymous, where former problem drinkers help those wishing to reduce their drinking. Numerous youth drug therapy and unwed mother programs use peers who experienced and solved similar problems as the helping agents. The New York Harlem Youth program, for example, is based on the idea that people not only meet their own needs to be helpful but also solve their own problems while helping others. The Samaritans, a movement originating in the United Kingdom, consists of unpaid volunteer helpers available at all hours to assist lonely, distraught, and confused people in urban communities. They apply a kind of first aid at the time when people need help most. The Fish program in the United States, which is organized largely around churches, has similar on-the-spot helping services. Peer helper support groups are especially helpful in grief work. Parents who have been through the poignant experiences of sudden infant death are powerful agents in helping other couples face this tragedy.

In the United States, renewed concern about neighborhoods is providing additional opportunities for informal helping. In the Netherlands an extensive government-sponsored program, translated as "neighborhoodship," was established to reinstate attitudes and structures of neighborliness once common in more agrarian societies. Most distressed people are not sick in a medical sense, but ignorant, deprived, deficient, or abandoned by the community. It is a blot on our humanity that we cannot look after one another more effectively in a caring manner. The helping groups cited are examples of progress toward community solutions of human problems.

The National Peer Helpers Association was organized in 1986 by school counselors seeking to extend their service potential to children and youth. There are state chapters and the national group holds annual conventions to expand the movement and improve on peer helper concepts and skills (Varenhorst & Sparks, 1988). Teenagers tend to go to their peers rather than to adults for help; so, training teenage peer helpers is crucial in a teen-helping setting.

Early investigators (Varenhorst & Hamburg, 1971; Varenhorst, 1972) reported the design and evaluation of a program to train youths from the seventh through twelfth grades in helping skills for fellow students. These volunteers were given information about youth problems and referral resources along with training in interpersonal skills. The evaluation indicated that this program was very effective in helping students with normal emotional and developmental problems. Dougherty and Dyal's (1976) and Dougherty and Taylor's (1983) review of peer counseling revealed the extensive and effective use of peer helpers in the elementary school setting. Peer helper programs in schools are commonplace today.

In elementary schools, peer helping has been shown to be effective with children who transfer between schools (Bogat, Jones, & Jason, 1980). Peer helpers can be influential positive role models for communication skills, academic behavior, and creative play (Downe, Altmann, & Nysetvold, 1986).

Dougherty and Taylor (1983) reviewed research studies and found that children in elementary schools with peer-helping programs improved in self-esteem, classroom behavior, and school attitudes.

In middle schools, the peer helpers seemed to benefit as much as those they helped (Bowman, 1986). When carefully selected and trained, peer helpers can help one another traverse the difficult middle-school experiences in areas such as self-concept, prevention of drug abuse, improved grades, and increased maturity (Hedin, 1987; Gray & Tindall, 1987; Correll & Keel, 1986).

Students at the adult level can become effective peer helpers also, as indicated in a community college study by Pyle and Snyder (1971). These students were judged to be very effective in helping fellow students with a small amount of support during the difficult transition to college life, handling dependency and autonomy issues, learning how to learn, and making curricular choices. Those students from ethnic minority backgrounds were helped especially by those who understood their backgrounds and problems of adjustment. Locke and Zimmerman (1987) found that African American college students experienced greater growth in psychological maturity when in peer-helping relationships with African American peer helpers. As in other studies, a significant by-product was the personal growth of the student helpers.

It may be that persistent social problems can be alleviated by peer help also. In many major cities, for example, parents show great concern over busing children to achieve racial balance and to equalize educational opportunity. One of the more covert reasons for this concern is that many parents feel their children will be held back if mixed with children of deprived educational backgrounds. If the peer-helper principle could be put into practice, both the accelerated and the less able pupils could benefit from a diverse classroom.

Perhaps children can be helped more by helping others than by following adult models or listening to others whom they perceive as vastly superior to themselves. Although much work needs to be done on the usefulness of peer-helping relationships, enough is known to stimulate us to explore this helping resource more vigorously. A convincing rationale for the use of young peer helpers has been given by Bruner (1972). He regards the intermediate generation of teenagers and youths as new role bearers or models to bridge the gap between generations and to help youths and children enter the adult world. Bruner thinks these young role models should be given more responsibility for teaching the younger, less experienced children because they are key linkages between generations in periods of rapid changes. This process could become an endless chain of helping, with the helped becoming helpers of others. The possibilities for peer-helper effectiveness in education, rehabilitation, mental health, corrections, and poverty programs are vast indeed.

Self-Help Groups

Self-help groups and procedures for organizing and conducting helping groups have expanded rapidly (Gartner & Reissman, 1980; McCormack, 1981). These organized groups can be identified and located through the National Self-Help Clearing House.

There has been little research on why self-help groups are so effective in changing individual behavior. Hurvitz (1970) studied many groups as a participant-observer and concluded that much of their effectiveness was due to peer relationships among helpers and helped, inspirational methods, explicit goals, fellowship, and a variety of helping procedures. Hurvitz sees these self-help efforts as more effective in many cases than professional psychotherapy. Self-help groups use many sources of help that are outside conventional helping methods.

The helpful group in the context of this book functions without outside leadership, has a special focus, and usually is nonresidential. Some self-help groups develop extreme dependence on charismatic leaders and often develop a religious or cultic atmosphere that demands obedience to an authority. The "Jonestown Massacre" in Guyana is an example of a caring group gone amok under the influence of pathological leaders. Fortunately, most self-help groups are not in this extremist category. Those that are, however, garner a great deal of media attention for their unethical, sensational behavior.

Most groups organize for special purposes and often become institutionalized. Among the best known of this type are Alcoholics Anonymous and Alanon. Local groups organize around special concerns, such as adjustment to divorce or widowhood, teenage pregnancy, AIDS, illegal drug abuse, suicide, and family members with dementia. Urban areas have such special support groups for almost any human problem.

Another type of self-help growth group is spreading in the United States. While most self-help groups are organized around a specific need to change self-destructive behavior such as alcoholism, hard drug abuse, or overeating, these groups are developed by people who are already functioning reasonably well in society but who want to grow to higher levels of effectiveness. The groups are organized informally for purposes of spiritual and psychological growth, social enhancement, and mutual support in times of crisis. Such functions, formerly supplied by the extended family or small church community, are now largely absent from the impersonal urban scene. A current example is the men's movement in the United States: Men meet in self-help groups or go on retreats to find healthy connections for their internal and external needs of psychological wellness. It appears that this self-help movement will become stronger in our urban centers as residents discover its helping power.

Helpers Gain, Too

Helpers change in the process, too, as shown by the preceding evidence and discussion of peer helpers and motives for helping. They can receive as much or more than the helped. As a result of being asked to help, the helper's status is increased and his or her self-image is strengthened. Positive self-regard increases as a result of helping another person through giving rather than taking. Increased confidence in one's own psychological well-being comes from the awareness that "I must be OK if I can help others in need." There is growing evidence that helpers experience improved health through the act of helping (Luks & Payne, 1991). The helping process, furthermore, takes people out of themselves and into the perceptual world of others, thus diminishing concern with their own problems. Sharing feelings often results in strong mutual satisfactions for both people. We need to recognize this strong need to share and to be helpful to others so we can provide more opportunities for volunteers to train and serve.

Gartner and Reissman (1980) have surveyed the evidence on gains for the helper in nonprofessional and peer-helper studies. They concluded that the benefits for the helper come from demands of the specific helping role, increased feelings of prestige, and awareness of new ways in which the helper is perceived and treated. Reissman (1965) suggested also that placing persons who request help, such as drug users wanting to quit, in small helper roles starts a spiraling growth process whereby the helpers' motivations for self-improvement and the learning of helping skills gradually increase. Then they are added to the pool of people with high-level helping skills to be shared with others. Thus, the multiplier effect is actuated.

Helping Is Learning Self-Help Coping Skills

Helping is also a process of encouraging the helpee to learn how to learn. In the helping process helpees learn more effective ways of coping with their present feelings and environmental demands, as well as techniques for solving personal problems, methods of planning, and techniques for discriminating among value choices. Thus, by learning a process of self-help, helpees not only satisfy their present needs but also learn how to meet future needs. One of the most helpful services we can perform for others is to create conditions where they can learn how to solve problems with their own resources. People can be taught, for example, to make decisions and solve problems without the aid of a helper by following the steps listed under positive action in Figure 1-4 in the next section. This emphasis on self-management has grown appreciably in importance since the first edition of this book.

Coping is a process of actively solving personal problems that threaten a person's welfare. It is more than simply adjusting. It is bringing skills already in the person's repertoire to bear on the problem. Examples of such skills are support networking, problem solving, changing negative thoughts, managing stressors, and perceiving problematic situations constructively. Coping skills are listed in Figure 1-3. It has been demonstrated that these skills can be learned and applied by people in ordinary life transitions without individual coaching from helping professionals (Brammer & Abrego, 1981). Detailed presentations of these skills are made in Chapters 4 and 5.

Helping Skills Model for Understanding, Support, and Action

A Two-Stage Helping Model

Helping skills are used in various combinations to meet two major purposes—establishing a relationship and facilitating action. Many of the skills listed in Figure 1-4 under understanding and support are used early in the helping process to find out what the person wants and to create a climate for helping. Then, when a relationship of trust is established and the alternatives are more clear, more of the action methods come to the fore. Details of this process model are described in Chapter 3.

Classification of Skills

There is no standard classification of helping skills or common vocabulary. Goodman and Dooley (1976) surveyed a number of classification schemes for

---

1. Perceptual skills (seeing problematic situations clearly, as challenging or dangerous, and as solvable)
2. Cognitive change skills (restructuring thoughts and altering self-defeating thinking)
3. Support networking skills (assessing, strengthening, and diversifying external sources of support)
4. Stress management and wellness skills (reducing tensions through environmental and self-management)
5. Problem-solving skills (increasing problem-solving competence through applying models to diverse problems)
6. Description and expression of feelings (accurate apprehension and articulation of anger, fear, guilt, love, depression, and joy)

FIGURE 1–3   Coping Skills

For Understanding	For Support and Crisis Intervention	For Positive Action
1. Listening	1. Supporting	1. Problem solving and decision making
1.1 Attending	1.1 Contacting	1.1 Identifying problems
1.2 Paraphrasing	1.2 Reassuring	1.2 Changing problems to goals
1.3 Clarifying	1.3 Relaxing	1.3 Analyzing problems
1.4 Perception checking	2. Crisis intervention	1.4 Exploring alternatives and implications
2. Leading	2.1 Building hope	1.5 Planning a course of action
2.1 Indirect leading	2.2 Consoling	1.6 Generalizing to new problems
2.2 Direct leading	2.3 Controlling	1.7 Evaluation
2.3 Focusing	2.4 Developing alternatives	2. Behavior changing
2.4 Questioning	3. Centering	2.1 Modeling
3. Reflecting	3.1 Identifying strengths	2.2 Rewarding
3.1 Feeling	3.2 Reviewing growth experiences	2.3 Extinguishing
3.2 Content	3.3 Recalling peak experiences	2.4 Desensitizing
3.3 Experience	4. Referring	2.5 Shaping
4. Summarizing		
4.1 Feeling		
4.2 Content		
4.3 Process		
5. Confronting		
5.1 Describing feelings		
5.2 Expressing feelings		
5.3 Feeding back		
5.4 Meditating		
5.5 Repeating		
5.6 Associating		
6. Interpreting		
6.1 Explaining		
6.2 Questioning		
6.3 Fantasizing		
7. Informing		
7.1 Giving information		
7.2 Giving advice		
7.3 Suggesting		

FIGURE 1–4 Helping Skills

what they called "help-intended communications." These helping intentions were carried out in six "response modes," gleaned from several helping systems, as follows: (1) questioning, (2) advisement, (3) silence, (4) interpretation, (5) reflection, and (6) self-disclosure. The main question is, What categories are most meaningful in training helpers? All helping styles include skills that facilitate expression, awareness, or understanding of feelings and those that facilitate rational problem solving, decision making, and acting. Fig-

ure 1-4 contains a classification of these skills. The three categories of understanding, support, and action reflect the main helping process goals that are
translations of what helpees usually want. These three functional categories
are overlapping in the sense that methods for promoting understanding also
provide support and facilitate action.

The following chapters will present the basic helping skills, including outcome behaviors expected in the helpee. Although there is little research on
the relationship between helper behavior and consequent helpee behavior,
there is a body of experience and a set of hypotheses about the connections
from which to draw. Steps in the format for the three chapters on skills are:
(1) what the skill is; (2) purposes of using it; (3) illustrations of its use;
(4) outcomes expected for the helpee; and (5) summary of guidelines for
using the skill.

Outcomes Self-Check

After reading this chapter you can
(1) describe your own needs to be
helpful; (2) identify three sources of
personal gain to the helper from engaging in the helping process;
(3) identify the basic purpose and
point of view of this book; (4) identify
the nature of help in terms of fulfilling
needs and encouraging responsible independence; (5) identify three arguments supporting and three refuting
the value of professional and nonprofessional approaches to helping;
(6) describe and cite examples of self-
help, peer, cross-age, and community
helper projects; and (7) list thirteen basic skill clusters in the areas of understanding, support, and action. We will
look next at the personal characteristics of an effective helper.

Suggestions for Further Study

American School Counselor Association.
ASCA position statement on peer
counseling. *School Counselor* 26
(1979): 273–275.

Avila, D., and Combs, A. *Perspectives on
the Helping Relationship and the
Helping Professions,* 2nd ed. Boston:
Allyn & Bacon, 1985. (A series of
papers on what counseling leaders
have said about the helping process.)

Caplan, G., and Killilea, M. *Support Systems and Mutual Systems.* New York:
Grune & Stratton, 1976. (A collection
of articles on mutual support and
self-help programs.)

Carkhuff, R., *The Art of Helping.* 7th ed.
Amhurst, MA.: Human Development
Press, 1993. (A model of helping with
a program of skill development.)

Combs, A., and Avila, D. *Helping Relationships: Basic Concepts for the
Helping Professions.* Boston: Allyn &
Bacon, 1985. (Nature of helping from
a person-centered point of view.)

Gartner, A., and Reissman, F. *Help: A
Working Guide to Self-Help Groups.*

New York: New Viewpoints/Vision Books, 1980. (Includes information on a self-help clearing house in New York.)

Hattie, J., Sharpley, C., and Rogers, H. The comparative effectiveness of professional and paraprofessional helpers. *Psychological Bulletin* 95 (1984):534–541.

Ivey, A. *Developmental Strategies for Helpers. Individual, Family and Network Interventions.* Boston: Micro-training, 1991.

Kanfer, F., and Goldstein, A. *Helping People Change.* 4th ed. Boston: Allyn & Bacon, 1992. (An overview of different approaches to helping, each chapter written by a different specialist.)

Lieberman, M., and Borman, L. *Self-Help Groups for Coping with Crisis.* San Francisco: Jossey-Bass, 1979. (A guide to managing crises through group methods.)

National Peer Helpers Association, P. O. Box 335, Mountain View, CA 94942.

Rogers, C. Characteristics of a helping relationship. *Personnel and Guidance Journal* 37 (1958):6–16. (An early descriptive effort to define some dimensions of helping by a behavioral scientist.)

Schunk, D. *Learning Theories: An Educational Perspective.* New York: Merrill, 1991. (Educational applications of Maslow's hierarchy, pp. 234–237.)

Varenhorst, B., and Sparks, L. *Training Teenagers for Peer Ministry.* Loveland, CO: Group Books, 1988. (A detailed manual for conducting a peer-helper program in church settings.)

2

Characteristics of Helpers

Why Is Helping Effective in Assisting People to Grow?

A growing body of evidence indicates that the personal qualities of helpers are as significant for positive growth of helpees as are the methods they use. Effective and ineffective helpers cannot be distinguished only by their techniques, but they definitely can be contrasted on their personal beliefs and traits (Combs et al., 1969; Combs, 1982). In this chapter we will focus on helper attitudinal characteristics and their implications, and in the following chapters we will cover methods for communicating these helping attitudes to helpees.

Outcomes You Can Expect

From studying this chapter you will be able to (1) cite the key findings of three researchers on helper characteristics; (2) list and illustrate six general characteristics of helpers and five facilitative conditions determined by helper personal traits; (3) describe five levels of functioning; (4) describe the relationship between helper interview style and helper life-style; and (5) list motives for wanting to be a helper.

This chapter includes extensive lists and overviews of research on helper characteristics. To facilitate application of this material to your helping practices, keep a log of these traits and rate yourself. Thus you'll be able to judge yourself and receive feedback from friends on whether you possess the trait listed, whether it functions effectively for you, or whether it needs improvement.

Combs and his coworkers studied some basic beliefs about people and self-help by contrasting various helpers from counseling, teaching, and the ministry with nonhelpers. The helpers perceived other people as *able* rather than unable to solve their own problems and manage their lives. Other people were perceived also as *dependable, friendly,* and *worthy.* Helpers had self-perceptions and traits distinct from nonhelpers, such as identification with people rather than things, adequate *capacity to cope* with problems, rather than lack of problem-solving ability, and more *self-revelation* and willingness to be themselves than self-concealing.

Rogers (1980) concluded from his experience and reviews of research that the helper's theory and method were far less important for an effective helping relationship than manifestations of the helper's attitudes. Rogers noted also that it was the helpee's *perception* of the helper's attitudes that made a difference in effectiveness. Research has confirmed what the life experience of most of us has indicated, namely, that the helpful person needs to be an attractive, friendly person, someone with whom you feel comfortable, and someone whose opinions you value. The helpful person inspires confidence and trust.

There is a consensus among professional helpers that they must be examples of mature, actualized, well-functioning people themselves. They must care deeply about themselves as well as about others. Jourard and Landsman (1980) describe the healthy personality as compassionate, joyful, caring, possessing a deep sense of community yet enjoying alone time also. Such a person not only feels for others, but acts to remedy pain and injustice. There must be a balance between viewing the helper as a paragon of strength, maturity, and self-actualization with the humility and sense of vulnerability that come from tragic experiences of life. The helper's apparent vulnerability is a prelude to credibility and building trust.

Levels and Styles of Functioning

An important consideration is the helper's level of functioning in a helping relationship. Carkhuff and Berenson (1967) describe five levels of functioning for six interview dimensions. Level 1 on the empathy dimension, for example, means that no empathy is taking place. Empathy is that essential quality of putting oneself in the place of another, even to the point of experiencing feelings as the other does. Level 2 means empathizing very little and at a level that detracts from helpee functioning. Level 3 refers to the minimum level of feeling response necessary to be effective. Levels 4 and 5, according to Carkhuff and Berenson, mean high levels of helper empathy are evident. The same high level of functioning should be noted in the helper's ability to express his or her ideas accurately, to identify feelings correctly, and to communicate clearly. Respect or regard, genuineness, concreteness, and warmth can be scaled similarly from the highest of level 5 to the lowest, level 1.

Carkhuff (1969) presented convincing evidence that, if the helper is functioning at a high level in regard to *important* facilitative conditions, constructive changes will take place in the helpee. The converse is true also: A low level of helper functioning can have destructive consequences for the helpee. Similarly, if the helper is functioning at the same level as the helpee, no change is likely to take place.

All helper characteristics can be scaled. As a practical application of this concept on levels of functioning we suggest you develop a simple rating scale, similar to the following scale for the helper characteristics described in this chapter. As you learn to facilitate the growth of others, rate yourself on these scales. Ask your peers who observe your helping efforts to rate you also.

Facilitative Characteristic Levels

Level 5 Present consistently in helping exchanges
Quality of helper response consistently high

Level 4 Present most of the time in helping exchanges
Quality of helper response high 75 percent of the time

Level 3 Minimum and sporadic presence of helping characteristic—at least half the time
Quality of helping characteristic barely facilitative—minimal effectiveness

Level 2 Some evidence of helping characteristic present—at least 10 percent of the time
Quality of helping response extremely low

Level 1 No evidence of this helper characteristic in helping exchanges

It would be simple if we could relate facilitative characteristics to specific methods that the helper uses, but this condition is impossible at this stage of knowledge, especially considering the wide variations in style among individual helpers. The following facilitative characteristics, which have been identified in a wide range of studies, embody elements of many divergent helping styles and theories. As a result, they have wide application to many helping relationships. Rogers (1957), for example, stressed the essential contribution of helper personal traits to the broad helping process. Others, who emphasize behavior change, stress methods of changing the environment rather than helper attitudes, although the current trend is to emphasize both attitudes and the technology of behavior change.

Helping and Helper Life-Style

Another facet of the facilitative conditions described above is their natural out-growth of helper life-style. These conditions are not stylized traits that helpers turn on and off, but are characteristic of their lives outside of the helping relationship. If they are not living these conditions, they tend to be perceived by helpees as artificial and incongruous. The helper's life must thus be planned in a satisfying manner and lived according to the ideals of the effective and self-actualized person. In addition to enriching the everyday events of living, the helper must pay attention to continuous renewal and revitalization, periodically examining his or her life goals, clarifying personal values, setting new directions, and discovering new sources of energy. To avoid obsolescence, professional helpers must keep up with the rapid changes in the concepts and methods of helping. All helpers, however, need renewal experiences to counter the draining effects of continuous demanding contact with people.

Matching Helpers and Helpees

Although much research has been done on helper characteristics, helpee traits, and helping methods, very little has been done on the interaction of helper and helpee. Growing evidence from research supports our commonsense observations that the compatibility of helper and helpee personalities is a key factor in a successful relationship (Ivey, 1991). This compatibility applies especially to cultural and ethnic difference factors. While no compelling evidence exists that helpers and helpees *must* be of the same race, sex, or ethnic background, helpers must indicate that differences are understood, respected, and valued. Research on preferences for particular kinds of helpers indicates that choosing is a complex process, but it is clear on one point. Helpees tend to prefer helpers of the same ethnic background (Lopez, Lopez, & Fong, 1991; Atkinson & Matsushita, 1991). The important implication of this growing body of research is that we should be sensitive to these probable preferences and ask helpees whether or not they would prefer helpers of the same ethnic background.

Until the time in which there is more ethnic diversity in the ranks of professional or paraprofessional helpers, there will be more ethnic minority persons receiving help from majority helpers. Atkinsen, Morten, and Sue (1993, p. 62) suggest that there are both benefits and barriers to cross-cultural counseling. They summarize the research to conclude that cultural sensitivity on the part of the helper can help overcome some of the barriers that exist when the helper and helpee are ethnically different.

The Helper Personality

No cluster of traits describes a people-helper who is universally effective. Research on counselor and teacher effectiveness indicates that, although there is no fixed trait pattern for effective helping, there are strong indications of desirable conditions that facilitate constructive helpee changes (Carkhuff, 1968; Rogers, 1980; Combs, 1982; Combs & Avila, 1985). We include the essence of these findings and their implications to serve as a tentative template of traits and behaviors that you can place on yourself. You must realize, however, that this list of characteristics is a composite from research and opinions of experienced helpers rather than a model of essential qualities and conditions for all helpers. We will present first some general helper characteristics, to be followed by a list of more specific facilitative traits and growth conditions created by the helper.

Helper Personal Characteristics

A general dictum among people-helpers says that if I want to become more effective I must begin with myself; our personalities are thus the principal tools of the helping process. Combs (1982) used the term *self as instrument* to indicate that our principal helping tool is ourselves acting spontaneously in response to the rapidly changing interpersonal demands of the helping relationship. A teacher must react to new stimuli instantly, for example, with little or no thought ahead of time. How the teacher reacts is a function of who he or she is at that moment and how the relationship with that particular student is seen. We are behavior models for helpees, no matter how we construe our helping role. They imitate our behaviors, identify with our views, and absorb our values. Although we may try to be impartial and objective helpers, the facts indicate that we cannot be such and still remain involved in the relationship. The following helper characteristics determine the nature of this relationship.

1. *Awareness of Self and Values.* There is universal agreement among practitioners and writers that helpers need a broad awareness of their own value positions. They must be able to answer very clearly the questions, Who am I? What is important to me? What is the social significance of what I do? What are my beliefs about people? This awareness aids helpers in being honest with themselves and their helpees and assists them also in avoiding unwarranted or unethical use of helpees for their own need satisfactions.

Self-awareness provides some insurance, furthermore, against the tendency to project values onto others. In every human relationship a fantasy of the other person makes up a large part of our image of that person. For example, I may perceive the helpee from a few minimal cues as a very undependable person. The question is always, How much of this judgment is really descriptive of that person and how much is myself projected? Am I putting on others my own views of what is dependable? Dependability is a judgment; it is not a very descriptive term for behavior. Am I judging the person against some vague social norm?

To aid this self-awareness process, helpers need to know their basic assumptions about people. For example, do you believe that people are basically social, trustworthy, goal-oriented, and willing to change? If so, your helping behaviors will reflect these views. You will trust your helpees to take responsibility for their own lives. If you have grave doubts about the validity of the above assumptions, you should watch for inclinations to attribute blame to helpees for their problems, to be pessimistic about their inclination to change, or to become focused on correcting their erroneous behavior or thinking. Of course, there are some helpees who are so hurt by life that they defy our positive assumptions about human nature, but we need to be wary of tendencies to generalize to all people. It is understandable that if helpers are working in prisons, for example, their views of human nature could become jaded.

While we may have opinions about traits of people we like and want to associate with, one characteristic of effective helpers is that they try to suspend judgments of others. Although it may be helpful sometimes to confront helpees with our opinions, we should try to describe specific behaviors and to avoid labels, mainly because so frequently they are projections of our own social values.

Numerous helping situations test the helper's values. If a helpee is describing a sexual behavior that the helper finds unacceptable, or if the helpee is talking about divorce and the helper has strong convictions about the inviolability of marriage contracts, how does the helper behave? Can helpers maintain their own values and still accept the helpees? Can they empathize, yet be keenly aware of their own values as helpers and their tendencies to project those values?

How do helpers acquire this kind of awareness? Obtaining counseling for themselves or participating in awareness groups is a key source of self-awareness. Reflection and meditation are other means. Self-renewal workshops focusing on values, assumptions, and getting in touch with one's self are becoming sources of expanded awareness and renewed vigor to continue in demanding helping relationships.

2. *Awareness of Cultural Experiences.* A vital program of self-directed awareness training for helpers includes knowledge of populations other than one's own. For example, if a helper works with new immigrants with vastly different backgrounds, it behooves the helper to know more about their cultures. Knowing more about similarities and differences between helpers and helpees is vital to an effective helping relationship. People such as prisoners, drug abusers, children, older adults, those who are divorced, those with physical or mental disabilities, the poor, or racial minorities may all have life experiences different from those of the helper. Several obstacles fall in the way of helping people who are culturally different from the helper. Fear of not being adequate as a helper and fear of rejection by the helpee are key deterrents. These obstacles can be overcome in part through understanding helpees' histories and present problems, language and gender roles, neighborhoods of origin, religion, and family backgrounds. It helps also to be aware of the helpee's world view including perspectives on the goodness or badness of human nature, linear or hierarchical social relationships, the place of the natural order, and future, past, or present time orientation (Ibrahim, 1991).

A second helper task to be comfortable and effective with culturally different helpees is to confront our own ethnocentrism, racist tendencies, and stereotypic thinking. This means a deliberate effort to break out of our small cultural capsules. The starting point is keen awareness of our own cultural roots, biases, beliefs, and world views and our tendencies to project these views on others. When we know who we are, then we can see others more clearly as human beings like ourselves and can appreciate the differences.

Professional helpers study this topic in detail under cross-cultural counseling, but such detailed information about special helpee populations is beyond the scope of this book. We will point out some of the implications of these differences, however, under specific topics, such as listening skills. For helpers especially interested in this topic, we suggest Pedersen's (1994) *Handbook of Cross-Cultural Counseling and Therapy* and Atkinson, Morten, and Sue's (1993) *Counseling American Minorities.*

3. *Ability to Analyze the Helper's Own Feelings.* Observations of helping specialists suggest that one needs to be significantly detached from one's feelings. While effective helping implies awareness and control of one's feelings to prevent the projection of needs described previously, we must realize that helpers also are *feeling* all the time. They feel, for example, the elation of helpee growth toward independence. Similarly, they feel disappointed when their own expectations for helpee growth do not develop. They feel depreciated when their overtures of help are spurned by helpees. Knowing the reasons why helpee esteem needs require this kind of "rejecting" behavior is of some comfort, but helpers are inclined to respond with feelings of disappointment to others who do not value their efforts.

Even though the informal helper may not feel under the same pressure to be helpful as the professional counselor, there are fears about performing well enough to meet helpee expectations. We all want to look good and be appreciated, so there is that lurking fear that maybe the helpee won't like what I do, or that he or she will reject me as a bumbling incompetent. For example, it is discomforting at best when a person stares at you expecting you to say something helpful and yet everything you say or do falls flat. It is important to recognize these feelings of fear, disappointment, frustration, or disillusionment and then discuss them with a trusted friend or colleague.

It is necessary to promote a feeling of confidence in the helper, and there seems to be a nice balance between the stance of the know-it-all expert and the self-effacing attitude that says, "I don't have any special talent or skill; I'm just little old me!" Am I aware, for example, of my tendencies to depreciate myself as a helper, on the one hand, or my tendency to act like a "guru," one who has all the answers, on the other? Furthermore, why do I need to create a mystique about myself that promotes awe and dependency in the helpee?

One of the interesting phenomena of human interaction is the charismatic effect. Some people appear to have intense auras of energy that affect others around them. Some of this response is probably a placebo effect, meaning that through the power of suggestion, the helper's efforts or authoritative position brings results, no matter what he or she does. Weissberg (1977), after searching for an answer to the question, Why does counseling work? concluded that it was a "nagging" effect; by this he meant the active and challenging interventions performed by helpers that mobilize helpees into constructive action to solve their problems. Activities such as authoritative suggestions, assigned homework, and relentless urging are illustrations.

Helpers must learn to deal effectively with their confusion and value conflicts. When are self-assertion and expression of freedom important, for example, and when are conforming and adjusting the appropriate behaviors? The helper often is caught between liberating forces of growing independence and society's need to punish deviates, force conformity, and banish rebels. Helpers must learn to live with this basic human conflict in themselves and their helpees. Helpers also must face another great dilemma of life, namely, community and closeness versus autonomy and separation. Helpers must find the most productive and satisfying balance between these two positions in their own lives before they undertake helping others on this basic life issue.

Feelings of power over helpees come quite unexpectedly. Unless helpers are wary, they can be trapped into smug controlling feelings when helpees express strong dependence on them, or when they indicate their helper has influence over them. When our helpees express profuse gratitude, for example, we begin to wonder if we really provided a condition in which they felt they helped themselves, or whether they felt we did it for them. The latter feeling denies their own assertive self-help and personal power.

In addition to the personal power the helper may feel, it is important to be aware of the hidden dimensions of power in institutions. Governmental agencies, in particular, have certain regulatory responsibilities or legal mandates to offer services under specified conditions. Helpers in such agencies must be wary of identifying too closely with the power of the agency under the guise of carrying out the agency's mission. Often the helpee becomes lost in such settings, and the helping services tend to support the power of the organization. The result may be an exaggerated emphasis on adjustment or pacification rather than on actualization and liberation. An example in a school setting is a helping staff member taking the management side and supporting the school's power over the students rather than focusing primarily on what is in the best growth interest of the students. It would be useful at this point to focus on the suggested activity in Chapter 1 regarding assessment of your motives for helping. After your self-analysis and this discussion on power and dependency, to what extent do you find satisfaction in power over others, in seeing them dependent on and grateful to you, and in identifying with the power of your agency over its clientele?

Professional helpers label these unconscious feelings toward helpees as "countertransference effects," meaning that the helper's needs are expressed in behaviors such as dominating, overprotecting, loving, pleasing, seducing, or manipulating helpees. These feelings are "transferred" from the helper's own past relationships with significant people to the present relationship.

The only known antidote to the kinds of behavior described above is awareness of one's particular tendencies to "transfer" one's own needs, problems, and unrecognized feelings to the helpee. This awareness can be obtained primarily through feedback about one's behavior in individual and group counseling experiences. Furthermore, one needs to have one's personal life in such good order that one can take disappointment, frustration, demanding confrontations, and intensive encounters in helping relationships without projecting them onto helpees, or developing personal symptoms such as depression, withdrawal, or physical complaints. As a helper one needs a strong ego, meaning confidence in one's own worth as a person. Again, as stated earlier under helper life-style, possible protections against self-defeating conditions can be found in a counseling relationship for oneself occasionally, and in a satisfying personal life to provide continuous self-renewal. Helping is an emotionally demanding activity, even when done informally, and some provision must be made for helpers to "recharge their own batteries" occasionally. This will be discussed more in Chapter 7.

4. *Ability to Serve as Model and Influencer.* Helpers function as models and social influences to their helpees, whether they want to or not. Many research studies show the power of models for acquiring socially adaptive as well as maladaptive behaviors (Meichenbaum, 1977, 1985). It is more controversial, however, whether helpers must be models also of decorum, maturity, and effectiveness in their personal lives. We have two reactions to this issue. The first is that helpers must have fulfilling lives, or they will tend to use the helping relationship too much for satisfaction of their own unmet needs. A second reaction is that helpers' credibility may be questioned if they have chaotic personal lives. If their marital lives are stormy, for example, or if their children have constant brushes with police, the validity of their work is likely to be questioned.

Helpers often are caught in the squeeze between their personal desires to deviate from local community norms and to resist pressures to conform, particularly if they are employed by local agencies such as schools and churches. Our society is reaching a point, however, where wide variations in behavior are acceptable and where the private life of the prospective helper is respected. The final standard for judging the appropriateness of the helper's behavior is the helpee's judgment about the helper's usefulness in their present relationship.

Behaving like an "expert" helper in the eyes of the helpee is important to the helping relationship. Schmidt and Strong (1970) studied the behaviors seen as "expert" and "inexpert" from the helpee's viewpoint. Those helpers perceived as expert treated the student helpees as equals, with friendly attentive behavior. They spoke with confidence and liveliness. The "expert" helpers came prepared with knowledge about their helpees, their backgrounds, and their reasons for coming, and they moved quickly to the heart of the problem. Those perceived as "inexpert" were tense, fearful, rambling, uncertain, or overly cool and casual, communicating disinterest and boredom. Because of their more enthusiastic responsiveness to the helpees, the less experienced and less professionally trained counselors often were perceived as the "experts" by the student observers. To have influence with helpees, then, helpers must consider how they are perceived by their helpees and what kinds of models they are presenting.

The evidence about power and influence leaves no doubt that formal helping, in particular, is a strong influence process. Ivey (1994) and Egan (1994) see social influence theory as basic to the helping process. In a provocative article on therapy as manipulation Gillis (1974) made a strong case for the success of formal helping being due largely to the influence and assertiveness of the helper.

5. *Altruism.* We stated earlier that helpers have needs too and that they expect some satisfactions to maintain their helping behaviors. It is not too productive to engage in extensive self-probings about why one wants to help, but it is necessary to have some awareness that one is acting for one's self as well as for some assumed value for the helpee. It is evident, however, that the effective helper is very interested in people and in service. In their early studies of effective helpers, Combs and associates (1969) found that a central value was their concern with people rather than things and with an altruistic stance moving outward toward helping people rather than a more narcissistic focus on themselves. The effective helpers also identified with humanity rather than seeing themselves separated from people.

Granted, we could rationalize altruism quickly in terms of need theory or reward-punishment principles, but the love motive, in the Greek "agape" sense of nonerotic personal caring, is strong in most helpers. They believe they are helping out of deep love of humanity focused on a particular person. This motive has strong theological overtones and reflects the helpers' profound commitment to a special view of the world and their place in it. Although we subscribe to a considerable portion of this kind of motivation for helping we want to be sure our awareness "antennae" are tuned to feedback from our helpees so that we can check the validity of our views and the soundness of our motives. It is important to know, for example, when the helper's need to convert others to the helper's own way of thinking, valuing, and behaving, becomes too strong.

It is our opinion that the Judeo-Christian tradition has contributed in a solid way to the helping climate of our civilization through its ethic of unconditional service to others and its emphasis on the love motive. Yet, like knives, drugs, or machines, helping motives quickly can become destructive tools in the hands of naive or zealous users.

Findings from studies on altruistic behavior have relevance here (Baron & Liebert, 1971). Seeing a model of helping, that is, watching someone in the act of helping someone else, tends to elicit similar behavior in the watchers. A strong reciprocity principle operates in altruistic behavior also. People tend to help those from whom they have received help, since American society has a strong "give and get" norm and a subtle system of social debts and credits. There is also a social responsibility factor operating, since people tend to help those who are dependent on them, even when the rewards for helping seem to be remote. An example is the family caregiver who cares for a dependent older adult because he or she perceives the caregiving tasks as his or her responsibility.

Adults who find satisfaction in helping children are aware that their altruism begets altruism on the part of the children they help (Eisenberg, 1982, 1986). Children learn pro-social behavior such as generosity or kindness when they observe the modeling of adults or other children acting altruistically (Farver & Branstetter, 1994; Dodge, 1984).

Interpersonal attraction was a principle operating in some of the helping studies. Liking the person and being of similar background promoted altruism. A compliance principle seemed to explain some behavior where helping was expected in order to obtain social approval. This brief discussion indicates that altruistic motives are extremely complex; it is likely that a variety of socially conditioned as well as consciously chosen values motivate helping acts.

General helping acts often grow out of strong social support and change motives. From the standpoint of our collective self-interest, and perhaps survival as a race, it is essential that people support one another. When they do not, all are jeopardized in the form of crime, accidents, and pollution. We must have more people concerned about the welfare of others if our society is to survive. And we need activist-helpers who are concerned primarily with changing social conditions to meet human welfare needs, rather than merely helping individuals to cope with the demands of an ailing society. A growing number of help-oriented people are working to change large systems rather than encouraging people to adjust to the system. Examples are civil rights and justice groups and prevention of abusive behavior toward people and the physical environment. The popular bumper sticker "Think globally—Act locally" suggests this goal of creating a people-serving and growth-facilitating society rather than perpetuating the destructive practices of present society.

6. *Strong Sense of Ethics.* When outlined clearly, personal beliefs about people and society serve as conscious guidelines for action. When one values the helpee's welfare, for example, one will do nothing to harm him or her. If someone asks for personal information confided to the helper, it will not be divulged. The helper would regard that information as a symbol of trust. Chapter 7 will discuss this more fully.

7. *Responsibility.* Related to helpers' ethical behavior is the issue of how much responsibility they can assume for their own and their helpees' behavior. Responsibility is a judgmental term defined only in terms of a specific helping context, but there are common understandings about responsible helper behavior. These understandings will be discussed more fully in Chapter 7, focusing on the amount of helpee and helper responsibility for change and the relative amount of self-disclosure that is useful in sessions.

The issue of how much responsibility a helper can or should take for a helpee's behavior is very unclear. Some helpers move to one extreme of saying that the helpee is the only one responsible for the outcomes or consequences of the relationship. Others maintain a very accountable stance under the assumption that the helper is mainly responsible for what happens to the helpee as a result of the helping relationship. It is our observation that most authorities view this issue as a shared responsibility. They keep this question open and move along the responsibility continuum according to their best judgment of the specific condition and age of the helpee. Helpees are responsible for their own decisions, for example, including how much of themselves they are ready to reveal. The helper is responsible for presenting ideas, reactions, or support as deemed appropriate or as requested by the helpee. This responsibility continuum is not linear. Early in the process the helper assumes primary responsibility for providing structure, support, and energy to sustain the relationship. Responsibility shifts to the helpee for maintaining the helping process, as indicated in Figure 2-1. Thus, toward the end of the helping process the helpee takes primary responsibility for outcome and ending the relationship.

There is a misperception about responsible behavior in regard to how much personal data helpees reveal about themselves. It is commonly assumed that no harm is done if the helper just listens to the helpee; but listening has

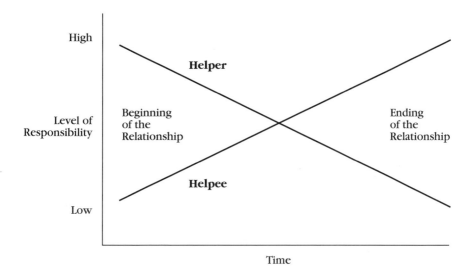

FIGURE 2–1   The Responsibility Continuum

a powerful uncovering effect on the helpee. Helpees often pull down their protective psychological armor while they become more open. The effect on the helpee is often a feeling of vulnerability and hurt, or, sometimes, fear over having revealed too much. One of the ways helpees tell us this is by not showing up for another session. Responsible helper behavior is knowing when to forestall these self-revelations or expressions of feeling. One of the great dilemmas of helping is that we can't be helpful if helpees are not open, yet the most helpful thing we might do is to discourage them from revealing too much about themselves.

Helper as Scholar-Researcher

Thoughtful helpers soon realize that they must have some framework for ordering their experiences with helpees. When they begin to question their assumptions about people, the effectiveness of their helping approach, or the validity of helping in general, they are *thinking* like behavioral scientists. When they systematically collect data about helping behavior, make valid inferences, generalize carefully, and form conclusions about those data, they are *acting* like behavioral scientists.

The critical helper sees the need for more information about the process, more effective skills, and more useful theories about people and the helping function. So the helper turns scholar by reading about others' experiences in helping and the results of specialized research reports.

Although not all helpers can or should become behavioral science researchers, they need to have the critical thinking and observational skills of the scientist. The actual research techniques for validating procedures and discovering new knowledge are part of professional helpers' education, but even they tend to leave the bulk of formal research to specialists. All people-helpers are scholars, though, when they read and apply results from books and journals.

While research and experience indicate that one can be an effective helper without extensive formal education, the helping function draws on the ideas of, and raises many questions related to, the disciplines of philosophy, biology, psychology, sociology, and anthropology, as well as literature and the arts. In other words, the helper's possibilities for flexibility and effectiveness increase as his or her own cultural awareness expands. For example, the issues raised in Chapter 1 about the nature of the helping act revolve around philosophical assumptions about what is real and worthwhile. Helping has political overtones also, as we talk about power, influence, responsibility, and self-determination. Helpers must be committed, in any case, to the ideal of lifelong learning to avoid obsolescence and to maximize their helping effectiveness. This commitment is expressed in the form of following a reading program, accepting feedback on skills, and working toward personal development.

As helpers become more involved, they develop increasing interest in the social context of helping. They find, for example, that the helpee's background as a racial minority member, an immigrant, or a resident of a particular urban subculture has a profound effect on the helpee's outlook and life-style. Understanding the helpee's background provides a sounder basis for empathy, understanding, and later interventions in the helping relationship.

Helper as Growth Facilitator

Since the principal helping function stressed in this book is facilitating achievement of helpee growth goals, some supporting data for growth facilitator characteristics are needed. This role of helper as growth facilitator is different from more traditional models of helping, such as the priest model, the medical model, and the behavioral engineer model. Of these alternate approaches, the *priest model* focuses on conducting ceremonials, interpreting sacred writings, and providing spiritual support. This help consists of supporting, prescribing rules for living, and providing outside intervention. The helper's goals are to make one's lot in this life more effective and to prepare for the next. Another traditional model we all know well is the *medical approach,* where diagnosis of complaints and application of treatments are the key features. The helpful elements include being told what is wrong and being given treatment, surgery, or prescriptions for correcting the disease condition. The *behavioral engineer model* stresses management of the environment. This help approach consists of changing the physical and psychological environment to meet essential human needs. Although these descriptions are oversimplifications of other helping models, they are cited as contrasts to our *growth facilitator model* of helping.

Rogers (1957) specified six essential interview conditions for helpee development. Among them are *congruence* (meaning consistency and genuineness) in the relationship, *unconditional positive regard* for the helpee, *empathic understanding* of the helpee's internal frame of reference, and *efforts to communicate* this understanding. Although there has been controversy over whether Rogers's conditions are essential and sufficient, there is wide agreement that the helper conditions he cites are very desirable. Most helpers agree, for example, that positive regard is important, but few assert that this regard must always be unconditional to be helpful. Several investigators have checked the relationship between these and other facilitative traits with helpee behavior outcomes. Some of the more productive are the early studies of Truax and Carkhuff (1967), Combs and associates (1969), and Carkhuff (1968). Results of these and similar studies are described in the remainder of this chapter.

1. *Helper Empathy.* Empathy is the principal route to understanding helpees and allowing them to feel understood. The helper attempts to see the world the way helpees perceive it, that is, from each helpee's "internal frame of reference." Helpers make an active effort to put themselves in this internal perceptual frame without losing their own identity or objectivity. They do this largely by thinking *with* rather than *for* or *about* the helpee. The word *empathy* derives from the German word *Einfühlung,* meaning "feeling into." It is related to the kind of response that sports spectators give when they lean forward with the jumper. Similarly, helpers tend to "feel into" helpees' feeling experiences as they talk.

Empathy has two stages. The first is the "feeling into" experience described above. Here, the helper experiences the same feelings of hurt or anger, for example, as the helpee. They may even cry together. This is not the same as having sympathy for the helpee. To have sympathy, one feels sorry for another's plight, yet remains relatively distant. To have empathy, one feels another's pain—while walking along beside.

The second stage is more of a cognitive awareness of being in the place of the helpee, seeing the world as the helpee sees it. It is putting oneself in another's frame of reference. In helping relationships the helpers minimize the first stage of exhibiting too much feeling, since this overly strong reaction could reduce their effectiveness. It could blur the distinction between the helper and the helpee. This issue has a paradoxical quality in informal helping, however, in that this emotional sharing develops a feeling of mutual closeness and trust. Both participants experience a common human level of understanding. For our purpose here it is important for helpers to be aware of these stages of empathy and respond according to their best judgment of what the helpee needs.

A key skill in judging what an appropriate response should be is reading nonverbal behavior. Body communication of feelings and needs usually is more revealing than words. Research on body language indicates that non-verbal channels convey more than half of the emotional message (Sweeney, Cottle, & Kobayashi, 1980). This skill involves an intentional effort to appre-hend the total cognitive-emotional message being transmitted.

In the second stage the helper tries to become an alternate self for the helpee, a kind of emotional mirror. The main criterion of success for helper empathy is whether helpees can use the helpers' empathic understanding for their own self-understanding and consequent confidence in their ability to solve their own problems. To function at a minimum level, the helper must respond accurately to covert feelings as well as to the overt content. Briefly, then, helpers manifest empathy through this ability to perceive what is going on in the helpee's feelings and to communicate this perception clearly to the helpee.

Helpers enter the internal frame of reference by listening attentively and asking themselves several questions: What is the helpee feeling right now? How does he view this problem? What does she see in her world? Conversely, the helper who is thinking from an external or diagnostic frame of reference is asking "why" questions, such as, Why is the helpee so upset? What is caus-ing the problem? Judgments are made, such as, He's upset and seems to be in bad shape; I've got to help him.

Since so much helping is done over the telephone in crisis centers and informal counseling situations, the question of face-to-face contact for empa-thy is significant. A study by Dilley, Lee, and Verrill (1971) in which face-to-face, confessional-type, and phone contacts were used found no differences in helpers' ability to communicate empathy in the three methods. This study suggests that more helping could take place effectively over telephones.

A helper tries to think and feel like the helpee. The helpee must be suf-ficiently open to allow the helper to direct a high proportion of attention and emotional energy toward the goal of working within the helpee's framework. This condition is difficult to achieve, particularly in helping situations in which the participants are far apart in race, age, experience, or socioeconomic status (Brammer, Abrego, & Shostrom, 1993). Operationally, empathy is demon-strated when the helper indicates that the helpee's message is heard accurately with no additions or deletions.

The converse condition of too much empathy on the helper's part could be a problem too, perpetuating a dependent immaturity. Helpers must main-tain a sense of independent direction in their own perceptual tracks as they attempt to get within their helpees' framework. If they move too fast and too completely into their helpees' frame, they are likely to lose their objectivity and sense of direction. Through this overidentification with the helpee, the helper is likely to be perceived as more sympathetic than empathic. Even when he or she maintains a strong empathic stance, there is the ever-present likelihood that the helpee's problem becomes the helper's burden too!

2. *Helper Warmth and Caring.* These related terms refer to key emotional qualities in the helper, and they often accompany empathic responses. Warmth is a condition of friendliness and considerateness manifested by smiling, eye contact, and nonverbal attending behaviors. Showing concern and interest such as offering a chair, looking after the person's comfort, and making the person feel valued are also means by which to show warmth.

Caring is a term closely related to warmth, but it is regarded as more enduring and emotionally intense; it means showing compassion and genuine concern about the welfare of the helpee. The act of caring has strong affectional overtones also, meaning that it is a way of saying "I like you."

Some helpers speak of warmth and caring as mild types of nonpossessive love for the helpee that meet needs for response and affection. Early in this century Freud and his followers emphasized warmth as a significant factor in therapeutic power. Warmth in the helper conveys a personal psychological closeness, as opposed to professional distance. Lack of helper warmth can have unwanted effects. Hadley and Strupp (1976) found that such helper qualities as coldness, need to analyze, excessive emphasis on helpee transformation, and hostility contributed to these harmful effects, such as communication problems, helpee getting "worse" (e.g., deeper depression, increased anxiety), or dependency developing between helpee and helper.

The helping skill involved here is how to convey this feeling of closeness, affection, and caring concern to the helpee without emotional entanglements, offensive forwardness, or threat of seduction. Some helpees, for example, have been so hurt by life that they cannot deal effectively with warmth when proffered, so alert helpers will adjust their behaviors to reduce the threat. Neither will they be embarrassed or upset when their helpees respond with cool detachment. In some social groups, emotional involvement with another makes one vulnerable to rejection and obligates one to the person offering the warmth.

A second helper concern is how much warmth to exhibit at different stages in the helping process. Although helpers do not turn warmth on and off, they are aware of the facilitative or debilitative effect of such emotional behavior on the helpee, and adjust accordingly. For example, showing warmth and caring is especially helpful in the early stages when the relationship is being built. They are helpful also when the helpee is going through a crisis, where the supportive value of helper warmth is especially desirable. Professional helpers for the past 80 years have written about the importance of warmth for a productive helping relationship. It is only recently, however, that research results have supported the facilitative effects of warmth and caring (Sarason, 1985; Rogers, 1980; Combs & Avila, 1985).

Helpers must also gauge their amount of expressed warmth and caring according to helpees' comfort level. From a multicultural perspective, overt expression of emotion must be used sensitively. Asian American helpees might be quite uncomfortable receiving strongly emotional care, especially early in the relationship. In the Hispanic American culture, overt warmth might be more acceptable between female helpers and helpees, but not so for males (Atkinson, Morten, & Sue, 1993).

3. *Helper Openness.* One of the principal goals in the beginning of a helping relationship is to encourage helpees to disclose their thoughts and feelings freely to their helpers. This self-disclosure is related to their helpers' openness, since helpers must be willing to reveal their own views to their helpees in an honest way (Jourard, 1968; Combs et al., 1969). The essential condition of trust, furthermore, is directly dependent on the extent to which helper and helpee are open to each other.

Like so many helper characteristics, openness is paradoxical in that too much self-revelation on the part of the helper confuses the issue as to who is helpee and who is helper. Helpers need to be aware when their needs begin to supersede those of their helpees. A general guideline to follow is that helpers should reveal only enough of themselves to facilitate the helpee's self-disclosure at the level of functioning desired. Helpers should reveal themselves in a progressively free manner natural to a developing relationship. Too rapid disclosure on their part may overwhelm helpees with unexpected behavior or threaten them with too much personal data.

A term that Rogers (1980) and other writers use in this context is *genuineness.* This is a state where helpers' words are congruent or consistent with their actions. If a helper says, for example, "I'm glad to see you," he or she reflects this feeling with body language and voice quality consistent with the words of welcome.

Another word used in helping contexts is *authentic*—the opposite of fake; the helper tries not to hide behind a professional role or facade. A certain amount of social game-playing behavior may be appropriate early in the process, when, for example, he or she says conventional things like, "Hello, how are you?" Effective helpers concentrate on listening and trying to understand what the helpee is feeling so that they can respond with appropriate and authentic feelings. The helper uses discretion in expressing negative feelings about the helpee at this stage, however, since such expressions may be destructive.

Carkhuff (1993) distinguishes between two stages of genuineness. The first involves a low level of functioning in recognition of the natural way trusting relationships develop. The helper is in a *responsive* set, listening to the helpee and responding to helpee messages. In the second stage of genuineness helpers are in an *initiative* set where they are more freely themselves as persons, thus enabling the helpees to be more expressive. The modeling effect of the helper is important in both stages. The open quality of communication exhibited by the helper serves as an example for the helpee and leads to a relationship where the helpee learns to be more open and genuine.

Congruence is another term used in helping professions to express the harmony between the helper's behaviors, such as words, and his or her basic attitudes (Rogers, 1961; Combs & Avila, 1985). Congruence affects helpers' credibility. They are perceived as more believable when their behavior and attitudes appear to "ring true" to the helpee. Perceiving helpers as congruent facilitates the helpees' own congruence between their words and feelings because of the modeling effect described above. When helpers, for example, say they are interested in the helpee's problem, their words should be consistent with their basic feelings; otherwise the discrepancy will be apparent to the helpees. The consequences very likely would be loss of confidence in the helper or annoyance at the helper's feigned interest.

4. *Helper Positive Regard and Respect.* This characteristic is an attitudinal set that expresses not only helpers' deep concerns for their helpees' welfare but also respect for their individuality and worth as persons. Rogers (1961) expresses this condition as "unconditional positive regard," meaning a nonjudgmental and deeply valued attitude. It says to helpees that they are free to be themselves and that they will be respected for it. The literature on helping shows that the term *unconditional* appears to be controversial. It means that no conditions or judgments will hamper the helpee's expression of feelings or ideas. We consider unconditionality relative to stages in the process of helping. In the first contacts it is important to convey through acceptance and warmth the attitude that "I neither approve nor disapprove of what you are saying. I want you to express yourself freely, and I will respect your right to feel as you please and to act as you feel within the limits of our mutual welfare. I want you to become your most real and effective self. Furthermore, I want to like you and respect you as a person." However, even at this initial stage, perfect unconditional positive regard is impossible due to our own worldviews and life experiences. It is an ideal of nonjudgmentalism toward which we may strive.

Later in the helping process, when the relationship is well established, the helper begins to experience a variety of feelings toward the helpee. Then the regard becomes more conditional. Helpers express more of their own approving and disapproving attitudes, thus tending to reinforce or diminish certain behaviors in helpees. The helper's spontaneous and authentic behaviors become more apparent as the trust level deepens and the helpee is more open to honest feedback from the helper.

The principal vehicles for expressing regard and respect are words matched with genuine nonverbal expressions of warmth, acceptance, and empathy. Helpers convey an attitude that their help is being given with the condition that the helpees express honest feelings and attempt to become their best selves on their own terms. The helpee is not required to please or conform to the wishes of the helper. This respectful stance is facilitated by conscious helper efforts to be freeing rather than controlling or manipulating (Combs and associates, 1969).

5. *Helper Concreteness and Specificity.* A key facilitating condition for accurate and clear communication in helping is the helper's attempt to be specific rather than general or vague. The effective helper models concreteness, but also confronts the helpee about specificity and clarity. When dealing with painful and unacceptable feelings, for example, there is a tendency to be abstract and circuitous to avoid direct confrontation with those feelings. Painful feelings tend to be stated in vague and elusive language in the beginning. In this instance the helper may say, for example, "You appear to be uneasy; most people seem to be uneasy in new situations." Another example is, "Please give me a specific example of what you feel right now." The strategy is to confront helpees with requests for *their* specific and present feelings stated in concrete terms. Using general phrases such as "most people," "they say," or "it seems we" detracts from the specific personal reference desired in the form of "I feel" or "I think that."

The helper assists the helpee in focusing more on present, rather than past or future, concerns and feelings through questions and reflections. Helpers also model good examples of specific communication by using clear "I" statements. That is, he or she speaks in terms of "I think" or "I feel" rather than "People say" or "They think that."

One problem in using and encouraging specific expressions is that they may tend to reduce the spontaneity and free association of helpee's expressions of feeling. So often helpees wander about, tapping sensitive areas cautiously. This issue must be resolved according to the helper's best judgment. Typically, helpers might encourage and model specificity and concreteness of expression early in the process. Then, when their helpees become more involved, helpers allow them more freedom to express themselves in their natural verbal style. Finally, when the process develops to the point of planning specific courses of action and when it demands a problem-solving approach, greater emphasis can then be placed on specificity and concreteness of expression and action.

6. *Communication Competence.* Since helping is so dependent on clear communication, it follows that a key characteristic of the effective helper is communication competence. Research in linguistics and explorations in cross-cultural communication, such as that by Bandler and Grinder (1982) and Ivey (1994), underscores this quality as essential to effective helping. Bandler and Grinder, for example, indicate how helping clarifies helpee sentences, gives helpees better ways to describe themselves, and provides them with sharper descriptive thoughts about their problems.

Awareness of the cultural basis for effective helping is an aspect of communication competence also, since helpers owe much of their effectiveness to being able to communicate within the verbal and nonverbal language framework of their helpees. Ivey (1994) observed from his studies of teaching helping skills in varied cultures that helping skills and attitudes have different effects in other cultures. For example, direct and prolonged eye contact in some cultures is considered rude, and a comfortable distance between helper and helpee is defined in each culture also. Expected techniques vary from culture to culture, as observed when some groups are offended by intensive questioning. Differences in showing affection nonverbally are apparent to even the casual observer. What all this means for the helper is that communication competence is enhanced by the conscious efforts to observe and appreciate these differences. How the helper chooses to react to these differences is covered in later chapters on helping skills, especially those of attending in Chapter 4.

7. *Intentionality.* Ivey's (1994) useful concept of intentionality describes a helper who is capable of choosing responses to helpees from a wide range of possibilities. The assumption underlying this trait is that there is no one right helping response to a person. The possibilities emerge from the helper's assessment of the whole situation, using information about the person's cultural background cited above, knowing the full range of methods appropriate to the goals of helping, and then selecting a response with confidence.

A Concluding Statement

After reviewing the ideal helper's personal characteristics, one is struck with their paradoxical simplicity, yet complexity, for facilitating growth in helpees. Most of the conditions described in this chapter are extensions of ordinary effective human qualities. The relevant research and cumulative experience of professional helpers point out the necessity, however, for examining continuously the amount and timing of these growth-facilitating conditions for particular helpees at special moments in their development.

Also important is the need to be flexible as a people-helper. At times one must be deeply personal, immersing oneself in the relationship, and at other times one must be an objective observer, studying the process carefully. Helpers must be able to move freely along the full range of these facilitating characteristics so that they can respond appropriately to helpee needs at different stages in the helping process. On the one hand this must be a natural intuitive artistic process, and on the other hand it needs to be a deliberate rational process of sizing up and meeting helpee needs. Although this artistry comes naturally to some, it is most often an outcome of intensive and extensive effort and criticism.

While you are in the process of learning to be a helper, it is important that you do not expect perfection of yourself. Helping skills are complex, but learnable. Research has taught us that if you do not expect immediate mastery, but give yourself flexibility and permission to make a few mistakes along the way, that the learning will actually come more easily and be more durable (Bandura, 1989; Cunningham, Davis, Bremner, Dunn, & Rzasa, 1993). So, relax and enjoy the process while you learn the art of giving of yourself to others.

However you construe the helping process—primarily as an art or as a science—it is essential that serious helpers take periodic looks at the assumptions they make about themselves, their helpees, and the helping process. This chapter focused on the helper as a person and how he or she uses this personhood as a helping tool. In Chapter 8 we will explore the idea of helpers as thinking beings who reflect on their work and develop a rationale for their help. Various models are presented for helper self-criticism and for describing what they are doing and why they are doing it.

While helpers need the fine human qualities described here, they must also possess a special psychological toughness and stamina to bear the stresses of constant and intense human contact. Results of helping efforts often are not apparent immediately. This condition leaves the helper wondering about his or her own effectiveness and worth. Occasionally, helpers must bear the burden of ridicule and disparaging labels such as "shrink" and "bleeding heart." Sometimes criticisms and expectations of giving more haunt the helper, especially those persons working with children and families. Therefore, burnout is a constant sword hanging over the helper's head. One characteristic of the strong helper is making time for renewal experiences and other burnout prevention strategies.

On the positive side, however, is the realization that service to others has its rewards also. The satisfaction of seeing students growing, patients recovering, employees working better together, and families functioning in a healthier way is intense. Helpers report that their sense of purpose and meaning in life was enhanced and their fulfillment increased as a result of their helping activities. Thus, the effective helper comes to realize more fully that he or she must find that ideal balance between giving and taking in a helping relationship. Finally, helpers must find joy and satisfaction in service to others. Dr. Andrus, founder of the American Association of Retired Persons, expressed this idea of sharing very well:

What I spent, is gone
What I kept, is lost
But what I gave away
Will be mine forever.

In summary, helpers need to be honest and forthright in their own self-criticism. They need to ask: What are my helping strengths and limitations? Am I aware of my vulnerable points and uncomfortable topics I tend to deny or avoid? Am I aware of my need to dominate, overpower, and push helpees in my direction? Am I as honest and forthright with my helpees as I try to be with myself? Do I look for the strengths in helpees as well as their problems and limitations?

Outcomes Self-Check

You can (1) name three research investigators of helper characteristics and cite their key findings; (2) list six general behavioral characteristics of helpers; (3) cite and illustrate five growth-facilitating conditions for helping relationships through helper personal qualities and values; (4) describe five levels of functioning; and (5) describe the close relationship between helper interview style and helper life-style and beliefs. The final criterion of successful mastery of the ideas in this chapter is your demonstrated ability to live a whole and creative life in and out of your helping relationships.

Suggestions for Further Study

American Counseling Association. *Ethical Standards.* Washington, DC: American Association for Counseling and Development, 1994.

American Psychological Association. Ethical principles of psychologists. *American Psychologist* 47 (1992): 1597–1611.

Atkinson, D., Morten, G., and Sue, D. *Counseling American Minorities.* 4th ed. Dubuque, IA: William C. Brown, 1993.

Brammer, L., Abrego, P. and Shostrom, E. *Therapeutic Counseling and Psychotherapy.* 6th ed. Englewood Cliffs, NJ: Prentice Hall, 1993 (Ch. 4 on the helping relationship and the characteristics of the therapeutic psychologist.)

Corey, G., Corey, C., and Callanan, P. *Issues and Ethics in the Helping Professions.* 4th ed. Pacific Grove, CA: Brooks/Cole, 1993.

Egan, G. *The Skilled Helper.* 5th ed. Pacific Grove, CA: Brooks/Cole, 1994. (Ch. 1 section on the portrait of a helper.)

Hamechek, D. *Encounters with the Self.* New York: Holt, Rinehart & Winston, 1971. (A comprehensive survey of principles and research findings on development and understanding of the self, especially Ch. 7 on developing a healthy self-image.)

Ivey, A. *Intentional Interviewing and Counseling*. 3rd ed. Pacific Grove, CA: Brooks/Cole, 1994. (Excellent discussion of counselor characteristics and motivation for helping.)

Pedersen, P., Ed. *Handbook of Cross-Cultural Counseling and Therapy*. Westport, CT: Greenwood Publishing Group, 1985. (A collection of comprehensive papers on cross-cultural counseling topics, especially Sections II and III.)

————. Ed. Multiculturalism as a fourth force in counseling. *Journal of Counseling and Development* 70 (1991): 5–250. (A special issue with 38 articles on various aspects of multicultural counseling.)

Rogers, C. *On Becoming a Person*. Boston: Houghton Mifflin, 1961. (A collection of Professor Rogers's papers on various personal aspects of the helping function.)

Sarason, S. *Caring and Compassion in Clinical Practice*. San Francisco: Jossey-Bass, 1985.

Sue, D. Counseling and the culturally different. *Personnel and Guidance Journal* 55 (1977): 422–425. (A set of guidelines for cross-cultural helping acts.)

3

The Helping Process

This chapter is intended as a map through the complicated pathways of helping. It will list typical sequential events in the helping process and cite some of the problems encountered at each stage. This process has two simple phases—*building a relationship* and *facilitating positive action*. This chapter presents suggestions for moving through these two phases, listing typical sequential events in the helping process and noting problems that may be encountered at each event. Methods for handling problems are covered in Chapters 4 through 6.

The term *process* refers to the sequence of events and their meaning to the participants. The helper uses different skills at each stage in this process. Initially, understanding and support skills are crucial in developing the relationship; in the second phase of the process, decision and action skills become more important.

The phases and stages in the process refer primarily to more formal than informal helping situations. The process steps become more identifiable as we move from friendships (with no identifiable process) to a contractual counseling relationship with clearer stages.

Outcomes You Can Expect

From reading this chapter you should be able to (1) describe the dimensions and stages in a typical helping process; (2) list the functions of a helping relationship; (3) act more confidently when facing some of the problems encountered in the two phases; and (4) develop your own cognitive map of the helping process on which you can place your ideas and methods about help. The ultimate criterion of successful study of this chapter will be your ability to understand and demonstrate how to initiate, maintain, and terminate a helping relationship.

Relationship

As implied in Chapter 1, the helping process takes place in a relationship. Within formal contexts this relationship takes the form of an interview, a structured helping relationship in which usually only two persons are involved. The variables contributing to the relationship are sketched in Figure 3-1. Informal relationships, on the other hand, grow naturally out of social patterns already established and need no formalities or rituals. Both formal and informal helping relationships have persons with individual backgrounds, worldviews, and experiences coming together in a new relationship. Helpees seek to share their current problems, which have grown out of past experiences, with a person who has life experiences that will allow understanding and help to occur.

The helping relationship is dynamic, meaning that it is constantly changing at verbal and nonverbal levels. The relationship is the principal process vehicle for both helper and helpee to express and fulfill their needs, as well as to mesh helpee problems with helper expertise. Relationship emphasizes the *affective* mode, because relationship is commonly defined as the inferred emotional quality of the interaction. Thus we speak, for example, of warm relationships.

All authorities on the helping process agree that the quality of the relationship is important to effective helping (Sexton & Whiston, 1994). They disagree, however, on whether certain relationship conditions are essential, or only desirable (Gelso & Carter, 1985). All authorities agree also that it is important to have a good working relationship established early in the helping process. This good working relationship (at the center of Figure 3-1) is a product of genuine counselor attitudes, caring, and compassion. In addition, these real counselor attitudes interact with expectations and attitudes carried over by helpees from their past family experiences. These feelings are known in formal counseling writings as transference feelings and will be discussed later in this chapter.

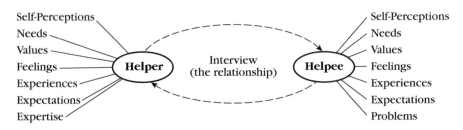

FIGURE 3–1   The Helping Relationship in the Interview

A third component of the helping relationship is described as the *working alliance* (Gelso & Carter, 1994). This term refers to the agreement of helper and helpee on the goals and tasks and the experience of an emotional bond in this mutual act. The working alliance is considered to be equal in importance to helper attitudes (Gelso & Carter, 1994). This aspect of the helping relationship will be discussed in the section on planning and structuring the helping process.

Dimensions

Brammer, Abrego, and Shostrom (1993) list the main dimensions of a helping relationship. One is *uniqueness-commonality*. Helping relationships generally are unique among human interactions. They have common features, yet they are as diverse and complex as the persons involved. An aspect unique to helping relationships is the helper's unusually extensive acceptance of the helpee. On the other hand, helping relationships have much in common with friendships, family interactions, and ministerial contacts. They are all aimed toward fulfilling basic human needs and, when reduced to their components, look much alike.

Another dimension is the relative amount of *intellectual and emotional content*. A relationship can be primarily an emotional encounter between two people with verbal and nonverbal emotional expression shared, or it can be a heavily verbal and intellectual exchange about the helpee's eligibility for services from the helping agency. Helping relationships typically range over the full spectrum of feeling and thinking. Usually there is a development in the depth of risk and sharing of emotion for both the helpee and the helper. Both parties spend time in and out of sessions thinking about what is happening, deciding what to do next, and wondering about the meaning of this helping relationship.

However, a helping relationship is different from a friendship. A helping relationship is not a reciprocal relationship. The focus is on the helpee's issues, both intellectual and emotional, and the helper must resist the urge to move the focus to his or her experience.

An important implication for helpers here is to be aware of the level of emotional involvement taking place and the consequences for the helpee of such involvement. The optimum level toward which to strive depends on one's goal. Helpers, on the one hand, can be so detached and intellectual that they are perceived as distant, disinterested, or afraid of feelings. Yet, if helpers allow themselves to become too emotionally involved, they may lose their objectivity and develop relationships such as those experienced by lovers or parents and children. Helpers need to deal comfortably with this paradox of involvement. They need to maintain their objectivity, so they remain in reasonable control of their own feelings and know what is going on in the relationship, yet remain enough of an emotional participant to keep the helpee involved at an appropriate feeling level. A helper can balance a helpee's approach to problem solving. If it is too emotional, then the helper can encourage more intellectual involvement, and vice versa. This requires the helper to be personally well balanced and not too easily drawn in by the helpee's approach.

An additional key to resolving the paradox of involvement is to clarify the nature of the implied contract. This means specifying reasons for the encounter, its limits, and particularly the roles of the helper. While professional helpers do this as a matter of course, it is more difficult for informal helpers since their roles are so ambiguous and often blend with friendships.

The dimension of *ambiguity-clarity* refers to the perception of the helping relationship as vague or structured. Initial ambiguity allows the helpee to project needs, concerns, and feelings into the relationship without constraint, whereas, if the relationship were structured initially as a precisely focused interview, the helpee would be inclined to respond to the narrowly perceived purposes of the helper. If the relationship were too ambiguous in terms of purpose and identity of the helper, the helpee would be likely to react with considerable anxiety, or would drift into social conversation. The key to resolving this dilemma is that the helper and helpee must decide what this helping relationship is designed to accomplish and choose a level of ambiguity consonant with this purpose. If the purpose, for example, is to explore helpee feelings or to discover what is on the helpee's agenda, leave the relationship and your helper role deliberately ambiguous so that the helpee can use the relationship as a screen on which to project his or her feelings, ideas, and goals.

A crucial relationship dimension is that of *trust-distrust*. Helpees are willing generally to accept help from people they trust. For trust to develop, helpees must have confidence in their helpers and must be able to believe what they say. Certain specific helper behaviors, such as clear motives for helping, create trust. The motives of the helper must be apparent and attractive to the helpee, and they must not be a cover for helper efforts to control, manipulate, or punish. Helper openness, or self-disclosure, is another characteristic leading to a climate of trust. Thus, helpers model the risking behavior expected of the helpee. To disclose one's self risks rejection, ridicule, or betrayal; so helpees want to feel safe.

Under conditions of trust helpees perceive themselves as being accepted and valued people. They feel warmly received. They perceive their helpers as sincere in their efforts to give of themselves and their willingness to reveal their own feelings honestly. The helpee experiences the relationship as a shared and confidential effort to achieve growth, as a mutual problem-solving and learning activity. Yet, the helpee feels free to accept or reject the relationship and the implied help.

Conversely, distrust often causes the helpee to reject offers of help, as when the helpee thinks the helper wants to change him or her. The helpee may feel dependent, inferior, helpless, or depreciated, and thus resist the helper. These reactions become a circular series of events, since helpers sense this resistance and feel unappreciated and possibly even rejected. The helper may then attempt more intensive or retaliatory efforts to change the helpee. He or she may cool, and eventually end, the relationship, with residual feelings of disappointment or anger in both persons. One of the most insidious guises for helping another person is the rationalization that the helper is acting for the helpee's own good, whereas in reality he or she is doing it for manipulative or punitive reasons to fulfill the helper's own needs.

Although little research has been done on trust, two studies have given us a clearer picture of the nature and effect of trustworthiness. Schmidt and Strong (1970) studied the effect of perceived trustworthiness on the helper's influence. They used interviewers trained in trustworthy and untrustworthy behaviors. Trustworthy behavior was defined as showing genuine interest in the helpee as well as absence of ulterior motives, nonconfidentiality, and boastfulness. It was difficult to produce roles characteristic of significant untrustworthy and trustworthy behavior in this study, but they did clarify the nature of the trusting process. In later research Kaul and Schmidt (1971) studied the factors influencing perceptions of trustworthiness. They found that interviewer manner had a more significant impact on perceived trustworthiness than words. The key implication for our discussion of the trust dimension here is that we must attend more to the effects of our nonverbal communication. What we say with our bodies is related to our genuineness and honesty. Kaul and Schmidt's definition of a trustworthy person was one who respects needs and feelings, offers information and opinions for the helpee's benefit, generates feelings of comfort and willingness to confide, and is open and honest about his or her motives. Trust also came from the positive reputation of the helper.

In some situations, it takes time to build trust. LaFramboise and Dixon (1981) found that helpees of the majority culture attribute trust to the helper upon entering the relationship. However, minority helpees often suspend trust until helpers prove their trustworthiness. They stated, "perception of trust-distrust may be of particular importance in initial cross-cultural interactions and, in fact, may preclude further, sustained interactions."

There are other dimensions of relationship related to levels of personal-social responsibility, freedom-control, and ethical commitment, but these are discussed in other chapters. This section is an introduction to some general dimensions and relationship problems. The following discussion will describe, in more specific terms, two additional conceptual schemes for understanding the helping process. The first is an overview of the process as experienced typically by both helpee and helper. The second will list the specific stages in a typical model of the helping process.

The Helping Process as Experienced

The following sequence of events is typical of helpers' and helpees' experiences of moving from first contact through final outcomes. This general sequence is not dependent on helping style or theory of helping; it is an unfolding of a natural process of problem solving. Note that in Figure 3-2, the helpee's feelings, questions, and interpretations of what is going on are paralleled by those of the helper. The process moves typically from an initial statement of a problem by the helpee, to a covert translation of that problem into a broad awareness of the underlying message. Then the helpee moves to a further translation of the problem into a desired goal, on to an awareness of need for the problem-solving process, to experiencing the helper's strategy and method for reaching the goal or solving the problem. Finally, the helpees experience the outcomes themselves. This sounds like a complicated process, but it is a natural movement toward a goal, fulfilling a need, or solving a problem. The helper goes through a parallel process of experiencing initial questions, then forming some preliminary inferences and hypotheses about what is going on. Making working agreements with the helpee follows. Finally, the helper chooses a strategy of helping, and, in a facilitative role, moves toward the outcomes.

Stages in the Helping Process

The stages listed on the following page are typical of the process in the two basic phases—relationship and action. They do not always exist in this exact sequence, nor are all stages always present, since helpees typically determine the sequence and length of stages. Some helpees, for example, come with very vague requests, sometimes just with an uncomfortable feeling, whereas others come with specific requests, thoughtful expectations, and much experience. Some help takes the form of specific skill development, such as relaxation. Other help takes a more cognitive form—acquiring an educational and career plan. Often help is requested for managing intense feelings or resolving interpersonal problems. These diverse helpee needs and problem statements, therefore, call for some variation in the stages.

Another variable determining the sequence and emphasis given the stages in the helping process is the theoretical outlook of the helper. If helpers take a strongly behavioral stance, as described in Chapter 8, they will construe the process quite differently from the way a gestalt helper would conceive it. The helper leaning in the behavioral direction would see the process as discovering the problem, establishing the behavioral objectives, describing the interventions, managing the environment, evaluating the behavior change, and following up. The gestalt approach to process, by contrast, focuses on establishing the relationship, expanding awareness and self-support by use of confrontational methods, and enabling the helpee to decide on a course of action growing from the awareness of self and others. Both views emphasize the outcome of personal responsibility for decisions; but the behavioral view stresses the process of managing the external environment, whereas the gestalt and similar views emphasize the process of changing the internal environment (awareness).

From a generalist point of view, there are eight stages contained in the two basic phases of the helping process:

Phase 1: Building Relationships

1. *Entry:* preparing the helpee and opening the relationship.
2. *Clarification:* stating the problem or concern and reasons for seeking help.
3. *Structure:* formulating the contract and the structure.
4. *Relationship:* building the helping relationship.

Phase 2: Facilitating Positive Action

5. *Exploration:* exploring problems, formulating goals, planning strategies, gathering facts, expressing deeper feelings, learning new skills.
6. *Consolidation:* exploring alternatives, working through feelings, practicing new skills.
7. *Planning:* developing a plan of action using strategies to resolve conflicts, reducing painful feelings, and consolidating and generalizing new skills or behaviors to continue self-directed activities.
8. *Termination:* evaluating outcomes and terminating the relationship.

You may note that the above sequence is a general model of the helping process designed to incorporate problem-solving, skill development, life planning, and awareness models. Because case examples help to make this process explicit and more meaningful, we suggest you either imagine a person with whom you have worked, or consider yourself as a former or present helpee, and think through the process steps described in the next sections. How does your situation match this sequence of phases and steps? How would you conceptualize this helping process to fit your personal situation or work setting?

Stage 1: Entry

Readiness.   The goals of this stage are to open the interview with minimal resistance, lay the groundwork of trust, and enable helpees to state their requests for help comfortably and clearly. Helpees come to a helping relation-

FIGURE 3–2   The Helping Process as Experienced by Helper and Helpee

---

PHASE 1: BUILDING THE HELPING RELATIONSHIP

HELPEE BEHAVIOR
Initial statement of concern:
How do I state my desire for help?
"I need help...."
"I have a problem...."
"I'm unhappy...."
"Something is wrong...."
"I can't perform...."
"I can't decide...."
Can I trust this other person?
What am I getting myself into?

Initial statement translated into a basic message:
I can't cope with the demands of myself, of others, of the situation.
I need more information, more skill, more love, more understanding....

HELPER BEHAVIOR
Initial questions and reactions:
Why is the helpee here?
How does the helpee see his or her present situation?
What is the helpee feeling and thinking?
How am I and this relationship perceived?
What is the helpee's world like?
What does the helpee want of me?

Formulating inferences, hunches, and hypotheses:
What messages is the helpee trying to convey?
I see the basic problem as....Is this valid?
Can I meet the helpee's expectations?
What additional information do I need to explore?

HELPEE BEHAVIOR
Statement of a goal (usually in the form of "I want...." statements):
I want to decide....do....plan....
I want to feel more confident....worthy....happy....
I want others to like me....notice me....change to....get off my back....

Awareness of process needs:
I want a relationship to explore my feelings.
I want specific information about....
I want to talk over my various choices....
I want more choices to consider....

HELPER BEHAVIOR
Preliminary inferences and judgments about helpee need:
The helpee needs a process—planning, problem solving, decision making.
The helpee needs a relationship to work through feelings or obtain support.
The helpee needs information.
The helpee needs referral for specialized help.

Making an agreement or contract to meet helpee expectations:
I will (can)—
give information.
give time to listen.
give support.
I will not (cannot)—
relate to this person.
meet his or her expectancies.
I expect the helpee to—
do his or her agreed part.
take responsibility for any decisions or plans.

PHASE 2: FACILITATING POSITIVE ACTION

HELPEE BEHAVIOR

*Experience helper's strategy and
     methods:*
  I meet with the helper for the agreed
     purposes.
  I experience what we are doing as
     helpful (or not helpful) as evi-
     denced by....

Outcomes experienced:
  I feel better about myself.
  I feel better about others.
  My skills have improved.
  I feel better about my situation.
  I enrolled in....
  I obtained a job as....
  I experienced myself as competent
     in....

HELPER BEHAVIOR

Choosing a strategy of helping:
  I choose a specific interviewing
     method to meet helpee needs.
  I look for feedback from the helpee
     on the effectiveness of my help.
*Looking for evidence of achieving help-
     ing goals:*
  I see progress toward helping goals.
  I plan for termination of this helping
     relationship.

Outcomes perceived:
  I experience myself as helpful to this
     person.
  I see specific behaviors the helpee
     has learned, courses of action he or
     she has chosen, or plans he or she
     has made.
  I hear stated feelings he or she has
     experienced.

---

ship with mixed feelings about helpers and many attitudes that interfere with receiving help. On the one hand, they want whatever the helper has to offer; yet there is strong resistance in even the most highly motivated helpees. Basically, people fear change, and a helping relationship may intensify this fear.

One study of young adults in helping relationships found that 90 percent simply wanted to talk to someone and receive a personal response (Saccuzo, 1975). The three major factors leading these persons to a helping relationship were the need to learn more about themselves, release from troublesome feelings, and the need for encouragement. A key implication of this study is the necessity for helpers to ascertain, define, and reflect what the helpee wants *early* in the relationship. Inability to do so may risk termination of the relationship.

Resistance is a standard term in counseling literature used to denote helpees' conscious or unconscious reluctance to begin a helping relationship as well as their covert thwarting of the goals of the interview once the process is under way. There are several reasons for this resistance. In the first place, cultural norms in certain segments of society construe seeking help as an expression of weakness or incompetence. People are expected to handle their problems with fortitude and common sense, and this cultural pressure to be independent discourages involvement with a helper of any kind. In some cultures, such as the Chinese, personal problems are family issues. Hence, they are to be discussed in the extended family only.

Our tendencies to resist change in our style of living create further resistance to the relationship. We talk glibly about growth and becoming more effective people, but we really do not want to work up to our potential by going through the fearful discomfort of change. The following interview excerpt illustrates these points.

HR: Even though you say you want to apply for that new job, you have found reasons to put if off for two weeks.

HE: Well, I just can't seem to find the time.

HR: You really don't want that job?

HE: Yes I do. I guess I'm afraid I won't get it, so I don't try.

Fear of confronting our feelings is a strong deterrent for seeking help. The pain must be great in most of us before we will admit that we need a helping relationship. We may try all kinds of substitutes like drugs, for example, first. It is important for helpers to recognize this ambivalent, or mixed, feeling in all helpees.

We must recognize also that even those who have made a clear commitment to seek a helping relationship use all kinds of stratagems, of which they are unaware, to resist changing. Examples are talking excessively about irrelevant topics, leaving early or coming late, and making excuses. This resisting behavior also takes place long after the helping relationship is under way. Helpers constantly need to devise methods for dealing with resistance, such as confronting helpees with their behavior, as in the dialogue just described. Helpees may, for example, discuss matters at a high intellectual level to resist facing their feelings.

Helpers frequently ignore the milder forms of resistance, since these forms are protection for the helpee against intense feeling experiences. As the trust level develops, however, resistance tends to diminish. Helpers, therefore, need to focus on building the trust level of their interviews and must ask what in their own behavior might be contributing to helpee resistance. Examples would be demanding questions, judgmental attitudes, and high expectations. For a long time, professional helpers thought that reluctance of helpees to get involved or to change was a problem residing in the helpee. Current thinking places much responsibility for overcoming resistance on the helper also. Helpers should ask themselves, "What am I doing, or not doing, that contributes to the helpee's reluctance?"

Think for a moment about relationships in which you were the helpee. What was it like for you to ask for help? What did you feel? Was it easy or hard? What factors enabled you to overcome your resistance? Now think about the present prospects of going to a helping service. What are you experiencing? List the reasons why you would not want to get involved. This experience will provide a basis for understanding the nature of resistance.

The helper should realize some of the realities of a new relationship:

1. It is not easy to receive help.

2. It is difficult to commit oneself to change.

3. It is difficult to submit to the influence of a helper; help is a threat to esteem, integrity, and independence.

4. It is not easy to trust strangers and to be open with them.

5. It is not easy to see one's problem clearly at first.

6. Sometimes problems seem too large, too overwhelming, or too unique to share them easily.

7. Some cultural traditions deprecate giving and receiving help outside the family.

To assist helpees to determine their readiness for a helping relationship, helpers need to remind themselves that before a helping process can begin effectively the following conditions in helpees need to prevail:

1. Awareness of feelings of distress.

2. Desire for a change from the present painful situation or annoying behavior. (They want to help themselves.)

3. Awareness of the potentials and limitations of a helping relationship.

4. Voluntary desire to see a helper.

Setting.   The setting has something to do with ease of starting a relationship. This is an individual matter and should be an honest reflection of helper style. The clothes of the helper, the appearance and decor of the room, and the opening conversation should reflect the helper's nature and style. Most helpers agree with the obvious suggestion that distractions and interruptions should be eliminated, but here again helping can take place anywhere. The traditional formal office may even be a detriment, although it is a common setting for many helping relationships.

Even the distance of the chairs, assuming the helping is conducted while sitting, should be such that it facilitates communication and comfort. Distance between chairs generally varies during the interview depending on the involvement and comfort felt by the participants. Some work best "eyeball to eyeball," whereas other helpees are threatened by close physical proximity. They need the "safety" of a few feet of space. Although these are comparatively trivial considerations, the helper needs to perceive the implications of the setting for accomplishing the goals of the interview.

Opening an Informal Relationship

Inexperienced helpers often approach a relationship with some anxiety. If you haven't thought much about this topic before, it would be productive to imagine yourself being interviewed and note the qualities the interviewer exhibited to start the relationship off well. While it is difficult to make general rules about opening a helping relationship, the following guidelines should help to ease the early minutes of that first contact.

1. *Hello.* A greeting of some kind is a suggested natural starter since it affirms the presence and acknowledges the worth of the other person. A pleasant greeting also begins the relationship on grounds familiar to the helpee.

2. *Why Are You Here?* If the contact is helpee-initiated, he or she will begin usually by saying why your help is sought. If the helpee does not start, then a simple request to "Tell me why you are here" or "How can I help you?" suffices. Note that the lead is vague so as to allow helpees to pick it up any way they wish. Do not imply that they have a problem or that they have come into some kind of clinical setting where they are expected to act in a certain way. In less formal helping situations, even more natural conversational openers would be effective. When the helper has initiated the interview, an honest opening statement regarding why the person was asked to come is appropriate. Reticent helpees may need more encouragement to talk. Suggestions along this line follow later in this chapter under stages of the formal interview. More ideas on starting relationships are presented under leading skills in Chapter 4.

Stage 2: Clarification

The goals of this stage are to clarify helpee statements of why they want help and to get a better feel for how helpees see their problems and general life situations. It is not necessary to assume that all helpees come with defined "problems," a general descriptive term for helpee concern.

Use of Questions.   It is a common tactical error of helpers at this point to begin asking questions. Helpees often feel interrogated, and, as a result, threatened. They may perceive this interview as a problem-solving session in which, if all the facts were brought out, the solutions would be apparent or forthcoming from the wisdom of the helper. Asking questions reinforces the kind of "help set" that physicians model when symptoms and complaints are described to them. Physicians usually offer a diagnosis after such elaborate questioning. The history and diagnoses are followed with suggestions and prescriptions. Our goal in psychological help is to discourage this passive-receptive set by resisting the temptation to ask many questions and mainly by active listening and by reflecting the feelings expressed by the helpee. We try to suspend judgments and to limit diagnostic thinking, especially in the early stages, although as indicated in the experience list of Figure 3-2, the helper is thinking about the experiential world of the helpee and is trying to get into his or her perceptual framework much of the time. *Diagnosis* is an important step in some kinds of specialized helping with very disturbed people, but within the framework of helping described in this book it has no place.

The helper encourages helpees to elaborate and clarify their statements about the nature and kinds of help they seek. This process is not belabored, however, because helpees often do not know *why* they want help. Frequently, they are aware only of some behaviors and external conditions that make them uncomfortable, ineffective, angry, or anxious. Sometimes they are aware only of vague feelings of discomfort. It is not fruitful, therefore, to ask "why" questions, even though this tactic is tempting. It is so easy, for example, to engage in a questioning routine around "Why do you feel this way? Why did you do that? Why don't you try...?" It is more productive to keep helpees focused on both feeling and cognitive levels by dealing with "what" questions; for example, "What are you feeling right now? What is going on in you? What did you do?" usually are productive questions that keep the helpee exploring his or her thoughts and feelings.

"How" questions can also help clarify issues. For example, the helper might say, "How does that suggestion help?" "How do you feel right now about this interview?" "How does your wife's behavior affect you?" Helpees can amplify such topics in their own way and clarify and focus their responses at the same time. Additional ideas on questioning strategies may be found in the Suggestions for Further Study section at the end of this chapter.

Where Do We Go from Here?   Informal relationships ebb and flow with the natural inclinations of the two persons, although the general goal is to keep the helpee talking about personal concerns with as few questions as possible from the helper. Helpees are encouraged to move in their own ways and discuss topics they choose while the helper listens actively according to the methods detailed in the next chapter. In the meantime there are only two thoughts in the mind of the helper: What is going on in this person's world right now? How does this person see his or her life now? This stance aids in achieving the understanding goals of that first contact. Our sincere interest in the helpee's story is a way of showing concern and caring for the other person also.

If the helping relationship shades into a more formal interview, then other considerations need to be faced, such as: What are our goals? What are my obligations and responsibilities to this other person? What is my role as a helper? How much time can I agree to give? What is the nature of the helping contract between us? These questions set the stage for the detailed process discussion to follow.

Planning the Helping Process.   As the helping process proceeds through Stage 2, much information is being gathered about helpees and their world-views. While the questions cited above are not designed to diagnose the person's problems or give them a label, they elicit information useful in planning what to do next and where to go for the remaining stages in the helping process. In formal helping settings this is called *treatment planning.* In informal helping settings, the focus is on what the helpee continues to experience in the present. There is less attention on where the process is going in the future. The process flows along naturally.

A few general principles are gleaned from a formal planning procedure to assist the helper toward a more productive helping process. The alternative to planning is trusting the helper's intuitive moment-to-moment judgments about what to do next. Often this approach is reliable, but for most of us planning helps to prevent problems, especially if several people are involved. With threats of possible litigation, even for informal helpers, it seems prudent to have a rationale for one's helping process.

A key part of the plan is to have a clear conception of the process, such as the stages listed in this chapter. These stages, while variable from person to person, are a kind of road map through the process. If the stages appear to fit this particular helpee, then they become process goals and steps in the plan. In addition, the planning of the helping process includes attention to helpee goals. Early in Stage 2—clarification—it becomes apparent why the person wants help and what he or she wants from the helper. When the helpee's goals become clear, these can be summarized and reflected back to him or her. These goals then become part of the helping plan and are used, not only as guidelines through the process, but as indicators when to stop helping as goals are reached.

Helpers should be alert to the obvious possibility that the helpee's goals will change in the process and that the helping process plan will need to be adapted to these revised goals. For more information about details of planning in more structured helping relationships see Seligman (1986) in the Suggestions for Further Study section at the end of this chapter.

Ownership of Problems.   Another consideration at this opening level of problem statements is to assist helpees in determining who "owns" the problem. Is the problem that of the helpee exclusively, such as feeling depressed? Is the problem owned by two people involved in a relationship, or does it merely appear to belong to two people when it actually belongs to only one of them? For example, a parent may come for help with his or her child. The parent then talks mainly about the child, but actually the parent owns the problem because he or she feels the concern; the child does not. Or perhaps a teacher refers a child to a school counselor "for help." It soon becomes apparent that the teacher is the helpee because he or she has the problem, not the child. Stage 2 goals, then, are to make clear who the principal helpee is and to clarify the helpee's reasons for coming or being referred.

Perceiving problems clearly is crucial to continuing a helping relationship. Helpees do not continue the counseling if they think that the helper did not hear their concern or perceive their problem accurately (Epperson, Bushway, and Warman, 1983). So, if the goal of the helper is to see the person again in a helping relationship, it is important that helpers communicate clearly to their helpees that they understand the problem and the goals for which they will work.

Stage 3: Structure

As helpees explain their reasons for seeking help, or helpers explain why they are offering help, the principal question becomes, What are the conditions under which the relationship will work? The goal for Stage 3 is to decide whether to proceed with the relationship and, if so, on what terms. To reach that goal, the following sequence of questions must be answered, at least tentatively, by the two parties of the helping relationship:

Helper Questions

1. Am I able to work with this person? (skills, knowledge)
2. Do I want to work with this person? (comfort, compatibility)
3. Can I meet his or her expectations? (given my skills and knowledge)
4. What kind of structure do we need to proceed? (informal understanding, counseling contract, leave the issue open)
5. What am I expecting of this person? (time, place, effort, commitment, responsibility)

Helpee Questions

1. Is this a person I can trust?
2. Will this person be helpful on my terms?
3. What will the helper's terms be?
4. Will this relationship get me more involved than I want to be?
5. Am I willing to commit myself to a relationship agreement on the other's terms, or will we work it out together?
6. If I agree to a "contract" to do specific things, can I get out if I want to?

Stage 3 structures vary considerably in complexity and formality; however, most helping relationships are formed at a very informal level where either

person may withdraw easily at any time. Neither person has a very firm commitment to the other, as in casual friendships. People handling crisis center
phones and interviews, for example, do not quibble about the niceties of relationship building. They deal with the current crisis. Structuring questions such
as the above are worked out later if a relationship is indicated. Helpers who
take their work seriously feel the need for more commitment and structure,
yet they want to maintain a close informal relationship with the helpee. Most
helpers, therefore, engage in a process called *structuring*.

Structuring the Relationship.   Structuring defines the nature, limits, and
goals of the prospective helping relationship. During this process the roles,
responsibilities, and possible commitments of both helpee and helper are outlined. The helper generally indicates the steps to reach the helpee's goals so
that both have a clearer idea of where they are going and about how long it
will take. This does not mean that the process is planned and that it is precisely predictable, but there are enough general principles and fairly predictable stages for helping relationships to give helpers a rough idea. Helpees
should know where they are (type of agency and type of help offered), who
the helper is (qualifications, limitations), why they are there (purpose of the
interview), and what their option for future choices may be. If these points
are not made clear in the referral process, the agency brochure, or the opening comments of Stage 1, they need to be faced before proceeding. Helping
specialists often are required by law to give this preliminary information as
part of their professional disclosure statement. This level of structuring is often
called an informal contract when both parties agree.

One view of structuring indicates that structure is implicit and that it
evolves naturally; therefore, it need not be discussed formally. Helpers must
develop their own styles, and they must be flexible in adapting to different
helpee circumstances. The main point here is that attention must be paid to
the understanding of why this particular helping relationship exists. Lack of
such structure may precipitate unnecessary anxiety in the helpee because the
relationship is too ambiguous. On the other hand, the anxiety level of the
helper may be so high that a compulsive need to structure frequently is felt.

Some of the advantages of agreements on structure are that the *time* to
be spent will be clear, both for the first interview and for the total process.
Any *fees* involved should be discussed frankly at this stage. *Action limits* can
be discussed when an incident takes place. In working with young children,
for example, it may be necessary to point out that they can attack the toys or
say anything they wish, but they cannot attack the people present. *Role limits*
are usually discussed in the early stages because roles may be contradictory.
One may offer help unconditionally on the one hand, yet one may exercise
some kind of judgmental authority over the helpee on the other hand. An
example is the teacher who is often in the position of helper but who also
exercises authority over the students. Many agency workers who administer

public programs are in similar positions. These are called dual relationships and will be discussed in Chapter 7.

Structure Helpee Behavior.   If help is to proceed efficiently and constructively, helpees must accept their share of responsibility for the interview, and they must know how to express themselves in a manner that allows the helper to be most effective. In other words, in Stage 3 they must learn how to be good helpees. Examples of such process values and norms are that present feelings are important data to bring out, that talking about oneself freely and honestly is expected and accepted, that taking responsibility for any choices and actions is necessary, and that, although the interview may start on a vague and ragged note, things become more specific and clear as the interview progresses. Much of this process structure comes out naturally from events in the interview, and much comes from the helper's effective modeling of these behaviors. The exact form of these process norms depends largely on the helper's theoretical view of the helping process—again, a reason for considering seriously one's own theory. The nature and timing of structuring are controversial issues among helpers. The range of possible views on process structure has been presented here so helpers can experiment and develop the style most effective for them.

Formal Contracts.   Helpers inclined toward a more behavioral approach to the helping process speak of a formal event in Stage 3, called the *contract*. This is an agreement between the helper and helpee that they will work toward certain goals, that each will carry out specific responsibilities to achieve the goals, and that certain specific outcomes will be taken as evidence that the help was successful. An example is the helpee who sees his or her problem as one of making a career change. The helpees agree to seek certain kinds of information, to keep a log of homework on planning, and to consider the helping process successful when they arrive at three options for choice with confirming and limiting data for each choice. In a more interpersonal problem area, such as excessive shyness, a helpee may agree to spend about ten hours with the helper and follow a prescribed set of exercises possibly involving relaxation methods, trying assertive social behaviors, and agreeing to make two new acquaintances each week. The helping interviews then are devoted to discussing the helpee's feelings about the homework tryouts, learning new skills, revising goals, and looking at evidence of progress. Chapter 6 includes more detail on formal and informal contracting techniques.

Stage 4: Relationship

The discussion on structure and contracts assumes that the decision has been made to give a formal helping relationship an extended test. The goal of Stage 4 is to increase the depth of the relationship and the intensity of helpee commitment. It is understood clearly that either the helper or the helpee may bring up the possibility of terminating the relationship by mutual agreement. Stages 1 through 3 usually take place in the first contact so that helpees know when they leave what will happen next and what is expected of them if the relationship is to continue. During this time also increasing trust and openness have deepened the relationship. By the end of Stage 4, the relationship should be firmly established and the helpee should be ready to work specifically toward goals announced upon his or her arrival.

Silence.   The function of the pause, or silence, is of concern at all stages, but it is of particular significance in the relationship and exploratory stages. Pauses have many meanings that require different handling. Helpees may stop talking as a resistive act because they don't feel comfortable about revealing themselves further. The trust level may not be sufficiently strong, as indicated by awkward glancing about, flushing, and abrupt changes of topic. If this hunch turns out to be valid, then further discussion of the relationship between helper and helpee is indicated.

A pause may mean the helpee is temporarily stopped in the ongoing exploration. Helpees appear preoccupied with their thoughts and sometimes distressed, mainly because they feel blocked in their desire to go on. They may need some quiet time alone to pull their feelings together before they explore further. This is often a very productive time, and the most helpful thing to do is to wait quietly until the helpee is ready to go on. Sometimes, inner struggles take place during these silent periods which may last several minutes; occasionally the helpee will emerge with a significant insight or expression of feeling.

A pause may mean the helpee has come to the end of a thought or discussion unit. Helping interviews are characterized by these natural pauses, much like conversation. The helper and helpee then work out a new topic direction. The helpee, for example, may mention several things on his or her mind, and the helper responds with silence or attention to one item, thus starting a new topic. The helper's attention has a rewarding effect that encourages the helpee to explore that new topic further. The helper may suggest several possibilities from which the helpee chooses. Usually this is a natural process with attention by both helper and helpee to the nonverbal cues of the other.

Stage 5: Exploration

In this working stage the helper becomes more active and assertive. During the first stages helpers are attempting, through listening, clarifying, and structuring methods, to understand how their helpees see themselves and their worlds. The helpee has been taking the lead. By Stage 5, the helper has a clearer grasp of who the helpee is, what is wanted, and how help can be given. There are two key questions at this exploration stage: What changes in helpees' behavior are appropriate and needed to achieve their goals? What strategies for intervention will most likely produce these outcomes? The term *intervention* is used commonly in formal helping circles to designate techniques that helpers initiate.

It should be noted, however, that the term *intervention* has two different levels of intensity in the helping field. The most common definition of intervention is any intentional act or technique the helper uses to initiate change in the helping process. A simple confrontation question or homework assignment could be an intervention. The second meaning is primarily in the drug and alcohol field, and indicates a meeting called to confront an individual who is evidencing some harmful addictive behaviors. This is a one-time, intense session, usually resulting in admittance to a treatment facility. For the purposes of this book, we are using the former definition.

What is done at this stage and beyond is tailored to the kind of problem the helpee brings, whether primarily planning, problem solving, interpersonal conflict, or intrapersonal feeling problems. The methods of intervention described in the following chapters are designed to give the helper a wide spectrum of skills and strategies that can be applied selectively to specific helpee problems and expected outcomes. The specific *process goals* for the helper at this exploratory stage, however, are as follows:

1. Maintain and enhance the relationship (trust, ease, safety).
2. Deal with feelings in helper and helpee that interfere with progress toward their goals (examine resistance).
3. Encourage the helpee to explore problems or feelings further (clarify, amplify, illustrate, specify), so helpee's self-awareness is expanded.
4. Encourage helpees to clarify and further specify their goals.
5. Gather necessary facts that will contribute to the solution of helpee problems.
6. Decide to continue or terminate the relationship.
7. Teach skills required to reach helpee goals (demonstrating, modeling, coaching).
8. Initiate helpee homework activities that move them toward their goals (tryout, evaluation, progress).

In the exploratory stage helpees tend to turn inward while describing feelings and delineating problems. This tendency is expected, but the helpee should understand that exploration of feelings and problems is primarily a prelude to action for the consolidation and planning stages. Here helpees move outside themselves once again toward putting their expanded awareness and new insights into action plans.

Sometimes helpees feel so good after the exploratory stage that they think their problems are solved. Some helpers think this is the time to terminate, and it may well be an appropriate time; but this may merely be a good feeling or relief of tension with no specific behavior change in sight. This condition is a critical point in a helping relationship because the goals and process still may be so unclear that the helpee thinks it is over. This is likely to take place in grief problems, for example.

Another critical point in the exploratory stage arrives when helpees who are involved in extensive exploration of their feelings experience discouragement. They may want to terminate the relationship out of sheer exhaustion and disillusionment with the process. At this point discussion of their feelings is appropriate, followed by several options: (1) reduce the intensity of exploration by moving to another topic; (2) continue exploring feelings in greater depth; or (3) terminate exploration with this helper and consider building a relationship with another. The third option is especially appropriate when the helper's discomfort with intense feelings becomes apparent.

Another issue is how assertive helpers should be. In the early stages helpers usually are fairly unassertive, and they encourage helpees to explore on their own initiative. Helpee responsibility for the direction and content of the interview is emphasized by helpers of all theoretical views and styles. As the process lengthens and moves closer to the planning and action stages, helpers generally become more active partners and use all their helping skills of informing, suggesting, and interpreting. Helpees should not be pressured to continue, however, and should feel free to leave.

Transference and Countertransference Feelings. As a result of increasing intensity of interaction, helpees experience specific feelings toward helpers that they may have felt only vaguely in the early stages. These feelings range widely from admiring and affectionate to angry and rejecting. Some reactions may be due to specific behaviors of the helper, but it is more likely that a condition called *transference* is taking place. This reaction is a common event in all human relationships where feelings once felt toward someone close to us are now projected onto the immediate helper. Examples are feelings about a parent carried over from childhood. Helpees may see their fathers symbolically in the helper, who now has a position of some authority and power, and they may respond to the helper in the same way they responded to their fathers in earlier years.

Helpees are unaware, of course, that transference is a likely explanation for their feelings. Unless this phenomenon is understood and discussed, much effort is expended that is not related to the problem at hand. A frank discussion of authority problems growing out of the present relationship between the helper and helpee could become a growth experience; helper judgment and the specific goals for the particular relationship affect how transference problems are dealt with. When discussing a planning problem with a helpee, for example, it would be inappropriate to spend the limited time talking about transference feelings. It is important to realize, however, that they exist.

Helpers similarly may have strong reactions toward their helpees, which come from the helpers' unresolved personal relationships. This is called *countertransference*. For example, a helper may see the helpee as an ungrateful child. Helpers too may be unaware of the source of their own feelings of annoyance or discomfort with a particular helpee. They may get sleepy, have difficulty attending, tighten up, sympathize with the helpee, or become argumentative.

To understand countertransference events we suggest you take some time here to recall incidents when you were talking with or interviewing another person. What in your behavior surprised or embarrassed you, such as lapses of attention or yawning? Did you find yourself becoming irritable or angry with the helpee? Of course, you may have had cause to be angry or been very fatigued, but why at that moment and with that person? What happened outside the interview to remind you of that person, such as dreaming about him or her? In severe form we may want to avoid other people who make demands on us.

The important question is not whether countertransference occurs, but what helpers can do about it. If they view these behaviors as signals of unresolved difficulties in their own lives, they can take care of the matter by discussing this possibility briefly with the helpees, so they know at least that the problem resides more in the helper than in their relationship. This honesty should help to resolve some emotional difficulties in the present relationship. For the long term, however, such helpers should think about a personal growth experience for themselves to expand their own awareness and to change their behaviors. Discussing the matter with colleagues is one possible solution. Studying videotapes of one's work with the help of a colleague and reflecting on what one sees there is another. Finally, a personal counseling or encounter group experience where helpers can explore their feelings, obtain feedback on their behavior, and try out new forms of responding may be an answer.

Helping, especially in its more formal aspects of counseling and psychotherapy, is a powerful interpersonal influence process (Corrigan, Dell, Lewis, & Schmidt, 1980). Strong's early studies (1968) showed that helpers who present themselves as attractive and trustworthy experts are much more influential with helpees than those who do not present themselves as experts. Helpers, in turn, react in a variety of ways when helpees treat them as influential experts. Since you, as a helper, must be aware of your style of response on this issue, it would be productive to stop at this point and get in touch with your views on expertise. How do you respond to experts in any field when you choose to consult them? Identify your basic feelings about experts and authorities. What role does trustworthiness play for you? How do you measure up to your own criteria for trustworthiness? How do you respond when others treat you as an expert? Identify your basic feelings about being treated as an expert. To what extent do you judge your self-inventory of these feelings as facilitative or nonfacilitative in a helping relationship?

Stage 6: Consolidation

Whereas the bulk of the helping time usually is spent in the work of Stage 5, the task of settling on alternative choices and plans or of practicing the new skills is an important part of the helping process. That inevitable point comes when helpees must decide or act and stop talking about themselves, their problems, or their possible plans. This consolidation stage flows from the exploratory and blends into the planning stage to follow, but its distinctive process goals are to further clarify feelings, pin down alternative actions, and practice new skills.

Occasionally helpees are so committed to their tasks and have been through the exploratory stages so many times before that they move quickly to the consolidation and planning stages. In such cases, the bulk of the time is spent in decision making and planning.

Stage 7: Planning

This stage is characterized by rational planning processes where plans for termination and continuing alone are formulated. The process goals for this stage are to crystallize discussions of earlier stages into a specific plan of action and to decide that growth has proceeded to the point where termination of the relationship is indicated. Any tag ends of feelings are worked through, and bringing up new topics with feelings is discouraged. In helping processes that are heavily cognitive, such as career-planning interviews, this stage becomes quite lengthy since many action steps to accomplish the plan need to be formulated. For example, if the helping relationship has been focused on career transitions, it may be time to write a new resume and actually make appointments with future employers.

The discussion of Stages 6 and 7 has been comparatively brief since the strategies and methods most used in these stages are presented in Chapters 4 through 6.

Stage 8: Termination

Termination is a process that occurs at the end of each session and at the end of the helping relationship. The elements of each are similar. In this stage accomplishments toward the goals are summarized and progress is evaluated. If the goals were not achieved, hypotheses as to why they were not realized are made and discussed.

Termination can occur in many ways, and helpers must develop their individual techniques. Summarizing the process as indicated above is one effective method. A helpful procedure is to ask the helpee to summarize. If a number of plans were made or steps decided, a written summary developed jointly will help. Keeping the conversation at an intellectual level tends to discourage further exploration of feeling. If the process has involved several interviews, then spreading the last couple of contacts over a longer time span will tend to de-escalate the involvement. Reference to the agreed time limits along with the summary facilitates termination. In terminating the relationship, *referral* may be indicated if the helpee feels a sense of incompleteness and the helper is reluctant to continue the relationship. Leaving the door open for the possible follow-ups may make the termination less abrupt. Frequently in agencies such as schools or businesses, the helper may want to maintain a kind of *standby relationship* to observe and occasionally facilitate the helpee's further development.

Leave-taking is not the problem that is usually anticipated if the stages discussed have unfolded satisfactorily. There is a natural awareness that "this is the end." Helpees usually are eager to leave since they feel good about their new autonomy, plans, or solutions. Occasionally they even harbor some feelings of resentment (usually projected to the helper) that they needed help in the first place. Feelings of gratitude are expressed sometimes, but the helper should be wary of these since the goal was to have helpees feel that they solved their own problems. To have grateful helpees, though, expands the self-esteem of the helper. Sometimes helpees have lingering dependency feelings expressed as reluctance to leave. They bring up "just one more thing" or prolong the goodbye ceremony excessively. Some helpees literally need to be led out the door. Helpers may prolong the termination process too out of fears of separation or need for completeness. Helpers are usually comfortable with "hellos," but often they find appropriate "good-byes" uncomfortable. Helpers need to deal with their own grief after putting so much emotional energy into the helping relationship.

A Process Dilemma

In this chapter on the helping process a wide range of issues was discussed. Such a chapter presents a dilemma. On the one extreme are those helpers who say the helping process evolves. You do what comes naturally, as in developing a friendship; you trust your feelings since there are no specific cognitive guidelines. At the other extreme are those helpers who view the process as a highly structured enterprise that can be described in terms of precise objectives, steps, methodologies, and outcomes. The middle position presented here incorporates elements from diverse theoretical views about how the helping process works within the context of everyday helping events.

Outcomes Self-Check

You can now (1) list key dimensions of a helping relationship; (2) describe and illustrate the general sequence of events in the helping process as the helper and helpee experience these events; (3) identify eight stages in the helping process from entry to termination and cite examples of typical issues that must be faced at each stage. The principal outcome expected is that you have begun to develop your own "cognitive map" of the helping process, which is useful to you in facing the numerous issues of facilitating a helping relationship. The final test of your mastery of this chapter is your capacity to demonstrate your ability to initiate, maintain, and terminate a helping relationship that leads to specific helpee goals.

Suggestions for Further Study

Brammer, L., Abrego, E., and Shostorm, P. *Therapeutic Counseling and Psychotheraphy.* 6th ed. Englewood Cliffs, NJ: Prentice Hall, 1993. (Ch. 4 on process steps and critical points in the counseling process.)

Corliss, R., and Rabe, P. *Psychotherapy from the Center: A Humanistic View of Change and Growth.* Scranton, PA: International Textbook, 1969. (A humanistic view of the process, especially Ch. 2 on starting, Ch. 5 on growth, Ch. 6 on termination.)

Fong, M. L., and Cox, B. G. Trust as an underlying dynamic in the counseling process: How clients test trust. *The Personnel and Guidance Journal* (1983):163–166.

Ivey, A., Ivey, M., and Simek-Downing, L. *Counseling and Psychotherapy: Integrating Skills, Theories and Practice.* 2nd ed. Englewood Cliffs, NJ: Prentice Hall, 1987. (An overview of theories of counseling, description of the intentional counselor, and practical suggestions for helping.)

Kanfer, F., and Goldstein, A. *Helping People Change.* 4th ed. Boston: Allyn & Bacon, 1992. (A collection of papers on practical aspects of a helping relationship.)

Krumboltz, J. D., and Thoreson, C. E., Eds. *Counseling Methods.* New York: Holt, Rinehart & Winston, 1976. (A collection of articles on the helping process from a behavioral viewpoint.)

Long, L., Paradise, L., and Long, T. *Questioning Skills for the Helping Process.* Pacific Grove, CA: Brooks/Cole, 1981. (Suggestions for asking questions in an interview.)

Martin, D. *Learning-Based Client-Centered Therapy.* Pacific Grove, CA: Brooks/Cole, 1972. (An approach to the helping process based on a blend of behavioral and client-centered views.)

Seligman, L. *Diagnosis and Treatment Planning in Counseling.* New York:

Human Sciences Press, 1986. (Suggestions for planning a formal helping process.)

Watkins, C. E., & Terrell, F. Mistrust leveland and its effects on counseling expectations in Black client-White counselor relationships: An analogue study. *Journal of Counseling Psychology* 35 (1988):194–197.

Zaro, J., et al. *A Guide for Beginning Psychotherapists*. New York: Cambridge Press, 1977. (An introduction to many issues of consultation and counseling, addressed to the beginner.)

4

Helpers Skills
for Understanding

This chapter focuses on skills that promote understanding of self and others. These skills fall into seven clusters:

1. Listening skills
   Attending—noting verbal and nonverbal behaviors
   Paraphrasing—responding to basic messages
   Clarifying—self-disclosing and focusing discussion
   Perception checking—determining accuracy of hearing
2. Leading skills
   Indirect leading—getting started
   Direct leading—encouraging and elaborating discussion
   Focusing—controlling confusion, diffusion, and vagueness
   Questioning—conducting open and closed inquiries
3. Reflecting skills
   Reflecting feelings—responding to feelings
   Reflecting experience—responding to total experience
   Reflecting content—repeating ideas in fresh words or for emphasis
4. Confronting skills
   Recognizing feelings in oneself—being aware of helper experience
   Describing and sharing feelings—modeling feeling expression
   Feeding back opinions—reacting honestly to helpee expressions
   Self-confrontation
5. Interpreting skills
   Interpretive questions—facilitating awareness
   Fantasy and metaphor—symbolizing ideas and feelings

6. Informing skills
   Advising—giving suggestions and opinions based on experience
   Informing—giving valid information based on expertise
7. Summarizing skills
   Pulling themes together

Outcomes You Can Expect

The outcomes you can expect from studying this chapter are competencies to (1) identify seven helping skills that contribute to self-understanding; (2) cite subskills in each skill cluster and give examples from helping interviews; and, with practice, (3) use seven basic skill clusters effectively in helping relationships.

The final criterion of success will be your demonstrated performance of the skills such that the helpee feels understood and confirms this feeling with appropriate verbal or nonverbal behavior. You may expect helpees to respond positively to you when they feel you understand them. You can expect that they will talk about themselves and you more freely. They will share their new understandings with you. Later, you may expect helpees to try to change themselves or their circumstances on the basis of their new understandings, skills, and changed environments.

Rationale for Skills Training

The skills described here and in Chapters 5 and 6 are based on the idea that, by learning the components of a skill, one can then put them together into a complex performance. By looking at specific helping skills, we can explain the total interview interaction. This approach, described in more detail in Chapter 7, is known as microskills training and is analogous to skills training in a sport such as golf, in which one learns the fundamental skills of stance, grip, and swing. Research supports the validity of this approach, but the principal problem is putting the components together into a smooth, flowing, and natural performance (Ivey, 1994). The integration of these skills is essential for helpful interpersonal interaction in fields ranging from education to health sciences to management sciences (Levasseur, 1991).

Skill Cluster 1: Listening

At first glance the term *listening* implies a passive act of taking in the content of the helpee's communication, but actually it involves a very *active* process of responding to total messages. It includes not only listening with your ears to helpee words and with your eyes to your helpee's body language, but a total kind of perceptiveness best described by Reik's (1948) phrase "listening with the third ear." It means also that we are silent much of the time and that the helpees talk. When helpers can answer in considerable detail the question, What is going on in this person right now and in his or her life space? they are listening with all their perceptual capacities. Listening skills are basic to all interviewing whether the purpose be for gaining information, conducting structured in-depth interviews, or helping informally.

Attending

Attending has several components, which have been studied intensively by Ivey (1994) and others. It is important initially to emphasize the cultural context of these skills. Each culture, for example, places its own norms and meanings on eye contact and distance. In a Middle Eastern setting public eye-to-eye contact is permitted between two men but not between a man and a woman; sustained eye contact is considered offensive to some Native American groups. Helpee nonverbal behavior should be watched for signs of stress or discomfort when eye contact is made. The following descriptions of attending skills are based largely on experiences with middle-class Americans and should be adapted with care to other cultural settings.

The first component we will consider is *contact,* principally through the eye. Looking at other people, usually at their eyes, is a way of indicating intense interest in them, because eyes are one of our key vehicles for communicating. This does not mean that eye contact must be a fixed stare to be effective. If the helper is honestly interested and at ease, he or she will look naturally at the helpee while the person is talking. Simply writing about eye contact does not do justice to the power of the eyes to communicate caring and understanding as well as to maintain attention. Think of your own experience when someone looked at you intensively. Sometimes it was done in a vacuous way just to hold your attention. At other times the person said with his or her eyes in a warm way, "Look at me; I hear you; I understand," so that you felt the person genuinely cared about you and understood how you were feeling. At the same time the helper is picking up nonverbal messages from the helpee's eyes.

Distance between helper and helpee needs experimentation before the most comfortable distance for the two is discovered. Some helpees are very uncomfortable, for example, if the space is less than three feet or so, because they are so socially conditioned against close contact. In American culture a comfortable helping distance is three or four feet.

A second element of attending is *posture.* Usually, the interested helper leans slightly toward the helpee in a relaxed manner. Relaxation is important because tenseness tends to shift the focus from the helpee to the helper, in addition to provoking an empathic tension response in the helpee.

A third related element of attending is *gesture.* The helper communicates much with body movements. If helpers flail wildly with their hands, or if they cross them over their chests in a pontifical manner, they will very likely communicate some unintended messages. Try to be aware of the messages your gestures and posture send to helpees. Are the messages ones you intend to communicate?

The helper's *verbal* behavior, a fourth attending component, relates to what the helpee has said. The helper does not ask questions, take the topic in a new direction, or add to the helpee's meaning, but the helper might, for example, mention a word or reflect a phrase from the statements of the helpee to focus further on an idea. Some confirming, yet not too personal, comment such as, "I see what you mean," "I can appreciate what you went through," or "That certainly seems to tie things together," often helps to keep helpees exploring and assures them that you are listening. Verbal attending behavior has the effect of encouraging a helpee to keep talking. Often a simple comment "hmm" or "oh" paired with an empathic facial expression will facilitate this.

Why does attending behavior work so well? It is very rewarding according to studies, and helpees like it. The effect on helpees of attending behavior is to encourage them to verbalize their ideas or feelings freely. It has a powerful *reinforcing effect,* in other words. It rewards helpees' communications and tends to build a sense of responsibility for the interview. This is one difference between helping and conversation; in social interaction there is more give and take of opinions, questions, and feelings. Conversely, *selective inattention* by the helper can serve to discourage further exploration of the topic. For example, the helpee may be on a rambling intellectual description of an historical event. You may think it more productive to have him focus on how he feels now about that event, so you attend when he focuses on feelings and ignore him when he is on a story-telling trip. You can see how controlling attending behavior can be. Helpees control helpers, too, by giving them verbalizations that hold their attention.

If a helper is relaxed, the helpee will tend to be more at ease also. One of the most difficult tasks for the beginning helper is to let helpees tell their stories without profuse questioning and jumping from topic to topic in a tense manner.

Attending behavior, furthermore, is a kind of "fail-safe" method for opening an interview because it furthers the goals of helpee self-exploration and minimizes the chances of making destructive interventions. Even if an awkward silence takes place, the helper can acknowledge what has just been stated or refer to some earlier comments.

Taking notes during a helping interview is a controversial issue, since notetaking reduces attending behavior. Any notes deemed necessary to maintain continuity or meet legal requirements should be made immediately after the interview. Helpers who feel compelled to take notes during the helping interview should make the effort sparse and unobtrusive so as not to disturb the flow and continuity of eye contact. The main case made for note-taking is that it demonstrates intense interest in what the helpee is saying and that it facilitates recall. Time between helping contacts often is insufficient to write adequate notes. In any case, the helper should be very forthright with the helpee about why notes are taken and what their disposition will be. One of the advantages of helpers who are not members of a formal professional group is less constraint to take notes for legal protection.

The following list is a summary of guidelines for effective attending behavior:

1. Establish *contact* through looking at helpees when they talk.

2. Maintain a *natural relaxed posture* that indicates your interest.

3. Use *natural gestures* that communicate your intended messages.

4. Use *verbal statements* that relate to helpee statements without interruptions, questions, or new topics.

Paraphrasing

Paraphrasing is a method of restating the helpee's basic message in similar, but usually fewer, words. The main purpose of paraphrasing is for helpers to test their understanding of what the helpee has said. (It is a practical test of your attending too!) A second purpose is to communicate to helpees that you are trying to understand their basic message and, if successful, that you have followed their verbal explorations. A paraphrase executed to the helpee's satisfaction is one objective definition of understanding.

The helper translates raw perceptions of what the helpee is saying into more precise wording, repeating only the helpee's message without adding any new ideas. To help in this process helpers should ask themselves constantly, What is this person's basic thinking and feeling message to me? The helper, at the time of a natural break in the flow of ideas and feelings, summarizes concisely what has been expressed. Usually the paraphrase has heavy cognitive content, although it includes feelings if these are an important part of the helpee's message. Helpers should look for some cues that their paraphrasing has been helpful. Examples of paraphrasing are:

HE: I really think he is a very nice guy; he's so thoughtful, sensitive, and kind. He calls me a lot. He's fun to go out with.

HR: You like him very much, then.

HE: I do, very much.

HE: I just don't understand. One minute she tells me to do this, and the next minute to do that.

HR: She really confuses you.

HE: Yeah, she sure does, and besides. . . .

Paraphrasing is especially helpful in exposing and clarifying the mixed or double message. When people apparently do not want to make a direct statement about feelings, they couch their statements in obscure language. The task of the helper is to pick up the two messages from both verbal and nonverbal cues and restate them in clear form. If this restatement does not result in increased understanding by helpees, then confrontational methods where the discrepancy is pointed out more directly may be appropriate. An example is:

HE: I really love my wife. She does many things for me constantly. She looks after my clothes, and she keeps track of where I am all the time because she says she's worried about me.

HR: You appreciate your wife's attentiveness; but I detect in your tone resentment over the constant attention she is showing.

HE: Yes. I have feelings both ways about her attention, I guess.

One problem in using paraphrasing and other listening component skills is that, if helpers are not careful, they develop a highly stylized way of responding that may annoy helpees. Helpers may say repeatedly, for example, "I hear you saying. . . ." Paraphrasing seems a bit artificial at first until the helper experiences some encouraging responses from the helpee. After a while it feels like a more natural form of communication than the usual questions, opinions, veiled threats, or bland conversation fillers.

Helpees feel understood as a consequence of paraphrasing. It may clarify their perception of what they have said and give a sense of direction to their rambling statements. Helpees tend to like the helper who paraphrases skillfully. The final effect of paraphrased statements is that helpees feel encouraged to go on. When learning paraphrasing skills in a laboratory setting, students should practice until the "helpees" indicate that the paraphrase is accurate to their satisfaction in at least two out of three trials.

Here is a summary of guidelines for paraphrasing:

1. Listen for the *basic message* of the helpee.
2. *Restate* to the helpee a concise summary of the basic message.
3. Observe a *cue,* or ask for a *response,* from the helpee that confirms or denies the accuracy and helpfulness of the paraphrase for promoting understanding.

Clarifying

Clarifying brings vague material into sharper focus. It goes beyond simple paraphrasing in that the helper makes a guess regarding the helpee's basic message and offers it to the helpee. A helper also may ask for clarification when he or she cannot make sense out of the helpee's responses. The message may have been so vague, the wording so confusing, the reasoning so circuitous, or the style so complex that it is a strain to try to paraphrase. Examples of what might follow a rambling helpee monologue are: "I'm confused, let me try to state what I think you were saying." "I lost you there; I'm not clear how you feel about your job; could you give me a brief repeat and an illustration?" "It seems to me you were trying to focus on something there, but the ideas just seemed to tumble over one another." "I'm not sure I understand; could you tell me more?"

This method has a touch of interpreting or explaining how the helper sees the situation, and this interpreting need is one of the strong temptations to which helpers must not submit in the early stage of the relationship. The clarifying remarks are stated in terms of the helper's feelings of confusion to avoid implications of criticism at this tender stage. After all, the confusion may be due to the helper's inattention rather than to confusing helpee statements. Clarifying responses or requests should result in clearer helpee statements, such as efforts to rephrase, to summarize, or to illustrate.

General guidelines for clarifying are:

1. *Admit confusion* about helpee's meaning.
2. Try a *restatement* or *ask for clarification,* repetition, or illustration.

When the intent of helpers is to clarify helpee communications by giving some of their own reactions, the act is often termed *self-disclosure.* Here the helper takes some risks in giving personal reactions to what is going on, but does not do so as strongly or directly as in confrontation methods.

Perception Checking

Perception checking asks helpees to verify your perceptions of what they said, usually over several statements. It actually involves the chaining together of several skills. Ask for feedback about the accuracy of your listening. The reason that perception checking is so effective as a listening skill is that it is a method of giving and receiving feedback on the accuracy of the communication. Assumptions that understanding is taking place are checked out with the helpee. Here again, ordinary social conversation differs from a helping interview. In conversation we often, intentionally or unintentionally, obscure our intentions and central meanings. We expect the hearer to be confused or to take the effort to clarify the communication. We are conditioned socially to chatter onward, even to deliberately confuse the meaning with innuendo, humor, irony, and metaphor. We rarely check with one another about what we intend to say. In helping relationships we reverse this process and put a heavy premium on direct and clear communication aided by frequent perception checks of our understanding of what the helpee meant.

Examples of helper perception checks are: "You seem to be very irritated with me; is that right?" "I was wondering if the plan you chose is the one you really want. You expressed some doubt; did I hear correctly?" "I want to check with you what I'm hearing. You said that you love your wife, yet in the last few minutes you said that you can't stand to be with her. I detected strong contradictory feelings toward her; is that the way it appears to you too?"

The effect on the helpee is likely to be a feeling of being understood in a way that is rare in other relationships. The helpee may perhaps feel truly understood for the first time. Listening, followed by perception checking, is a method of clearing up confusing communications quickly. Perception checking thus serves to correct misperceptions of the helper before they increase to misunderstandings.

In summary, guidelines for perception checking are:

1. *Paraphrase* what you think you heard.

2. *Ask for confirmation* directly from the helpee about the accuracy of your perception of what was said.

3. Allow the helpee to *correct your perception* if it was inaccurate.

Listening is the key skill in this cluster. To use it naturally and effectively, helpers must want very much to understand their helpees, to communicate meaningfully with them, and to relate to them with acceptance and trust. Effective listening requires much confidence in helpees' abilities to solve their own problems and to establish their independent identities.

Skill Cluster 2: Leading

The purpose of leading is to encourage the helpee to respond to open communication. Although leading skills are used throughout the helping process, they are useful particularly in the opening stages of a relationship to invite verbal expression. The helper anticipates slightly the helpee's direction of thought as a method for stimulating talk. It is analogous to the football passer who anticipates the receiver's path so that the ball and the receiver arrive at the same point. The helper's interventions thus appear to their helpees appropriate to where they want to go.

Leading sometimes is described in helping literature as the helper's degree of impact on, or thinking ahead of, the helpee. All helping skills can be rated on the amount of leading involved in their use, but for purposes of this discussion leading will mean the more specific act of anticipating where the helpee is going and the act of responding with an appropriately encouraging remark.

More specific objectives of leading are (1) to encourage helpees to explore feelings and to elaborate on those feelings discussed already; (2) to allow helpees freedom to explore in a variety of directions and to respond freely to what is going on; and (3) to encourage helpees to be active in the process and to retain primary responsibility for the direction of the interview.

Questioning

Encouraging helpees to actively explore their issues often involves the use of questions. Questions serve a variety of purposes. Helpers use questions to ask people to expand on points, start conversations, obtain specific illustrations, check perceptions, and obtain information. They are used more frequently early in the helping process. As a general rule, questions should be used purposefully and sparingly; otherwise, they tend to become substitutes for making statements. Asking a question such as "Don't you think divorce is a good solution in this instance?" is a safe but indirect way of making a statement. More risk is involved when the helper says directly, "I think divorce is a good solution in this instance," since he or she must take responsibility for the statement and its consequences. Think of your personal reaction to a barrage of questions. How did you feel toward the helper?

Some of the unpredictable effects of too many or poorly phrased questions are that they:

1. Offend the helpee, who often feels interrogated.
2. Reduce personal responsibility for the helping process.
3. Increase helpee dependence on the helper.
4. Encourage socially acceptable answers rather than honest responses.

"Why" questions are especially accusatory and are difficult to answer candidly. It is hard to answer a question such as "Why did you say that?" since it asks for speculation about motives and often implies criticism.

Questions fall into two basic categories, which have differing effects and purposes. An *open* question is one that requires a complete answer; it cannot be answered "yes" or "no." Skillful questioning involves asking open questions that leave helpees free to explore and to take the interview where they wish. Open questions avoid most of the problems cited above, because they lead to assisting helpees to understand their issues rather than simply supplying information to the helper. An example of an open question is "What is your relationship with your parents like?" not "Do you get along with your parents?" Other examples are "What do you mean by 'failure'?" "How do they indicate their feelings toward you?" Note that questions beginning with "how" or "what" tend to elicit elaborated responses.

The effect is different with a *closed* ("yes" or "no") question. These usually start with "are," "is," or "do." Examples of closed questions are "Do you like school?" "Are you angry with your boss?" "It is difficult for you to relate to that patient?" Closed questions have the effect of shutting down or limiting conversation.

The following list summarizes guidelines for questioning leads:

1. Ask *open questions* that cannot be answered with "yes" or "no."
2. Ask questions that lead to *clarification for the helpee* rather than information for the helper.
3. Do not fall into a pattern of asking too many questions.

Indirect Leading

The main purposes of indirect leading are to get helpees started and to keep responsibility on them for keeping the interview going. One common use of this idea is to open an interview, for example, with: "What would you like to talk about?" "Perhaps we could start by your telling me where you're at now." "Please tell me why you are here." Later interview examples are: "Tell me more about that." "You were saying (pause)." "What do you think that means?" "How did you feel?" "What else would you like to discuss?" The generality of these leads allows helpees to project their own ideas and direction into the interview. Sometimes, pausing and looking expectantly at the helpee serves as an indirect lead.

Helpees recognize indirect leads as invitations to tell their stories or elaborate on what has been said. This lead is encouraging to most helpees, because they experience more responsibility for the relationship. To others it is threatening or annoying since they often expect the expert to be more active and to do most of the talking, advising, and questioning. More ideas for opening interviews are discussed under Stage 1 of the helping process in Chapter 3.

The following are guidelines for indirect leading:

1. Determine the *purpose* of the lead clearly.
2. Keep the lead *general* and deliberately vague.
3. Use *open* questions.
4. *Pause* long enough for the helpee to pick up the lead.

Direct Leading

Direct leading is a method of focusing the topic more specifically. This method also encourages helpees to elaborate, clarify, or illustrate what they have been saying. Sometimes a strong element of suggestion is included. Some examples are: "Tell me more about your mother." "Suppose we explore your ideas about teaching a little more." "How do you mean—funky?" "Can you think of an illustration that happened recently?"

The behavior of helpees in response to a direct lead usually is to comply with the specifics of the lead, particularly if the helper's attitude manifests interest to match his or her words. The main long-range consequence, however, is to enhance helpee awareness and later understanding, through more elaborate exploration of feelings.

The guidelines for direct leading follow:

1. Determine the *purpose* of the lead.
2. Express the purpose in words that elicit *specific elaboration.*
3. Use *open* questions.
4. Allow the helpee *freedom to follow* your lead.

Focusing

Focusing the talk on a topic that the helper thinks would be fruitful to explore is used when the helpee is rambling vaguely or citing multiple problems. Often in the early stages, helpees will wander over numerous topics, sometimes in circular fashion. Occasionally, the helper's indirect leads have encouraged this wandering, which, if allowed to continue for several minutes, tends to become confusing for both. When helpers think that their helpees have explored the main topics of their concern, then the helpers may stop the helpees and ask them to focus on one aspect, since another purpose of focusing is to emphasize a single feeling or idea chosen from a vast array of possible intellectual verbiage. Focusing is also a way of aiding helpees to get in touch with their feelings.

Some illustrations of focusing leads are "Please elaborate more specifically on those feelings about your mother." "You have been discussing many topics the last few minutes; could you pick the most important one to you and tell me more about it?" "Can you choose one word to describe the last five minutes' talk?" "We have been talking about words, words, words, but I haven't detected much feeling yet; could you name a feeling you have right now?" "What were your feelings as we've been talking?" "Let's not talk for awhile. I suggest you close your eyes and try to get in touch with what you are feeling."

Focusing can sometimes be done by picking out one word or a short phrase from the helpee's talk and repeating it with a question mark or with emphasis. For example, after a helpee has been talking about how confusing her relationships with her supervisor have been, you might say, "Confusing?" The effect is, "Tell me more!" The one-word focusing method can be effective in keeping the helpee going. The helper can say, for example, "And?" "Then, what?" or "But?"

Focusing tends to reduce the helpee's confusion, diffusion, and vagueness. Again, the ultimate expected outcome is more meaningful verbalization and, eventually, increased understanding. Another immediate outcome expected from leads focusing on feelings is that helpees will talk more about their feeling experiences. This skill, like all others in the leading cluster, has a controlling effect on the helpee, so the helper should exert cautious judgment about the degree of his or her leading. Additional consequences of excessive leading are erosion of trust, irritation, and perhaps cessation of productive conversation.

In summary, guidelines for focusing are:

1. Use your *own feelings* of confusion and sense of helpee direction as a guide to decide when to focus.

2. Be alert to *feedback* from the helpee about priority of topics.

3. Assist the helpee to *focus on feelings* that may be hidden in the discussion.

Skill Cluster 3: Reflecting

Reflecting is one way of expressing to helpees that we are in their frame of reference and that we affirm their deep concerns. There are three areas of reflecting—feeling, experience, and content. From the helper's viewpoint, the main purpose of using reflection is to understand helpee experience and to tell helpees that we are trying to perceive the world as they do.

Reflecting Feelings

Reflecting feelings involves expressing in fresh words the helpee's essential feelings, stated or strongly implied. The purpose of reflecting feelings is to focus on *feeling* rather than on content, to bring vaguely expressed feelings into clearer awareness, and to assist the helpee to "own" his or her feelings. So often helpees talk about their feelings as "it" or "them," as if feelings were not part of themselves. This is why we usually begin the reflecting method with "*You* feel" as an attempt to help him reown the feeling. You will know when your reflection is accurate because the helpee will tend to respond with something like, "Yeah, that's it."

Skillful use of reflecting depends on the helper's ability to identify feelings and cues for feelings, from body cues as well as words. It is inappropriate, generally, to ask directly, "And how does that make you feel?" Most of the time, the answer should be fairly obvious. Helpees will probably respond like Louie Armstrong did when someone asked how to know good jazz—"If you have to ask, you'll never know."

Helpers must themselves experience feelings and be in touch with those feelings. Feelings are more subtle than emotions, such as anger, love, disgust, fear, or aggression. Examples of feelings would be affection, pleasure, hostility, guilt, or anxiety. When a helpee is expressing strong emotion, it is so obvious to both that reflecting is unnecessary. The more subtle feelings, however, are often disguised behind words. The helper looks for these hidden feelings and enables the helpee to recognize them more clearly.

The English language is notoriously deficient in varied designations for feelings. A productive activity for helpers is to list common feeling words to make them more accessible when helpees are groping for descriptive terms. Imagine a number of emotional situations and brainstorm all the feeling words you can think of. Compare your list with others and compile a common list to broaden your descriptive language. Groups completing this activity frequently come up with over five hundred words describing various shades of feelings.

The steps in reflection of feeling, then, are to determine what feeling the helpee is expressing, to describe this feeling clearly, to observe the effect, and to judge by the reactions of the helpee whether the reflection was facilitative or obstructive. Sometimes, inaccurate reflections can have a facilitative effect, inasmuch as the helpee will often correct the helper and state feelings more clearly. Examples of reflecting feelings are: "In other words, you hate his guts." "You've always wanted to be a doctor." "Around him you feel guilty all the time." "It really hurts to be rejected by someone you love." Sometimes two contradictory feelings are expressed, and a reflection clarifies this condition, as, "You feel angry when he punishes you; yet, you feel relieved about it, too."

Reflecting Experience

This reflection is descriptive feedback that indicates broad observations of the helper. It is done without editorializing, unlike confronting skills, described later, in which the helper tells what he or she thinks about the behavior.

Reflecting experience goes beyond verbalized feelings in that the helper also reads the implied feelings of nonverbal body language. The helper notes, for example, rapidity of speech, heavy breathing, sighing, flushing, changing postures, and darting glances as cues to the helpees feeling. When reflecting feelings implied in body language, it is a good idea to describe some observed behavior first, then reflect the feeling. Examples are, "You are smiling (behavior description), but I sense you are really hurting inside" (reflection of feeling). "You say you really care about her (paraphrase), but almost every time you talk about her you clench your fists (description); it seems you strongly resent her" (interpretation).

Reflecting Content

Reflecting content is repeating in fewer and fresher words the essential ideas of the helpee and is like paraphrasing. It is used to clarify ideas that the helpee is expressing with difficulty. Helpees lack vocabulary, for example, to express ideas simply and clearly, so reflecting content is a skill to give them words for expressing themselves. Sometimes it helps to repeat a helpee's statement, emphasizing a key word. The helpee says, for example, "His remark really cut me." The helper responds, "It *really* hurt."

In actual practice the three reflecting skills blend into one another. The helper is paying attention to *what* the helpee is saying (content), but also *how* he or she is saying it (feeling tone). Helpers usually respond with a mix of feeling and content to suit their process goals at that moment. They may judge, for example, that the helpee is not ready to face the deeper feelings implied in his or her body language, so they will emphasize content. Reflecting is a way of controlling feeling awareness and expression in the helping interview. On the other hand, in the early stages helpers may wish to emphasize recognition of the total feeling impressions they get from feeling words and observations of body movements and postures.

Helpees experience the reflecting helper as a person who understands what they, the helpees, are experiencing. This favorable reaction increases the possibility that the long-range goals of understanding self and others will be reached. A more immediate outcome is that helpees will be able to identify and express feelings more effectively. Furthermore, they will be able to own their feelings, as indicated by more "I feel" statements. In other words, they will be more ready to continue expressing feelings.

Common Errors in Reflecting

Some common errors in using reflecting methods are, first, stereotyping your responses. This means that helpers tend to begin their reflections in the same monotonous way, such as, "You feel," "You think," "It seems to you," "I gather that." This repetitive style gives the impression of insincerity or an impoverished word supply. We thus need to vary our styles of reflecting.

Another error is timing. Beginning helpers sometimes get into a pattern of reflecting after almost every statement the helpee makes, or they wait for a long monologue to finish and then try heroically to capture the complex feeling in one statement. It is not necessary to reflect every statement, yet it is effective to interrupt the helpee occasionally to reflect. Usually it helps to nod acceptance or give a slight "uh huh" or "I see," to encourage continuation until a reflection seems appropriate.

Overshooting with too much depth of feeling for which the helpee is unprepared may retard the interview. We may read more interpretations into statements than are there. The helpee says, for example, "I don't know if I can stay overseas for a year without her." The helper who reads more depth of feeling and content than is there might respond, "You feel you would be so frustrated that you think you couldn't function at all unless she were with you."

The language must be appropriate to the cultural experience and educational level of the helpee. For example, the helpee might say, "I can't make it with girls; I'm so shy." An inappropriate helper response would be, "Your inferiority complex really shows with girls, then." At the same time, the language of reflection must be natural for the helper too. If he or she is a traditional type, for example, the helper would appear as a phony to attempt to use the latest slang terms.

It may be reassuring to realize that helpees usually are not as critical as these illustrations imply. As helpers, we can reflect incorrectly, but if our sincerity and interest shine through, helpees are amazingly tolerant of bungled efforts. Occasionally, an inaccurate reflection will elicit a correcting response from the helpee so that the net effect is clarification and progress even though the reflection was not accurate.

A summary of guidelines for reflecting is as follows:

1. Read the *total message*—stated feelings, nonverbal body feelings, and content.
2. Select the best *mix* of content and feelings to fulfill the goals for understanding at this stage of the helping process.
3. *Reflect* the experience just perceived.
4. *Wait* for helpee's confirming or denying response to your reflection as a cue about what to do next.

Skill Cluster 4: Confronting

Constructive confrontation involves a complex cluster of helping skills:

1. *Recognizing* feelings in oneself as a helper.
2. *Describing* feelings in oneself and sharing them with the helpee.
3. *Feeding back* reactions in the form of *opinions* about his or her behavior.
4. *Self-reflection* as a form of self-confrontation.

The idea of confronting is to recognize honestly and directly and to point out to helpees what is going on or what you infer is going on. The effects are challenge, exposure, or threat. Resulting emotional effects are sometimes anxiety when challenged with feedback from the helper, and sometimes pleasure with his or her honest opinions and expressions of caring. In other words, confronting skills involve risk—resulting either in unwanted resistance from helpees or in desired openness of communication. It is a "telling it like it is" method that may threaten or thrill, depending on the timing and readiness of the helpee to be confronted with feedback honestly offered. We will look at the subskills of the confronting skill cluster in more detail next.

Recognizing Feelings in Helpers

It is very apparent that one's ability to recognize and respond to feelings in helpees is based on the ability to recognize feelings in oneself. What do tenseness, sweating palms, twitching muscles, and fluttering eyelids say about one's own anxiety, guilt, anger, pleasure, or pain? Helpers must be aware of fine shades of feelings in themselves, which frequently are reactions to what the helpee is saying and can serve as guides to responses. For example, if helpers experience annoyance at what their helpees are saying, they must decide whether the goals of the relationship would be enhanced or retarded by expressing those feelings. As indicated in earlier discussions of countertransference feelings, the helper must make two judgments: Does this annoyance indicate problems I have as a person, or is it a reasonable reaction to what the helpee is saying? Depending on their theories of what is helpful, helpers usually *express* feelings they are aware of experiencing since their helpees sense them anyway from cues such as frowns and agitation.

Describing and Sharing Feelings

Sharing personal feelings about the helpee is a more intense form of self-disclosure than clarification responses. The principal value in describing feelings in oneself as a helper is that such a description helps to clarify how the helper feels. It also serves as a model for helpees to recognize and express their feelings. Helpees frequently do not understand the idea of expressing feeling, especially to near strangers—as helpers often appear to them initially. The condition of trust is dependent on an open sharing of feelings. Again, helpers can accelerate the process of building trust by sharing their own feelings. This "sharing of experience," as described in Brammer, Abrego, and Shostrom, (1993), is one of the best ways to model the idea of "being a person." Some examples are the helper saying, "I feel angry when you talk so much about wanting to hurt other people and not giving a damn about them." "It makes me feel good when you talk about yourself that way." You can see that this kind of response could have a reinforcing effect on helpees, because they are getting some rewards in the form of helper response for expressing feelings even when that response has a critical tone.

The values for helpees of sharing feelings are considerable. They experience relief from tensions (sometimes called emotional catharsis), satisfaction that they had the courage to face the feelings, and release of new creative energies.

The limitations of free expression of feelings by helpees are that they feel so good afterward that they consider it unnecessary to go on actively solving their problems. Sometimes, as we will see in the next chapter, expression of feeling is a goal in itself to provide relief from suffering. Most helpees have protective mechanisms for preventing them from revealing more feeling than they are able to tolerate, but helpers should be alert to occasions when helpee defenses are overwhelmed, and where their behaviors deteriorate under prolonged emotional catharsis. Helpers offering their services need colleagues, or specialist referral resources, to call on in such emergencies.

Some guidelines for knowing how far to let helpees ventilate and some cautions to observe follow. Be cautious about free expression of feeling if:

1. they are known to have severe emotional disorders—hysterical tendencies, delusional thinking, extreme anger, for example.

2. their lives are fraught with crises and emotionally demanding pressures such that discussing them mobilizes more feeling than they can handle.

3. their past history in dealing with emotional crises is known to be shaky.

4. strong resistance to exploration of feelings is noted.

5. the adequacy of your own experience as a helper of disturbed people is doubtful.

6. your own emotional life is in turmoil.

7. the time available for working through the feelings all the way is not adequate.

8. specialist support services are not available or adequate.

9. the policies of your agency discourage exploring the intense emotional life of clients.

10. the attitudes and expectations of parents or guardians of young helpees are not explored.

These guidelines are included to enhance your awareness of possible hazards in free expression of feeling, not to discourage you or make you fearful about dealing with helpee feelings; they are included also because of the common idea in helping circles that sharing strong feelings always has desirable outcomes. In addition, there are growing legal constraints and narrowing definitions of what is harmful or prudent helping behavior. If you find that sharing your own feelings, or working with helpees who are sharing their feelings, is uncomfortable or interferes with your effectiveness, it is a signal to do more work on your own feelings through means described in earlier chapters.

An issue more common than excessive sharing of feelings is the helpee's underexpression or ignoring of feelings. This condition is manifested when the helper focuses on content or when the helpee uses the phrase "I feel" when referring to an idea rather than a feeling. Thus, helpees are unaware that they are avoiding feelings. An example is "I feel that the best thing to do is not to go to college at this time." Depending on the tone, this statement expresses an opinion or a conclusion rather than a feeling. A feeling statement would be more like "I'm afraid of going to college now. High school was such a bore." The principal goal of the helper in using the confronting skill is to challenge helpees to include honest feelings in their statements. One of the keys to this condition is to model expression of feeling yourself.

One way to get helpees to express feelings is to ask them to do so. Some examples are "What are you feeling right now?" "You've described some facts about your situation; how do you feel about it?" "You have been saying what you think about your job, but I haven't sensed your true feelings about it yet. How do you feel about it?"

In summary, guidelines for describing and sharing feelings are:

1. *Share* your own feelings as a model.
2. *Ask* helpees to share their feelings.
3. *Be cautious* about the depth and extent of sharing.

Feedback and Opinion

Feedback is a term borrowed from electronics and physics where information is fed back into a system so that corrections can be made. Examples are thermostats that use information about temperature to activate the furnace switch, or guidance systems in space vehicles that feed information into the navigation equipment to correct the astronauts' course. Similarly, we give information in the form of opinions and reactions to helpees. As a result, they have a better idea of how they are performing, and they can use the information, if they so wish, to change their behavior.

One of the most valuable confrontational skills for developing understanding is honest feedback to helpees on how they affect you. We acquire our definitions of who we are by the reactions of other people to us. Our personalities are the total of our parents' opinions, chidings, and praises. Our helping relationships merely continue this basic process in a more focused fashion. Effective feedback from people they trust and know to care deeply about them can assist helpees to fill in gaps in their self-awareness. Reflect for a minute on a situation when you received feedback from another person. What were the factors that made it useful or not useful for you?

The main guidelines for giving feedback are:

1. *Give opinions in the form of feedback only when helpees are ready.* This means that in most cases they will ask for feedback, but, if not, the helper will ask if they would like some reactions. An example is, "We have been talking about your plans for the future; while you were listing your limitations I had some reactions." (Helpee's interest is aroused and the usual response is, "Oh? Tell me.") "Well, I'm convinced from what you have told me about yourself that you are vastly underestimating your capabilities here; from my observations I think you express yourself very clearly and concisely, for example."

Feedback may be in the form of critical commentary, also, as in the following illustration: "We have been talking about your problems in getting along with people. You may be interested to know that I have been feeling increasingly irritated with your persistent quibbling about almost everything I say. I feel that I don't want to listen to you anymore. Do you think my reaction is typical of those of other people you know?"

Giving opinions without helpee readiness to make use of them is only likely to arouse resistance, resentment toward the helper, or outright denial since it would not fit the helpee's current self-opinion.

2. *Describe the behavior* before giving your reaction to it. Note in the illustrations above that the helper described the specific instance and then gave his or her feeling about it. This description keeps the responsibility for opinions on yourself. Often it is difficult to determine when the feedback is a projection of your personal prejudices and problems and when it is the kind of reaction that the helpee would get from most people. Feedback must be given cautiously, and with the clear understanding that the helper is offering his or her personal reactions to the helpee's behavior. Keeping reactions descriptive rather than evaluative leaves helpees free to use them as they see fit. Emphasizing strengths is another starting point.

3. *Give feedback in the form of opinions about the behavior* rather than judgments about the person. It may seem like quibbling to separate the behavior from the person, but it is vastly different to say, "I don't like the way you constantly interrupt me," from "I don't like you because you are constantly interrupting me."

4. *Give feedback about things that helpees have the capacity to change.* It is not helpful to give feedback about physical characteristics or life circumstances, for example, which they would find very difficult to change.

5. *Feedback should be given in small amounts* so that helpees can experience the full impact of the helper's reaction. Too many items may overload them and create confusion and possibly resentment. An example of such an overload would be, "I didn't like the way you spoke to me; I felt put down. Besides, you have been late consistently to our staff meetings and your progress reports have been getting skimpier, which has been irritating me even more." Feedback given in this cumulative manner serves more as ventilation of hostility for the giver and less as a helpful gesture to the helpee.

6. *Feedback should be a prompt response* to current and specific behavior, not unfinished emotional business from the past. Being told, for example, that one is "too forceful" is not as helpful as saying, "Just as we were about to decide what to do, you pushed your idea and seemed not to hear the other suggestions. I was conflicted about whether to resist you or just give in."

7. *Ask the helpee for reactions* to your feedback. How do you react? Was it helpful or not? Did it enhance the relationship or diminish it?

The main attitudinal pitfalls in giving constructive feedback are:

1. A subtle demand for change.
2. A patronizing implication that "I'm doing this for your good."
3. A judgment about the goodness or badness of the person.

Praise, under the guise of positive feedback, often is interpreted as a judgment about the person. Negative feedback, such as admonition or reprimand, is not used in a helping framework. However, it has its place in supervisory relationships when the person conveying the feedback on performance has power over the other person (Ivey, 1994).

Self-Confrontation

Self-confrontation involves disciplined self-examination. The process takes motivation and courage since it requires questioning of cherished beliefs and assumptions and creates the discomfort of realizing that one's thoughts and values have been flawed. The helper's role is to offer suggestions and then let the helpee's initiative and motivation for self-improvement take over. Most methods of self-confrontation are part of advanced psychotherapy and should be managed under the supervision of a professional helper. The illustrative methods will be described here because of their usefulness in many informal helping situations.

Changing thoughts is a useful confrontation method. It is described by Meichenbaum (1985) as "cognitive ecology." This means clearing out self-defeating negative thoughts and substituting more self-enhancing positive thoughts. Examples of such thoughts are "I'll never be able to find another satisfactory relationship;" "This experience is more than I can bear;" "This is just one more event that proves how inadequate I really am." Statements such as these usually are based on deeply entrenched beliefs about one's adequacy, power, and control that are developed over a lifetime. Hence, they are difficult to change. It is possible, however, to change some of this negative thinking and consequent self-defeating behavior through a five-step process.

The first step is to remind yourself that you are in control of your life and that this control includes your thoughts.

The second step is awareness of what one is saying to one's self through rigorous self-examination questions like, "What am I telling myself that is making me upset?" Being clearly aware of the self-message is the beginning step. To make this topic more relevant, write down two messages you have given yourself this past week that were self-critical and had self-defeating results.

Step 3 is to examine the statements for flawed or distorted reasoning. For example, have you exaggerated by using such words as "never," "always," or "every"? Have you overgeneralized by drawing a false conclusion from one incident? Were your perceptions of the situation overly simple or did you overlook an important aspect of the situation?

After these self-confronting questions Step 4 can be undertaken. This is a restructuring or reframing of the negative statement in Step 2. For example, a reframing of the first illustration above might be "Even though it will be difficult for me to leave this relationship, I will probably find others in the future." Note that this statement does not exaggerate in the positive direction, but puts it in the framework of possibilities.

Step 5 is to keep trying. Changing deep-seated negative thinking takes effort and practice. If negative thoughts persist, it would be helpful to apply thought-stopping procedures. This is done mainly through the self-command to "stop it" whenever negative thoughts come into my mind. If these steps do not work after reasonable effort, or if negative thoughts are accompanied by depressive feelings, it may be necessary to consult a helping professional.

A summary of the five guidelines for self-confrontation by restructuring thoughts is:

1. Reassert beliefs about *personal power and control* over one's life and thoughts especially.
2. Identify specific forms of *self-defeating thoughts.*
3. Examine the thoughts for *distortions.*
4. Restructure the negative thoughts to more *functional positive statements.*
5. *Keep trying* since thoughts and beliefs are difficult to change.

Meditating is a form of self-confrontation with ancient origins. It is a method that focuses on body states rather than thoughts. It is a method of dampening thoughts. Many philosophical groups such as Zen, Yoga, and Sufi, along with the Christian, Hebrew, and Moslem traditions, emphasize the values of self-understanding inherent in meditational forms. The main feature and principal value of meditation for the helping process is that it stops the active flow of ideas and actions and allows helpees to get in touch with themselves. The goals are relaxation and psychological as well as spiritual well-being. Meditation also opens the possibilities of awareness of self in relation to the world, which is a different process from the usual rational sensory types of awareness. Our Western languages have few forms in which to express these nonrational or esoteric experiences. Zen, for example, emphasizes awareness through a state of "no mind" where the flow of consciousness stops. Various styles of meditation are aided by special postures, mantras (repeated vocalizations), contemplating an object, or breathing exercises, but the basic idea of stopping action and thought to allow other forms of experience is the same among them. Finally, meditation practiced diligently is a vehicle for transformation to higher levels of consciousness (Walsh, 1983).

If you decide that this meditational form of self-confrontation would be useful to your helpees for enhancing their self-understanding, you should become familiar with at least one of the styles mentioned above and experience it first yourself. A few general principles can help, even if you are relatively unsophisticated about specific meditational forms. Helpees who flit from topic to topic and who have difficulty relaxing or getting in touch with their feelings, for example, might be helped through some kind of meditation. You can ask your helpees to stop talking, close their eyes, get in a comfortable position, and just be quiet awhile. You might ask them to focus on their breathing—how they inhale and exhale—and to let the ideas flitting across their awareness just fade away.

The value for helpees of this method is that it should open new doors to their feelings and awareness of themselves in relation to others and their physical environment. If nothing else, it should help them to calm down and should prepare them for a new approach to their problems. To obtain maximum value from meditational methods, helpees should practice them in everyday life also. Some helpers assert that this form of self-confrontation is too advanced for an introduction to helping skills. There are many levels of meditation from simple relaxation and quieting thoughts to highly stylized forms taught by disciplined experts. The simple approach here emphasizes breathing exercises that promote awareness of body states and relaxation responses.

Here is a summary of guidelines for using a simple meditational form of self-confrontation:

1. Be familiar with one or more styles through *personal experience.*
2. *Explain* the value of the method to the helpees.
3. Ask them to assume a relaxed *comfortable position* with eyes closed.
4. Ask them to be *quiet* and to let their thoughts fade away.

5. Ask them to focus on their *breathing* as a means of getting in touch with their body processes and feelings.

Skill Cluster 5: Interpreting

Interpreting is an active helper process of explaining the meaning of events to helpees so that they are able to see their problems in new ways. The main goal is to teach helpees to interpret events in their lives by themselves. In *paraphrasing,* the helpee's internal frame of reference is maintained, whereas through *interpretation* the helper offers a new frame of reference. Interpretation is used more in formal psychotherapy than in simple styles of helping because of therapists' needs to think diagnostically. They must be formulating hunches all the time about what is going on and what might be a logical explanation for their helpees' behaviors. They do not always share these thoughts, since they serve primarily to help them understand what is going on in their helpees. Many helpers feel this kind of thinking hinders the helping process because the helper becomes preoccupied with thinking *about* or *ahead* of helpees rather than *with* them. This shift to an external frame of reference in the helper is one of the main limitations of using interpretive skills.

Interpretations often are given in terms of some special theory of personality change held by the helper. Usually these explanations are expressed as hypotheses, or hunches, about what is happening. The best method of becoming familiar with the many styles of interpreting is to watch films or listen to tapes of different helpers.

Interpreting is similar to reflecting, but interpreting adds the helper's meanings to the helpee's basic message. When you decide that an interpretation might be helpful, look for the basic message of the helpee (as in reflecting and paraphrasing), restate it in capsule form, then add your understanding of what the helpee has said (the interpreting). If the interpretation makes sense to the helpee, it will accelerate the interview. If the interpretation is not meaningful, try again. You must also be confident that your interpretation was essentially accurate, since it may take some time before its significance to the helpee sinks in. Interpreting means that you are leading helpees to seek wider understandings of their feelings and broader perceptions. You must recognize that occasionally you will be too far removed from the helpee, and then you will need to aim a little closer to the helpee's level of awareness. It should be understood clearly that the goal of all interpretive effort is *self-interpretation* by the helpee and increasing the helpee's ability to act effectively.

Some examples of interpretation at a simple level without an elaborate theoretical rationale are: "You have told me about your family as if you were a disinterested observer. I gather you have no specific feeling about them."

"It is possible for people to both love and hate their fathers at the same time."
"Perhaps you can see that your feelings of hostility toward men might be at
the root of your marital difficulties."

Interpretive Questions

Some interpreting is done in the form of questions such as, "Do you think
then that you distrust men because your father treated you so badly?" This
questioning form implies a more tentative quality than the declarative statements and makes interpreting less risky for the helper. Interpretive questions
have a focusing effect also, such as in the following illustration where the
helpee has been avoiding discussion of his self-concerns.

HR: When are you going to be concerned about yourself, too?

HE: That is a selfish attitude.

HR: So, what's wrong with that?

HE: I don't like selfish people.

HR: Because . . .?

HE: Selfish people aren't very popular.

HR: So, popularity is important to you; and if you are too self-centered, people won't like you. Is that getting close to where you are?

Fantasy and Metaphor Interpretations

Another stylized way of introducing an interpretation is to put it in the form
of a fantasy (daydream), even using the picture language of a metaphor. An
example is, "I have a fantasy about what you have just said. I picture you
walking down a path in the woods, coming to a fork in the path, and being
undecided which one to choose. You unconcernedly flip a coin and run joy-
fully down the path chosen by the coin. How does this fit?" If the fantasy is
close to the helpees' awareness, it will trigger new ways of perceiving themselves. The limitation is that in using this skill helpers shift into their own
frame of reference, thus forcing helpees to deal with them (or their fantasies).
Sometimes it is useful just to give one's reaction in the form of a metaphor,
such as, "Most of the time I perceive you as a great big soft teddy bear who
stays in any position he is placed." A meaningful metaphor for helpees is the
"box of life." It is useful to help them understand the difficult situations in
which they find themselves. For example, the helper might say to a helpee
who feels restricted, frustrated, or exploited, "It appears to me that you have
allowed others to put you in this cramped little box. How long are you going
to stay there? What are you going to do to get out?"

A second skill in using metaphors is to observe the special action words used by helpees to describe their experiences. They tend to use certain images consistently. Some of these images are visual ("I see the light"), while others are auditory ("That sounds right"), or kinesthetic ("That idea grabs me"). Some helpees use gustatory words ("a sour project"), or olfactory images ("a stinking mess"). Many people have a dominant sensory mode, while others tend to have a mixture of sensory images in their language. The point in helping is to listen for the sensory metaphors used by the person and then match your helping language to the helpee's dominant sensory mode. For example, if the helpee uses primarily visual verbs and images, such as bright, shining, looking, and drawing, then the helper tries to use this modality in his or her own responses. The purpose is to get into helpees' experiences to promote their self-understanding and to put the helper in a position of greater influence with helpees.

Another goal is to broaden the helpee's sensory language base by asking, for example, how the person's life is *going,* how the person *sees* his or her past, and how the future *rings.* The research base for this work is in psycholinguistics, or the psychological study of language (Bandler & Grinder, 1975, 1982).

Levels of Interpretation

We have mentioned the idea of levels of interpreting several times. Interpreting could be placed on a continuum from reflecting, where you stay at the meaning and feeling level of the helpee, through elaborate theoretical explanation of behavior in depth interpretation. Even in so-called depth interpretation we do not dig deeply into the helpees' psyches and come up with brilliant insights that unfold the mysteries of their personalities. This is a popular view that came from distorted perceptions of psychoanalytic methods.

The solution to most psychological problems comes down to understanding the meaning of the problem for the person. Interpreting is explaining or suggesting ways to construe the meaning of a problem or its solution. The basic underlying assumption is that if the meaning is more clear the person will be better able to work through present and future personal problems. The following illustration offers a few of these ways of responding at different levels of meaning. The helpee says, "I was at a party last night where I drank too much. I broke into tears and cried and cried. I acted like a child who wanted to go home to mother. I feel so ashamed." Your response, at different levels, might be one of the following:

1. "You drank to the point where tears came freely. You're ashamed now as you talk about it." (content paraphrase)
2. "You feel very bad about what happened last night." (general feeling reflection)

3. "You feel bad that you lost control of yourself last night." (mild interpreting—adding the idea of control)

4. "You drank until you lost control of your feelings. As you look back on the evening now, you want to punish yourself for acting that childish way." (interpreting—adding the idea of punishing and reverting to childhood patterns)

5. "Your drinking, crying, and mentioning mother makes me wonder if you want to go back to mother—like being dependent on her for comfort and feeling you can't stand on your own two feet." (deeper level interpreting—desire for a comforting mother and dependency)

6. (Interpreting the helpee's statement according to some theoretical framework, like gestalt, which might explain in terms of giving up dependency on others and substituting self-dependency; or the rational-emotive approach for getting rid of self-defeating and self-punishing feelings about behavior; or psychoanalytic interpretations about wishes to go back to the womb. Behaviorally oriented helpers might inquire about the helpees' desires to change their drinking or crying behavior.)

The myriad verbal forms for couching interpreting skills are really too complex to cover in detail in this basic helping skills book, but it would be wrong to understate the significance and usefulness of interpreting skill for the average helper. We should know not only the possible uses but also the implications for misuse. Further readings in the Suggestions for Further Study at the end of this chapter will add to your understanding of various styles of interpretation.

The main consequences for helpees of being confronted through interpretation are broadened perceptions of meanings of their behaviors and different ways of viewing their problems and possible solutions. Generally speaking, helpees can expect a deeper understanding of their problems as a result of the added perspectives of the helper. If you get the "Suddenly I realized" reaction, you know your interpreting has been successful. Interpreting also has the effect of intensifying the emotional involvement of helpees so that they will take more responsibility for their own interpreting.

Guidelines for interpreting are:

1. Look for the *basic message(s)* of the helpees.

2. *Paraphrase* these to them.

3. Add *your understanding* of what their messages mean in terms of your theory or your general explanation of motives, defenses, needs, styles.

4. Keep the *language simple* and the *level close to their messages*. Avoid wild speculation and statements in esoteric words.

5. *Introduce* your ideas with statements that indicate you are offering *tentative ideas* on what their words or behaviors mean. Examples are "Is this a fair statement?" "The way I see it is," "I wonder if," or "Try this one on for size."

6. Solicit *helpee reactions* to your interpretations.

7. *Teach helpees* to do their own interpreting. Remember, we can't give insight to others; they must make their own discoveries. When helpees make interpretations that you gave them earlier, but they act as though it is original, pat yourself on the back, but say nothing about the source of the idea. You have done your work as a helper well!

Skill Cluster 6: Informing

Giving Information

This skill of information giving is so commonplace that it needs little elaboration. It is included here to indicate that sharing simple facts possessed by helpers is sometimes the most helpful thing they could do. Some kinds of information in the expertise category, such as information from test instruments, require special skills for planning and decision making that are beyond the scope of this general helping book. Further information on skills for informing about interests, aptitudes, and personality traits may be obtained from the Suggestions for Further Study section at the end of this chapter.

Another category of information about services concerning financial planning, retirement decisions, caregiving resources, career planning, and family planning needs to be handled by specially informed people through referral skills to be described in the next chapter.

Advice

Giving advice is a common type of informing activity by helpers. Helpees, expecting some kind of expert pronouncements in the form of sound advice on what to do, often thrust the helper into the role of expert. Beginning helpers, too, often perceive their function as giving "common sense" advice. Before reading further we suggest you formulate your own ideas about giving and receiving advice. How do you feel when people advise you? Under what conditions in your life has advice been helpful? What were the characteristics of the adviser? Do age or experience make any difference? Conversely, how do you feel about giving advice? Are there differences between giving advice and offering information?

There is a long tradition of giving advice in the helping folklore. It is a common occurrence between persons who know and trust one another. This time-honored function among friends is often beneficial. Issues arise, however, when helpees consult helpers in their larger environments at work, church, or school. These institutions have many natural self-styled advice givers who often have attractive charismatic qualities. As a consequence, they are sought out by confused and troubled people, largely because they are attractive people with a reputation for being helpful. These persons could just as well be bartenders, janitors, or clerks as well as those with helping titles such as ministers or teachers. Helpees without serious emotional disabilities often do not want psychotherapy or counseling, but seek advice mainly on a particular problem. What they often search for is an empathic listener who will not attempt to "psych them out," "play the therapy game," or treat them like disobedient children.

In an informal study of what Korner[1] called "indigenous counselors" he found that almost all bureaucratic organizations had such an informally appointed advice giver in the small-group structures. This person's function, according to Korner's data, is to become the organization's human behavior lay expert. His data from people who consulted these indigenous advisers indicate that such advisers enjoy talking to people, appreciate the respect and confidence people place in them, appear self-confident and dignified, and are very willing to give of their store of accumulated problem-solving experience in a no-nonsense neutral manner. They had an unusual quality to get to the core of the matter and inspire confidence and trust. The advice was offered in a manner that did not obligate the receiver to follow it or seek subsequent meetings for further help. Receivers were careful to indicate that this adviser did not offer solace and support to reduce psychic discomfort. The main contributions of the indigenous advice givers were to crystallize and focus issues, to clarify decision processes, and to move beyond the impasse. It appears that persons perceived as helpful advice givers use helping skills far beyond sheer conventional advice. These findings suggest also that such indigenous helpers in organizations are performing useful services to people informally and could probably enhance their effectiveness with additional work on helping skills. Unfortunately, Korner's data did not reveal the nature or the consequences of "bad advice."

Giving advice in the traditional manner is a controversial topic in helping literature. Some writers claim advising reflects the arrogance of helpers who assume they are so all-knowing that they can advise other persons on a course of action. Critics also claim advice is ineffective and fosters dependency. Yet others assert that advice giving is helpful under some circumstances. Advice can be helpful if it is given by trusted persons with expert opinions based on solid knowledge of a supporting field such as law, medicine, or child rearing. Sometimes helpees need a recommended course of action supported by wide experience and, it is hoped, by facts. There is a place for suggestions that leave the evaluation and the final decision about courses of action completely

[1]Korner, I. Unpublished paper, "About Advice Giving."

open to the helpee. You can suggest hypotheses that need checking before acting upon them. Examples are situations in which parents are exploring ways of handling rebellious children or students are weighing choices about courses. The use of considered suggestions is appropriate when the contact is short and the decision relatively inconsequential in the person's life.

Advice is often appropriate in crisis situations where several people must cooperate to prepare helpees for major readjustments of their life circumstances. Examples are family reorganization after hospitalization, divorce, imprisonment, unemployment, or financial loss. Advice is wholly inappropriate for dealing with major individual choice questions, such as, "Should I get a divorce?" or "What career should I enter?"

Most people object to advice given in the form of "father knows best," or offhand suggestions tempered with strong persuasion. Usually, persons giving advice have a strong stake in the helpee's following that advice, and their persuasive attitude often generates hostility in helpees. Every parent knows this!

The principal limitation of advice giving is that helpees usually don't follow it. They often seemingly ask, or even beg, for advice but they are most often asking themselves the rhetorical question, "What shall I do?" They may be expressing dependent feelings, knowing full well what to do. If helpers fall into this trap, they justifiably incur the wrath or contempt of the helpee. A more productive strategy, especially if there is time, is to deal with the feelings involved first. The main task is to distinguish between the honest and direct request for information or suggestions and the expression of indecisive or dependent feelings. When in doubt, it is more productive to try a reflecting approach with the presumed feelings first, and then deal with the request itself.

Some other limitations of giving advice are that it reinforces dependence on experts, which shifts responsibility to the helper for solutions. Frequently, helpers who take the "If I were you" approach are projecting their own needs, problems, or values into the advice rather than keeping the helpee's needs foremost. Experience in group forms of helping indicates that often participants begin giving advice because they unconsciously perceive the other person's problems as their own; therefore, they are really speaking to themselves. Another limitation, furthermore, is that the helpee may take the helper's advice and later find that it was invalid. The helper then is blamed when things don't turn out right in the helpee's life.

A summary of guidelines for informing skills is as follows:

1. Be *informed,* or know the sources of information, in your area of advertised expertise.

2. Do not use educational or psychological test instruments without thorough *training* in their uses and limitations.

3. Don't use advice unless it is in the form of *tentative suggestions* based on solid expertise.

Skill Cluster 7: Summarizing

Summarizing skills include attention to *what* the helpee says (content), *how* it is said (feelings), and the *purpose, timing,* and *effect* of the statements (process). Most helping interviews wander widely over many ideas and feelings. This may be part of the helpees manner of showing discomfort by resisting direct discussion, or of keeping the helper at a safe emotional distance for awhile. It may reflect also the helpee's unwillingness to terminate the interview. Summarizing involves tying together into one statement several ideas and feelings at the end of a discussion unit or the end of an interview. It is much broader, therefore, than paraphrasing a basic message, as indicated in the following example. Following a discussion of the helpee's vague feelings of inadequacy the helper says, "From your talk about family, school, and now your new job of selling, you appear to have experienced feelings of personal failure in all of them."

Summaries of an interview, or a series of contacts, may include a long paragraph, but the idea is to pick out the highlights and general themes of the content and feelings. Summaries of *process* include statements of where the helping process has been going and where it is now. The helper may say, for example, "You've been discussing your ideal jobs and what things you have liked and disliked about your past work; you've also talked about your plans for more training. Are you ready to take a look at some other considerations in planning for a new career?"

The main purpose of summarizing is to give the helpee a feeling of movement in exploring ideas and feelings, as well as awareness of progress in learning and problem solving. Summarizing also helps to finish an interview on a natural note, to clarify and focus a series of scattered ideas, and to clear the way for a new idea. It has the effect also of reassuring helpees that you have been tuned in to their messages all along. For the helper it serves as an effective check on the accuracy of perceiving the full spectrum of helpee messages. Summarizing the previous sessions at the beginning of an interview often provides needed continuity.

The helper tries to get helpees to do the summarizing, if possible. This is a test of their understanding as well as a method of keeping responsibility on them. The helper may say, for example, "How does our work look to you at this point? Try to pull it together briefly." "Let's take a look at what we've accomplished in our time today; how does it appear to you?" When a relationship is terminated, summarizing will probably be a joint effort to capture the essential points explored, progress achieved, and next steps planned.

Guidelines for summarizing are:

1. *Attend* to the various *themes* and emotional *overtones* as helpees speak.
2. Put together the key ideas and feelings into *broad statements* of their basic meanings.
3. *Do not add* new ideas to the summary.
4. Decide if it would be more helpful to state your summary or ask them to summarize the basic themes, agreements, or plans. In deciding, consider your *purpose:*

> Was it to *warm up* helpees at the beginning of the interview?
> Was it to *focus* their scattered thoughts and feelings?
> Was it to *close* discussion on this theme?
> Was it to *check* your understanding of the interview progress?
> Was it to *encourage* them to explore themes more completely?
> Was it to *terminate* the relationship with a progress summary?
> Was it to *assure* them that their interviews were moving along well?

Outcomes Self-Check

After reading this chapter you should be able to (1) list the seven main clusters of skills for promoting awareness of understanding self and environment; (2) cite subskills in the clusters and illustrate their uses and misuses with examples from helping interviews; and (3) apply the skills, after practice and feedback from associates.

Suggestions for Further Study

Benjamin, A. *The Helping Interview.* 2nd ed. Boston: Houghton Mifflin, 1982. (Ch. 5 on the use of questions and Ch. 7 on leading and reflecting.)

Brammer, L., Abrego, P., and Shostrom, E. *Therapeutic Counseling and Psychotherapy.* 6th ed. Englewood Cliffs, NJ: Prentice Hall, 1993. (Ch. 5 on building a therapeutic relationship, Ch. 7 on strategies for facilitating therapeutic change, and Ch. 9 on group methods of helping.)

Carlton, J. Working it out. *Successful Meetings* 42 (1993):102–109. (Use of help-ing skills language during business meetings, including how to productively share anger.)

Egan, G. *The Skilled Helper.* 5th ed. Pacific Grove, CA: Brooks/Cole, 1994. (Helping models and skills in Chs. 3–9.)

Gordon, D. *Therapeutic Metaphors.* Cupertino, CA: Metapublications, 1978. (How to construct and use metaphors to increase helpee understanding.)

Gordon, T. *Parent Effectiveness Training.* New York: Peter H. Wyden, 1970. (Chs. 3–7 on listening methods with children.)

Johnson, K. L. How to gain your client's trust—fast. *The CPA Journal.* (1993, Sept.):40–42. (Trust building in the accounting industry.)

Long, L., Paradise, L., and Long, T. *Questioning Skills for the Helping Process.* Pacific Grove, CA: Brooks/Cole, 1981. (Ch. 3 on the inappropriate use of questions.)

Rogers, C. *Client-Centered Therapy.* Boston: Houghton Mifflin, 1951. (Description, rationale, and illustrations of reflecting skills.)

Supervisory Management (1991, July). (A special issue on communication in the workplace.)

Williamson, T. M. From interrogation to investigative interviewing: Strategic trends in police questioning. *Journal of Community & Applied Social Psychology* 3 (1993):89–99.

5

Helping Skills for Loss and Crisis

One of the most common helping functions is providing relief from psychological suffering. Social service literature contains many practical ideas for dealing with specific types of situational crises, and traditional religions have had much to say about human suffering, hope, and existential crises. After surveying the scanty crisis literature spanning forty years, we have found little systematic information for the general helper. Only in the past decade have helping professionals become systematic about crisis intervention and research (Aguilera & Messick, 1994; Gottlieb, 1983; Slaiken, 1990). This chapter summarizes these findings about crises and skills for giving support during times of loss and stress.

In general, dealing with people in crisis calls for flexibility of response, rapid and active intervening with alternatives, and setting limited goals for getting the person functional. Although there are some special skills available for providing comfort and managing crises, the personhood of helpers is a more important consideration. Their values, experiences, and personality traits have a profound impact on helpees' ability to face stress conditions and crises. Thus, helpers cannot depend only on their personal experience, but must draw on a variety of sources—including religion, philosophy, behavioral science, and the helping professions—for their values, ideas, and skills. Behavioral scientists alone, though they produce most of the concepts and methods for testing helper effectiveness, cannot offer belief systems, values to live by, or hope to suffering persons.

Many of the skills described in the previous chapter can be applied in loss and crisis situations since they provide support as well as promote understanding. This chapter will (1) define and discuss terms used in loss and crisis work; (2) describe strategies for helping people in crisis; (3) describe skills to facilitate support in times of stress and crisis; and (4) list suggestions for further reading.

We recommend that, before delving into strategies and methods developed by helping specialists, you stop to think over events in your own life where you experienced suffering during a transition, and perhaps a crisis in bereavement, illness, or unemployment. What sources of help were available, and which did you seek? What coping strategies or coping methods were helpful to you in working through your crisis? What comforting characteristics did the helper exhibit? Which were most useful among your self-help approaches? To what extent did you include writings from religion, philosophy, and the behavioral sciences? How helpful were these self-directed readings?

Outcomes You Can Expect

From studying this chapter you will be competent to (1) identify skills and strategies useful in situations requiring support and comfort; (2) identify understanding skills that also have a supportive function; (3) use the terminology for describing loss, transition, crisis, and stress; and (4) exercise judgment on strategies to be used with stressors and crisis situations. The ultimate degree of your effectiveness will be measured by helpees' improved ability to cope with crises and by their demonstrated ability to translate crises into growth opportunities.

Human Conditions of Concern

Stressors and crisis conditions can be divided into three categories: loss due to outside factors, internal distress regardless of cause, and transitional states that demand adaptive responses. Causes and effects are difficult to separate. Some illustrative conditions are:

Severe Loss (External Factors)

Bereavement	Disability
Unemployment	War separation
Disaster	Terrorism
Surgery	Crimes against person
Imprisonment	

Internal Distress

Hopelessness	Post-traumatic stress
Despair	Bad drug reactions
Depression	Suicide impulses

Transitional States

Job changes/Retirement	Family conflict/Divorce
Relocation	Family member absent
New family member	Illness

Life Transitions

Life changes are experienced as a sense of loss. Even positive changes, such as vacations, involve losses of familiar surroundings, people, and comforts. Such changes sometimes are stimulating and are sought for this reason. Nevertheless, the sense of loss usually is experienced as a spectrum of feelings from uneasiness to depression and helplessness.

This awareness of loss thrusts people into a grieving process. Grief follows a generally predictable series of stages, most apparent in severe loss but visible even in ordinary life transitions, such as moving and retirement.

A transition is a special kind of change, characterized primarily by a discontinuity or break with the past. It also brings out strengths and coping skills from the person's life experience. Transitions follow the general steps of grieving, but not as dramatically as the literature on death and mourning suggests. If the transition is unexpected or has a crisis quality, there is a response of shock that is experienced as numbness and disorganization, as described later under grief. The helping strategies used here are discussed under crisis intervention.

The second stage experienced in a life transition is expression of feeling, sometimes of anguish but often of relief. Again supportive helping skills are needed here, because following shortly is denial of the severity of feeling or meaning of the event. Responses of "I'm OK, this isn't so bad," or general denial of feelings experienced about the loss, are typical.

Often people move shortly into experiences of sadness and losing their self-esteem. Self-blame, catastrophic fears of the future, or a sense of helplessness and being out of control emerge. While shoring up the person's self-esteem is an important helping step at this stage, one view is that this period of sadness and detachment is a healing process to allow the person to reflect on the experience of change, to let go of the past, and to take hold of a new value, goal, or relationship.

The length of this stage of sadness, and sometimes depression, varies with the person and the loss event. It is a time for healing and letting go of the past. Generally it lasts long enough for the person to recover optimism, hope, and motivation for planning new life directions.

The final stage of taking hold of a new way of life is characterized by emergent optimism, functional problem-solving skills, and personal goals for the future. This final acceptance of the change and working through this transition process puts the person back on a functional level ready to tackle the next life transition. Hopefully, the helping strategy during this last stage includes some discussion of what was learned from the experience of working through the recent transition. The results would allow the person to cope more effectively with the next one. An additional helping strategy here is to assist the person to understand the process clearly and to realize how the person coped and utilized his or her strengths.

The term *coping,* as used frequently in this book, means an active problem-solving approach to change and other stress-producing conditions. Coping is not a passive adjustive process. Coping means that the helpee is taking charge of his or her own life and is seeking the resources needed to solve current problems. An example is the disabled accident victim who is learning new everyday living skills and is taking the initiative to discover new ways to make life more livable. We describe such people as "hardy copers." Studies of successful copers (Kobassa, 1979) reveal that they view change as a challenge, or opportunity, to solve a difficult problem or to exercise some creativity. For example, the helpee fired from his job can now consider the career he has always wanted. Hardy copers also believe that they can control their lives. Even though they suffer accidents beyond their control, they, like the accident victim cited above, believe that they can control their reactions to the event and can take charge of their rehabilitation.

While not a rigid sequence, typical reactions to transitions can be summarized as follows:

1. Shock and disorganization.
2. Expression of anguish and/or relief.
3. Experience of denial and minimization of the loss.
4. Sadness and lowered self-esteem.
5. Taking hold of a new way of life and letting go of the past.
6. Final acceptance of change and planning for the future.
7. Reflections on learning from the transition experience.

Family Crises

Families, by their nature, are always experiencing change. Some changes are so sudden or so significant that they are considered by that family to be a crisis. From a family therapy perspective, there are two kinds of change in families: first order and second order change (Becvar & Becvar, 1988, p. 86).

First order change is something new that happens in the family that causes a mild rearranging of the way that family operates. *Second order change* causes major disruption and a need to reevaluate the family rule system.

The degree of help a family needs to deal with these changes varies from family to family. For example, a married woman with one child plans for another and gives birth. While this family will likely need help adjusting to the change, it likely would not be defined as a crisis. On the other hand, if a woman with two grown children has just started graduate school, her husband, with whom she is not getting along, has just lost his job, and she finds out she is pregnant, the birth of that child may be seen as a crisis. The whole family will need to reevaluate how they are going to deal with the situation. It is important to know that families, just as individuals, define each crisis in their own way and have different coping skills for managing. Helpers must look at the family's perception of the problem, not just how the helper would feel in the same situation. Often a family in a crisis can benefit from professional help, but the skills of this chapter are of a general nature and useful in *any* support system, professional or otherwise.

Definitions of Terms

Stress

A stress reaction is a condition characterized by physiological tension and persistent choice conflict. The helpee feels under pressure to reduce the tension and achieve comfort or equilibrium. Often the resolution takes a maladaptive form, such as illness, without awareness in the helpee. A stress experience is a more pervasive and less intense condition than crisis, but it may continue for unlimited time, with or without the provoking stimulus (Janosik, 1994).

Tension from changes is cumulative, and, though individual events appear to have little impact, the cumulation over a year can contribute to major crises, such as illness. Holmes and Rahe's (1967) original studies on the effects of such cumulative change events in relation to health, found that a person with a high cumulative point index, based on events scaled in intensity from death to parking tickets, was likely to suffer a major health problem that year. Numerous studies have confirmed the close relationship between stress and ill health (Monat & Lazarus, 1991).

One should not be tempted to think that it takes a major life change to cause stress in a person's life. In fact, some of our greatest stress is caused by the accumulation of what Lazarus (1984) calls *daily hassles*. These hassles include daily running of a household, health, time-pressure, inner emotional concerns, environmental worries (e.g., crime, noise), finances, work-related stress, and insecurity about the future.

People must be helped to an awareness of the nature and power of stressors in their lives as well as the buildup of minor stress reactions to crisis proportions. Helpees need to realize that the transitional states between periods of relative stability—school to work, marriage to singlehood—are normal conditions that require specific self-help skills and, sometimes, helper support to cope with the consequences of change. As Meichenbaum (1985) states, people must learn stress-management skills to inoculate themselves against the effects of stressors.

In the business community, for example, there is gaining acknowledgment of the influence of stress and its relationship to health concerns of its workers. When counseling is made available and paired with other stress preventative measures, workers stay healthier (Kellerman, Felts, & Chenier, 1992; Cooper, Sadri, Allison, & Reynolds, 1990; Erfurt, Foote, & Heirich, 1991).

Crisis

Crisis is a state of disorganization in which helpees face frustration of important life goals or profound disruption of their life cycles and methods of coping with stressors. The term *crisis* refers usually to the helpee's feelings of fear, shock, and distress about the disruption, not the disruption itself. Crises are limited in time, usually lasting not more than a few weeks (Janosik, 1994; Slaiken, 1990). Crises, therefore, are defined primarily by the helpee since the emotional responses cited previously vary in intensity during any wrenching life transition. Crises usually are provoked by such dramatic events as suicide of a family member, assaults, surgery, or accidents, but crises may also develop from cumulative ordinary life transitions such as moving, retirement, job change, illness, or travel. The crisis point on that continuum is reached when coping resources fail, and the point of extreme disequilibrium or dysfunction is reached. It is also that critical turning point where people may rally their coping resources and move on to new heights of growth or may deteriorate further into disorganization eventuating in severe illness or death. The crisis intervention tasks of the helper are clear in providing psychological first aid as outlined in this chapter.

In summary, crises:

1. Are temporary.
2. Result in distress and often dysfunction.
3. Involve loss of coping capacity.
4. May have long-term negative or positive consequences.

There are normal *developmental crises,* such as birth or a child going off to school. *Situational crises* are associated with severe loss of status, possessions, or loved ones. *Existential crises* refer to the conflicts and anxious feelings experienced when facing the significant human issues of identity, purpose, responsibility, freedom, and commitment. Although this existential type of crisis is a normal part of human existence, it becomes a true crisis when one becomes aware of the discrepancy between old forms of constricted being and new possibilities for action. For some, these pressures to choose and to act assume crisis proportions. If they are not resolved in a constructive way through normal living or special helping processes, the crisis eventuates in feelings that range from detached boredom and purposelessness, to despair over forced responsibility for choice, and finally to panic and disintegration. An example is the sense of purposelessness, feelings of dread, and loss of energy often experienced in mid-life.

Four phases of a crisis period have been described by Caplan (1964). An adaptation of his phases follows: (1) Initial tension is experienced, which arouses habitual adaptive responses. (2) Tension increases under continuous stimulation, and lack of success is experienced in coping and tension reduction. This frustration is complicated by distress and inefficiency. (3) Tension increases until emergency resources, internal and external, are mobilized. The crisis may be eased temporarily through emergency coping mechanisms, seeing the problem differently, or relinquishing unrealistic goals. (4) An acute phase follows if the crisis is not eased in stage 3, or averted by denial or resignation. Tension mounts to the point where major dysfunctions in behavior develop, and/or emotional control is lost.

The helpee can be highly influenced in crises. The values of crisis can be realized if the person is now ready to reach for higher levels of self-realization, as well as calm equilibrium. Availability of the helping process is thus crucial at this early stage because the helpee is so malleable and ready for change. Parad (1965) cited many instances where agencies practicing crisis intervention have productive outcomes when help is offered and accepted early.

Most crises in the workplace are the result of employee personal problems such as alcoholism, marital stress, or financial obligations. However, each employer should also develop with the staff a plan for other possible crises or traumas that could develop and what would be the workplace response should these occur (Barton, 1992). Being prepared improves the helping response to the crisis and reduces employee anxiety about the workplace.

In addition to the availability of helping relationships, the psychological background and makeup of the person determine to a great extent his or her reaction to prolonged stress and intensive crises. We cannot assume when disaster strikes or when a family seems to be going through enormous stress that some kind of massive help is necessary. Some persons and families have enormous reserves to draw on. For example, they may have a large extended family or abundant financial resources. In addition, some families have dependable inner resources of courage, fortitude, and spirituality. Family crises tend to evoke these personality resources.

Through scrutiny of short case histories, Bloom (1963) investigated how helping professionals viewed crises. These family histories contained varying amounts of five elements constituting a crisis condition: (1) awareness of the precipitating event; (2) rapidity of onset; (3) presence of discomfort; (4) external evidence of behavior disruption; and (5) rapidity of resolution. Bloom found that helpers defined a crisis largely in terms of precipitating events and to some extent time of resolution, but a problem arose when trying to differentiate between those profound events that led to a crisis state and those that did not. This lack of precision in defining a crisis makes it very difficult to determine the effectiveness of a particular strategy or method.

A crisis marshals the coping skills outlined in Figure 1-3. How effectively a person manages a crisis is dependent in large part on the adequacy of his or her coping skills (Brammer & Abrego, 1981).

Support

Support is a condition in which the helpee feels secure and comfortable psychologically. It includes awareness of well-being and satisfaction of "affect hunger." Support offers a healing process—an integration of all parts of the person. It helps to counter experiences of "falling apart," being "at loose ends," or "pulled in many directions at once."

Support comes from three sources: (1) the relationship itself, where the helpee experiences the helper's acceptance and warmth; (2) direct counseling help in the form of reassurance or environmental support; (3) decisive and firm crisis management.

Whether support should be actively encouraged is controversial among helpers. Some claim that providing support is a necessary helping function, especially for persons in states of crisis. Helpees need comfort and security to recoup their coping forces, and the helping interview definitely should not add to this strain. Others assert that deliberately providing support reduces an opportunity for growth and induces dependency. They claim that helpees should take advantage of the "shaken up" condition following the crisis to explore new avenues of growth, take new risks, complete their "grief work," and make new plans. The psychological "first aid" should be the supportive quality of the helper's attentive and caring presence only. Where do you stand on this issue?

One value of providing direct support is the reduction of debilitating anxiety, and consequent psychological comfort and healing. Helpees who feel inadequate, unworthy, grief stricken, lonely, or fearful are given a supportive helper during the peak of their crisis, or the depth of their feelings, until they can marshal their strength to go on. In such a supportive relationship helpees can feel that they do not need to be strong and capable for a while; it is like feeling that they can "walk" before they need to "run." Support conditions allow them to express and face their dependency and security needs in a low-demand neutral environment.

Grief-stricken persons in a supportive relationship also feel that they are not alone, that someone understands, and that they are free to share their hurts. Similarly, a supportive relationship helps persons fearful of their impulses to express strong feelings of despair, frustration, and anger without being hurt more.

Helpers must resist the impulse to use expressions like "I know exactly how you feel." A helper may have had a situation similar to the helpee's current crisis, and it is often comforting to the helpee for that fact to be known. However, as stated previously, it is not the event, but the helpee's experience of the event that defines the crisis. Thus, one person cannot know exactly how another feels. A more helpful expression would be to briefly state, "I've been in a similar place once before. It hurts a lot, doesn't it?"

Proper support also assures helpees that they can help themselves, that they are capable, that they are worthy, or that they can plan. Realizing, for example, that they can save a marriage gives them the courage to keep trying for solutions. Although talking about one's grief and anxiety after a stressful event does not lessen the need for an extended healing process, emotional support goes far toward lessening the probability of suffering long-term stress reactions or extended grief.

Finally, a supportive relationship assures helpees that they do not need to take impulsive action that might increase their difficulties. They can take sufficient time to get their feelings sorted out and to explore alternatives before acting. An example is introducing "stop time" before initiating a divorce proceeding.

Some of the limitations of supportive relationships were implied above. Briefly, a major limitation is the creation of dependence on the helper as a source of support. Sometimes helpees feel resentful, or even guilty, when they are recipients of support. Occasionally they experience dependence on the helper. Some are threatened by too much warmth and closeness because they have not yet learned how to manage a close human relationship when they are hurting. Others feel that their suffering is minimized or trivialized by too much verbal reassurance.

Supportive efforts that come across as sympathy may be interpreted by helpees as insincere and gimmicky. Overuse of reassurance, for example, makes the helper sound shallow to the helpee. For example, helpees have often heard the platitudes that "everything will come out in the wash, so don't fret" or "every cloud has a silver lining." They know from experience that it is not true that things always turn out "right" or for the "best," especially if you or someone else has just given them some bad news. If a man has received negative evaluations of his work performance, he usually knows he has been unsatisfactory. Nothing is gained from "sweetening" the news, or from assuring him that some "miracle" is going to happen or that people do not understand him. A strategy likely to produce much more growth and restore self-esteem would be to help him to evaluate the feedback about his work objectively and to accept the validity of the judgments.

Hope and Despair

These twin concepts merit extended discussion in this context of support and crisis management because they are so central to helpees' recovery of equilibrium, management of stressors, and prevention of future crises. Korner (1970) has examined hope as a method of coping, a means of preventing crises, and as a route to healthy behavior. Helpers appear to have mixed reactions about the values of hope. On the one hand, they believe that hope makes stress conditions tolerable, but they are convinced also that it is foolhardy to rely on false hopes, or to use hope to avoid acting responsibly in the present. Few studies have been made of the helping functions of hope, but the general opinion among professional helpers seems to be that the elusive quality of hope is more a wishful panacea than a dependable aid to solving personal problems.

Instead of defining hope as expectations in the absence of verifiable facts, it has been more fruitful to look at its opposite, hopelessness or despair. The anguish and pain of this condition are well known. Despair implies that people have given up, that they have stopped trying to change the cause, that they feel dejected, and that they accept the inevitability of the feared outcome. Korner indicates that "hope induces a feeling of 'assumed certainty' that the dreaded event will not happen, that despair will not occur" (1970, p. 135). He goes on to say that "hope is an assumption which is clung to because it is of fundamental importance to the life of the individual" (p. 136). When helpees become aware of these assumptions, they may continue to use them as rationalizations to avoid despair, or they may see them as wishful thinking. In the latter case, they can manage them rationally in terms of their reality at that moment.

While hope remains primarily an emotional experience for helpees, they can think and talk about it also. Thus, hope involves expectancies that are different from simple wishes for events that might occur. The central characteristic of hope is a "quality of personal dependence on outcome" (Korner, 1970, p. 135), without building their actions "on 'expectations' that it *must* happen in order to avoid undesirable and disagreeable dreaded outcomes" (p. 135).

Some supportive values of hoping are momentary comfort and relief from suffering. Hope mobilizes reserve energy to meet present and future sources of stress. For some it means psychological, and even physical, survival. Medical folklore is full of instances where hope sustained, and apparently facilitated recovery of, the "incurably" ill.

A limitation that the helper should communicate is the tendency for hope to become an escape from unpleasant realities or responsibilities. It is also easy for hopes to be transformed into more superficial, unrealistic wishes. The consequences of giving up wishes are not as great as losing hope. If the former happens, the helpee may be disappointed, but, if hope diminishes, the person is vulnerable to doubt or, at worst, despair, insecurity, helplessness, and immobility.

Steps and methods to build and maintain hope are presented later under Strategies for Helping in Crisis.

Intensive Grieving

Grief is a normal emotional reaction to severe loss, usually of a significant person. An acute grief reaction may come considerably after the loss or traumatic event, or it may not come at all in the manner expected. Grief work following bereavement may take a normal, predictable course, as outlined earlier under transitions, or may be expressed in distorted and dysfunctional behaviors.

Lindemann (1944), one of the first to write about acute grief accompanying disasters, described the course of normal and morbid grief in a form currently useful for general helpers. Normal grief is characterized by (1) physical reactions—body distress in waves of twenty minutes to an hour, tightness and choking, sleeplessness, digestive disturbances, loss of appetite, sighing and shortness of breath, and weakness; (2) feelings of emptiness, tension, exhaustion, loss of warmth, and awareness of distance from people; (3) occasional preoccupation with images of the deceased; (4) occasional feelings of guilt over failure to do something or exaggerations of self-accusations over small incidents; and (5) change in activity patterns, restlessness, aimlessness, and searching for activity, yet lacking energy and motivation to follow through.

Morbid grief reactions are exaggerations of normal grief behaviors. They may take the form of underreaction or delayed grief, which may come years after the loss. Other grief reactions are prolonged isolation, flights into expansiveness and well-being, unusually strong irritability or hostility toward friends and relatives, and prolonged depression. These reactions require specialized care, and the bereaved should be brought to the attention of a specialist, preferably a psychiatrist experienced in grief work, since medication is usually one of the supportive treatments. All available human resources need to be involved, even more than in normal grief reactions. Depending on the specific individual's wishes and background, the involvement of ministers, with their traditional comforting rituals, reassurances, and relationships, could help persons accept and relieve their suffering.

Lindemann (1944) described the "anticipatory grief reaction" that complicates relationships when prolonged absence, as in wartime, takes place. After the separation, grief reactions sometimes occur and are worked through as if the absent person had died. When the absentee returns, as in the case of military personnel, both parties often are surprised at the emotional detachment of their reunion. The grief work had been carried out so effectively, probably as a protection in case of a death notice, that the spouse at home had little remaining feeling for the absentee. Such situations call for a delicate rebuilding of relationships or facing the decision to remain separated.

The normal course of grief work consists of (1) *accepting* the grief work process; (2) *expressing* the feelings of grief; (3) *dealing* with the memory of the deceased; (4) *readjusting* to the new environment without the deceased; and (5) *building* new relationships. An important element in the helping process is to enable the bereaved to accept and work through this grief process.

Although this section has dealt with intense grief and loss in terms of bereavement and disaster, the principles apply to less intense reactions to loss, such as employment, property, or reputation. The strategies to follow are applicable to the full range of loss reactions, from intense grief in bereavement to disappointment and anger over a missed promotion. These strategies also apply to crises other than loss, such as conflict, arrest, and persecution.

Strategies for Helping in Crises

The following discussions suggest general strategies for helping persons under sustained stress conditions or in a crisis. Simple formulas cannot ease human suffering, especially the sudden distress caused by uncontrolled traumatic events. Reactions to crises are highly individualistic and involve fundamental issues around the meaning of human existence. Even though it seems presumptuous to think of "helping" under such extreme conditions as life/death, some general helping principles apply to all types of crises. The first is liberal use of *emotional support* through close contact, reassurance, and listening to feelings. Often *changes in the environment,* such as taking the person to a safe and quiet place with nurturing and understanding people, are indicated. In addition, changes in the person's perception of the problem or changes in the meaning of the crisis follow emotional support.

Timing is an important factor in successful crisis interventions. The earlier the help after the crisis event, the more likely the positive outcome. This is why crisis centers in most communities are available for calls or drop-ins around the clock. Some centers have community outreach services to give help wherever the person is located. The basic idea behind early help is not only to reduce the person's danger to himself or herself but also to take advantage of the person's motivation to change or to grasp at any constructive solution.

Crisis Intervention Steps

Psychological first aid requires four crisis intervention steps. The helper first *appraises* (determines) the current condition of the person and the nature and severity of the crisis. An estimation must be made of the degree of risk or danger before emergency action is taken in a case such as a suicide threat. The appraisal of the person's situation includes how much disruption the person is experiencing, the person's strengths and coping skills, and what options are open. To obtain perspective on the present crisis, the helper may need to delve into conditions immediately preceding the crisis.

The helper must then *decide on the type of help* most needed at the moment based on an appraisal of the coping skills and resources of the person. The key question is, What resources are available to the person (such as a support group or a friend), and what personal strengths are available to help restore the person to a minimum level of functioning? The helper then puts the needed help in order of priority.

The third step is to *act* in a directly helpful way. The helper assists the person to vent present feelings of fear, guilt, or anger. In addition, the helper assists the person in expanding options for action, or at least acquiring an intellectual grasp of the plight. The helper assists people in crisis in mobilizing their defense mechanisms and coping skills. Through suggestions, the helper opens new possibilities for action and new relationships with people. These new options may include referral to a specialist for intensive counseling.

While working through the action steps, the person begins to *resolve the state of crisis* and to achieve renewed equilibrium. Here the helper reinforces the adaptive skills the person has mobilized to reduce tension and formulates a plan to reach new goals. The main goal for the helper in this step is to get the person back to a precrisis level of responding, not to work toward personality change or higher levels of growth. If the relationship continues, the helper may assist the person in gaining perspectives on the crisis experience such that it stimulates renewed growth, for example, toward independence and self-confidence.

Multiple Impact Support Strategy

Multiple impact strategy involves both an intensive and extensive support effort, usually combined with an active behavior change program. Teams of agencies and specialists generally are involved, each making an impact at the appropriate time and sequence. Environmental, or milieu, support is combined with relationship support. An example is a family in crisis that is given a minimum of two days' intensive round-the-clock attention in a residential or family service setting rather than in an agency, office, or the family's home. Thus, the family has the advantage of a fresh environment, a team medical-social-psychological approach, and individualized help in the form of groups and interviews. The assumptions underlying this strategy are that a family in crisis must be helped as a unit, or system, and that approaches to individual members separately would be ineffective. Total help in the early stages of a family crisis can be more effective than sporadic and progressive help later. The crisis can be used as a springboard for the family, or its members, to mobilize resources to deal with the crisis and to grow. In this process they learn how to prevent future crises.

This same multiple strategy is used with independent adults who face a crisis not involving a family. They may go to a retreat setting, or to a one-day program in a community mental health center, and receive intensive attention from a variety of professional and nonprofessional helpers.

An example of a multiple impact strategy in action is the support given to victims immediately after a traumatic event such as sudden death, rape, abuse, or community disaster. The victim is given an opportunity to describe the event and experience the remaining feelings associated with that event. This posttraumatic stress debriefing is designed to prevent the serious effects of the trauma from appearing later—known clinically as PTSD (posttraumatic stress disorder). The helping strategy here is to let the affected persons vent their feelings with an understanding helper.

While it is important to give aid to the victims of disastrous events, it is important also to give help to the rescuers and others involved with the event. A method called CISD (critical incident stress debriefing) has been instituted in many communities to get rescuers in groups as soon after the event as possible to describe their experiences and vent their feelings rather than deny or repress them. This debriefing, as it is called by Mitchell and Resnik (1981), is performed in teams consisting of a mental health worker, a police or fire-fighter representative, and a nurse or physician. It is a way to help emergency response workers from many services and to prevent stress responses and burnout after they take care of victims in disasters and traumatic events. In addition, families are included in these stress debriefings since they are victims also. An example is a student who comes to school with a gun and shoots the principal and injures teachers and students. In addition to the immediate responses to the crisis, a program of debriefing for the teachers, students, families, and other community members affected by the tragic event is necessary.

Building and Maintaining Hope

Since hopelessness, despair, and depression are such common components of stress and crisis, people depend heavily on helpers to deal constructively with these conditions. Hope is the main antidote to despair as well as the source of relief from tension and frustration of unmet goals and uncertain futures. Hope grants some satisfaction to the person to feel that the future may bring this relief. As Korner (1970) has indicated, hope includes strong emotional components akin to faith. People need faith and hope; "they resist losing them; they fight to maintain them" (p. 136). To protect these fragile feelings, people develop a "rationalizing chain" that is "formed from bits of reality accompanied by and held together by logic and reasoning" (p. 137). When stressors or crises come along, however, they are managed usually by strengthening the weak links with rationalizations. These rationalizations may clash increasingly with helpee perceptions of reality, until either they tighten the rationalizing logic in their chains or they revert to pure faith and feeling. Korner postulates a balanced condition, or "hope equation," between external sources of stress and a combination of faith and rationalizing that constitutes hope.

While hope is based largely on inner strength, especially cognitive skills, faith in forces outside one's own resources is helpful also. Drawing upon early religious training and spiritual resources developed over the years is very helpful. Helpers can encourage people expressing hopelessness and despair to draw upon these resources as a first step in building hope.

Another element in working with hope as a helping tool is to determine to what extent the nature and degree of disturbance are in the feeling component and to what extent in the rationalizing chain. If the feeling component is affected, the person may be depressed but is just as likely to have less visible feelings of hopelessness and the associated behaviors of passivity and detachment. In the case of sudden and severe loss, disorganized and dysfunctional behavior may be apparent.

After helpers have a better sense of their helpees' strengths, and how they are responding to the crisis, they can follow a general strategy of (1) expression of feelings; (2) cognitive integration; (3) mobilization of resources; and (4) action. The goal of this strategy is for helpees to begin functioning minimally so that their deteriorative tendencies can be arrested and their strengths mobilized.

The first step, then, is to get helpees talking about their feelings and hopes. If they feel helpless or numb, for example, let them talk about it. There is a role here for the helper who is not tied directly to the crisis event. Often the helpee needs to repeat the story over and over. This can irritate even the best of friends, especially those who are also experiencing the loss. The helper can listen multiple times, keeping the perspective that when not taken to extremes, this repetition is important to the grief process.

While it may assist helpees facing less severe stress to move quickly to Step 2—to clarify their situations through rational discussion of their false logic, to examine possible alternatives, and to engage in problem-solving activities—this approach generally is not useful when the stress reaction is severe and accompanied by feelings of intense hopelessness or helplessness. Ellis (1962) and Ellis and Dryden (1990) developed a Step 2 cognitive restructuring approach that they label *rational-emotive,* an attempt to examine the helpee's self-defeating assumptions and catastrophic logic. The idea is to look critically at the messages the helpee gives when he or she says, "I'm no good," "I'm a victim of circumstances," or "Isn't it awful?" A description of this method was given in Chapter 4 under Self-Confrontation. If you wish to understand this approach to changing helpees' thinking about themselves and their situations, also look at Ellis and Dryden's work listed under Suggestions for Further Study.

Most initial efforts toward helping people build their hope structures are neither rational nor feeling-oriented but are based on action. Loosening helpees from their lethargy and helpless feelings by encouraging activity aids their physical and mental well-being at this stage. Understanding skills should also be applied to provide an awareness of emotional support. The simple physical presence of a strong and understanding person as helpees talk about their feelings has some supportive effect. If these initial approaches fail to alter the despairing mood or passivity pattern, or if the condition seems to be deteriorating into feeling and thought disorders (delusion, hallucination, paranoia, fixed and unreal ideas, or severe depression), emergency referral measures would be appropriate.

In the specialized setting of a crisis center hotline, one study on effectiveness of direct advice compared with empathic listening strongly suggested that callers' immediate preferences were for the direct advice approach. This approach was preferred over a combination of approaches offered by paraprofessional helpers (Libow & Doty, 1976). One implication of findings such as these is that helpers dealing with crises must be prepared with a variety of approaches, including offering direct suggestions with firmness and confidence.

When helpees begin moving from their helpless feelings and passive behaviors, they can examine the "lost faith" and/or the missing links in their "rationalizing chain." The main helping strategy at this stage is to continue understanding support. Helpers should watch for opportunities to reinforce renewed hope, but they should also be aware of the limitations of too much approval of what the helpee is thinking and feeling. The choices about direction of the helpees' renewable belief system or reconstituted logic should be theirs, since these are value decisions. What should be reinforced is their effort to renew their hope and to take hold of new plans and ideas.

The other option that helpees face at this point is to stop thinking about hope temporarily and to face the situation or causes of the crisis directly. Or they may construct new hope structures better suited to their needs for security and more functional for controlling their anxiety. Regardless of which of the three options they choose, helpees need much supportive understanding at this stage. They need encouragement of efforts to reestablish their equilibrium and adaptive strength, as well as to act as responsibly as possible in this crisis. When helpees reach this stage of mastery in the resolution of their crises, they are in a position to explore renewal steps described in the next strategy. A significant factor in maintaining hope is the constant reminder that out of crisis comes new growth and opportunity for renewal.

Strategy of Renewal and Growth

Renewal and growth strategy is aimed primarily at identifying strengths in people, helping them to be aware of these strengths, and then helping them to develop a plan for releasing these growth potentials. It is not a strategy designed for helpees still in a state of crisis, however, because it "pushes" people into disequilibrium as a prelude to growth. This strategy requires skills in strength analysis and a whole array of competencies for facilitating awareness.

Much renewal work is done in the hundreds of residential growth retreat centers and institutes in the United States alone. These centers are not associated with formal educational structures, and they operate in a fairly unstructured fashion without courses, grades, or credits. Much use is made of encounter groups, sensory awareness, gestalt integration, communications training, meditation, and creative arts. A retreat setting facilitates concentration on developing the new skills and experiences apart from the realities and pressures of daily life. A laboratory approach enables the person to try out new experiences in the protected atmosphere of the group or growth center community without the risks inherent in real-life settings. The feedback under conditions of trust and safety is an invaluable contribution to personal growth. Participants establish their own growth goals and use the resources of the center to reach them. Renewal groups, for example, offer opportunities to reflect on values and purposes as well as to explore alternative life-styles and to discover hidden potentials. Examples are men's and women's awareness groups, gay life-style groups, widow and divorcee lifelines, professional development and burnout prevention groups.

For the helpee who has weathered a crisis and is at the stage of rebuilding, referral to such renewal groups reinforces hopes and strengths and facilitates commitment to action. The helpee experiences the warmth and support that come about from trusting others who are themselves on the personal growth quest.

The limitations of this movement, however, are that its popularity has attracted many helping opportunists who are poorly qualified to facilitate such educational experiences. There are few effective ways to control abuses and destructive outcomes of such irresponsible growth efforts. Like so many potential aids, these growth experiences are experimental and have side effects and misuses, as does use of medicinal drugs. It is a case of "let the buyer beware"; so it is essential to check carefully into the reputation of the growth center as well as into the backgrounds of the leaders before urging helpees to utilize this opportunity for renewal. Then too the leader may be highly skilled and may have an esteemed reputation, but the experience could be inappropriate for this helpee at this time. Participants who are ready to change are urged to take personal risks that enable them to move from their comfortable status to a higher level of functioning and joy. All helpers, therefore, need to become familiar, preferably in firsthand experience, with the possibilities and limitations of various styles of renewal opportunities.

The Crisis Center

For the helpee faced with continuing stress responses expressed as suicide attempts, drug abuse, or assault, the multiple approaches of a team of helpers often are needed. Most large communities now have such centers supported by community chests, private foundations, or public funds. Many are experimental efforts to meet community crises. They usually combine medical, psychological, and casework resources with peer helpers and volunteers. Examples are drug crisis clinics, rape relief, Traveler's Aid, and suicide prevention centers. Many centers operate telephone crisis lines that the person facing acute stress can call for supportive help and referral information. Many of these provide excellent free training in exchange for volunteer hours.

The Halfway House

The halfway house resource utilizes a strategy of facilitating transition from the crisis center or treatment facility to real life. Such houses are usually small homelike places with resident helping persons. The goal is to provide a semi-protected residential atmosphere where coping mechanisms and personality strengths can be developed before the helpee faces the demands of the real world. As the name implies, it is a facility halfway between the protective institution, or clinic, and the normal community. Work-release programs from prisons have the same rationale.

The Treatment Center

Treatment centers vary from the total environmental control of the conventional hospital, day-care center, and community mental hygiene clinic to small homelike residential centers (Lewis & Lewis 1989). An early model of a residential center was Synanon, which focused on drug rehabilitation performed by those who had been abusers of drugs but who adopted a different lifestyle and were willing to assist others who wanted to change their style of coping with stressors without the use of drugs. Similarly, substance abusers such as alcoholics have access to residential treatment centers that give psychological counseling as well as medical treatment. An example is the national chain CARE UNITS, usually affiliated with general hospitals. Another example is the camp or farm for children and teenagers who cannot cope with the stressors of family and community demands.

Therapeutic Counseling Strategy

Most of the strategies described previously involve multiple approaches in environmentally controlled settings. Much of the helping process for people under stress conditions or in crisis takes place in one-to-one interview formats, commonly labeled counseling. The usual strategy in counseling is to open the interview systematically with clarification of the reasons for the helpee's coming, establish mutual goals and responsibilities, then carry out a plan of action to reach the helpee's goals, and finally terminate the relationship. The counseling process varies according to the assumptions of the counselor about how behavior is changed and how personal problems are solved. Some counselors, such as Frankl (1965), use an existential framework that focuses on the meaning of existence. They see helping as a process of assisting helpees search for meaning in their lives and helping them to put tragedy and suffering in perspective. This "will to meaning" is not the same as faith or hope; it is a way of coping with the tension between what a person is and what he or she could become. "Logotherapy," as Frankl describes his view, is a means for dealing with the meaninglessness many persons feel about their lives and focuses on changing the way people construe their existence as a way of confronting directly the anxiety of living.

Behavioral counseling approaches, on the other hand, focus on helping people to change their habits and the environments that shape their behavior. It is concerned with behavior that leads to the feelings of discomfort and the consequences of acts to relieve that distress. Comfort derives from feelings of mastery over self and environment. Behavioral counseling writers have had little to say about utilizing crises, except in a general problem-solving framework.

Consoling Strategy

Consoling strategy is the traditional ministerial approach to comfort and crisis management and involves more than therapeutic counseling. For those persons who respond to religious ritual, writings, and assurances of life after death, it is a powerful supportive strategy, particularly in times of bereavement. Faith reestablishes hope. The person of the religious authority has a supportive effect also through whatever attributions of strength and protection are made to him or her. This religious tie may be some helpees' only means of managing grief so that they can move quickly through the healing process to new levels of growth, strength, and meaning in life.

Part of consoling strategies is to assist helpees to "accept the unaccept-able." Murgatroyd and Woolfe (1982) describe poignantly the problems faced by parents of a severely handicapped child. In addition to grieving over the loss of their "ideal" child, the parents must face the daily frustrations and prob-lems of care for the real child. Often, there is no end in sight for this care, since it may be a lifetime commitment. Crises in this context are recurrent. Similar issues arise with family caregivers for older adults. They must cope with the grief arising from loss of their "ideal" parent or spouse from their memories; yet they must face the daily tasks of caring for their real mentally and/or physically handicapped parent or spouse. Again, these tasks go on day after day, often with no respite or end in view.

The principal element in this aspect of consoling strategy is to be certain that the caregiver has accurate information (understanding) about the nature of the person's handicap or condition. The second element is building a sup-port system with other caregivers faced with similar kinds of handicaps. The third element is to help the caregiver become more aware of community ser-vices and the entitlements for which they may be eligible. Finally, the helper can provide a much-needed relationship to discuss the intense feelings asso-ciated with providing care without judgments or interpretations. These helping relationships can help caregivers not only cope with their own feelings but also become more aware of the tendency to overprotect the handicapped rel-ative or to deny the reality of the person's true condition.

Suggesting appropriate support literature for helpees often is helpful. Some illustrative examples from the myriad of special focus books are Hemfelt and Fowler's *Serenity* (1990) for assisting substance abusers through the twelve-step recovery program, Dean's *Nam Vet: Making Peace with Your Past* (1988) for recovering from war traumas, and Caine's *Widow* (1974). Helpers need to develop a special list of books to cover their areas of interest in death, divorce, rape, surgery, abuse, loneliness, poverty, war trauma, chemical dependency, illness, and disability. A general book that has helped many deal with grief and loss is Colgrove, Bloomfield, and McWilliams's *How to Survive the Loss of a Love* (1976).

Skills for Support and Crisis Management

It is difficult to speak of special skills for creating conditions of comfort. As indicated earlier in the chapter, comfort is due largely to the warm and caring personal qualities transmitted by the helper. Just being with the helpee in an attentive way during periods of stress is comforting. Thus, almost all the skills for understanding also convey support and result in comfort. Listening to the helpee ventilate feelings, for example, has a powerfully supportive effect. Sim-ilarly the skills for action to be described in the next chapter have implications for helping people move from passivity, so often characteristic of people in crisis, to action in building new relationships and planning for the future. The following skills can be used as supplements for those described earlier to produce conditions of comfort and to make use of the growth potential of crises.

Contacting Skills

Chapter 4 described *eye contact* as an essential ingredient in attending to the helpee. This nonphysical contact reassures helpees that the helper is with them. Physical *touch and hugging,* as we all know from our experiences with our families and friends, is another form of contact that has powerful comforting qualities. Among helpers, however, the question of touching helpees is very controversial. Putting a hand on a pupil's shoulder as a gesture of support and perhaps affection by teachers now is considered inappropriate by some helpers and parents. Americans seem to have strong touch taboos not present in many other societies. Southern Europeans, for example, are very demonstrative and kiss and hug profusely. Even though we recognize the power of touch to comfort, and even though many helpers favor its use, they must regard touch as a high-risk method at the present time because of potential lawsuits. The decision to touch depends on the context and structure of the helping relationship, as well as on local customs and legal constraints.

Touching is more permissible in the informal helping situation because it is more akin to friendship, where touching is encouraged. In more formal helping relationships touch usually is regarded as too intimate and seductive. In the final analysis, however, the appropriateness of touch depends on the judgment and ethical commitment of the helper. Because of child abuse practices, for example, children are being sensitized to and warned to be wary of any overtures from adults, no matter what the context. On the other side, popular discussions of touching and hugging among adults in the American cultural scene have legitimized this public behavior. Popular lectures and writings on love emphasize the healing power of hugging, even among strangers (Buscaglia, 1982).

In summary, this contact issue must be decided on the bases of:

1. The good judgment of the helper about the needs of this helpee.
2. Helpers' awareness of their own needs and ethics.
3. What is likely to be most helpful within the helper's rationale of helping.
4. What risks the helper is willing to take, having considered agency policy, local custom, professional ethics, and age, sex, and attitude of the helpee.

The issue of giving comfort by physical touching will be discussed further in Chapter 7.

Reassuring Skills

Reassurance is a method of verbally assuring helpees about the consequences of their actions or feelings. It acts as a reward since it reduces stress reactions and builds confidence. Reassurance fosters expectancies of future rewards. Examples of reassuring comments and suggestions are, "You are competent," "You can be reasonable," "You can solve your problem," "You can feel better." The goals of reassurance are to increase helpees' confidence, mobilize their strengths, reduce their anxiety to optimum working levels, or reinforce a desired behavior.

One reassuring skill is *expressing approval* of a helpee's statement. You say, for example, "That sounds to me like a good idea—very thoughtful." This process of agreeing, of course, reinforces helpees' expressions. Paradoxically, reassurance tends to fix the stated idea; the helpee, as a consequence, is less likely to change that idea or behavior if it turns out to be maladaptive.

A second reassuring skill is *predicting outcomes*. The helper says, for example, "You have been exploring your feelings pretty intensively today. You really have been spilling it out the last few minutes and now we have to go. You'll probably find yourself a bit moody the next couple of days; but this happens frequently, so don't worry about it." Another example is, "You have had a tough adjustment to face with your father's death, and it will probably continue to be rough for a while; but you will be able to handle it all right."

A third use of reassuring skill is *factual assurance*. Telling helpees that their problems have solutions, that people with this kind of difficulty make it, or that annoying symptoms disappear at fairly predictable times enables them to tolerate their momentary distress. Reassurance can be given at an even more specific factual level, such as assuring them that there are known steps to formulate sound career plans or to improve study performance, or to facilitate a life transition.

Some of the limitations and cautions in using reassurance are as follows: (1) It is easy to use, so there is a temptation to overuse it. (2) It may cause hostility in the helpee, who may feel the true nature of some serious condition was concealed or minimized. Helpees may feel that the helper is minimizing the seriousness of their feelings by remarks that indicate that "everything will turn out all right" or "it isn't as bad as you think it is." (3) Reassurance efforts come across often as insincere sympathy, which may jeopardize the whole helping relationship. (4) Dependency is often encouraged by the use of reassurance because people need periodic doses, which then act as a mechanism for avoiding change in their behavior. (5) If the reassurance is interpreted as agreement, helpees may feel *trapped* in their present thinking and action.

In summary, guidelines for reassurance:

1. Depend mainly on the positive quality of the relationship for supportive reassurance rather than relying on verbal forms of assurance.

2. Use verbal reassurance mainly to reduce distress through facts and predictions.

3. Use reassurance sparingly as a reinforcing agent to encourage continuing behaviors.

Relaxing Skills

Since stress reactions are usually accompanied by physical tension, one of the most direct forms of inducing comfort is to work on muscle tension. There are a number of styles of inducing relaxation through direct suggestion. Jacobson (1938) developed a form of progressive relaxation that is still used widely today. The helper systematically induces relaxation in large muscle groups by alternating the tensing and releasing of these muscles. Inducing relaxation is a simple skill to learn, and it has few hazards. Occasionally, hypersuggestible persons appear to go into a kind of hypnotic state, which may become a problem for the beginning helper. Simply telling helpees that when you finish counting to five they will wake up usually is sufficient.

Another way to induce relaxation is simple focusing on breathing, even counting slowly on inhaling and slowly on exhaling. One limitation is a condition called "hyperventilation" where the person may feel momentarily dizzy or faint after breathing too deeply. Certain body positions, such as those advocated in Yoga, induce relaxation also. Vocalizations, such as chanting, sighing deeply, and repeating expansive sounds, such as "a-ohm," help some people to relax. States of awareness, or consciousness, advocated by Zen practitioners also promote ease and physical relaxation. Hot baths with fast moving water have been used for millenia to induce relaxation. Since a detailed discussion of relaxation methods is beyond the scope of this chapter, helpers who desire to use these skills in their helping relationships should read basic works on physical relaxation, and the Eastern Zen and Yoga writers on awareness and meditation. See Suggestions for Further Study at the end of this chapter.

The uses of relaxation skills are varied. They may be used as a primary method to produce relief from tension precipitated by stressful conditions. Helpees frequently react with gratitude at the rapidity of relief that is afforded and thus feel more confidence in your ability to help them. Relaxation methods can be applied when you wish to reduce their anxiety and physical tension to sufficiently tolerable limits so that verbal skills can be utilized for understanding, comfort, or action (Cautela & Groden, 1986). Massage methods in the hands of an ethical and skillful operator can aid this process. Relaxation methods also are part of the sequence of systematic desensitization, a method for changing behavior to be described in the next chapter.

Guidelines on relaxing skills are:

1. Learn a verbally induced relaxation method that is comfortable for you.

2. Learn the importance of focusing on breathing as a quick relaxation method.

3. Become familiar with various psychological forms of relaxation and meditation as practiced by Eastern mystics, as an adjunct to your physical relaxation methods.

Centering Skills Cluster

Development of centering skills assumes that the helper regards the human personality as something beyond a collection of its components. Centering is a process of getting "in touch" and then "in tune" with one's person, or total self. Centering results in awareness of peace, harmony, unity, and strength. This skill cluster shows how different helpers emphasize different skills, depending on their personal experiences and assumptions about human personality. The helper has to view people as having an area in their psyches of private experiencing, called the "center," or the core of their being.

There are a variety of helper styles of centering and correcting overemphasis on one modality of existence, such as thinking, that come out of the Psychosynthesis tradition (Assagioli, 1973). One is a progressive awareness process where the helper tells helpees to close their eyes, get comfortable, and breathe slowly and deeply. Then the helper goes through a few verbal suggestions to guide their awareness to the center of being. Say, for example, "Your body is part of you . . ., but your body is not the total you; what else is there? You have feelings; they are part of you . . ., but your feelings are not the total you. What else is there? You are a thinking being; you have ideas . . ., but your thoughts are not the total you. You have a center where all of these parts of you come together, a center of your being where you experience peace, wholeness, strength . . .; this center is an important part of you. . . ."

Centering methods such as this one are used to help people who feel frustrated, out of tune, or even at war with themselves. Parts of their personalities are working at cross-purposes and consuming enormous amounts of energy. Their bodies, for example, may be out of phase with their thoughts. The aim is to promote an awareness of smoothness and unity as a means toward comfort. The method is designed also to get the parts back into balance. Some helpees, for example, seem to have an exaggerated awareness or valuing of their bodies, to the exclusion of other aspects of existence. Conversely, people who have denied body experience find great comfort in rediscovering their bodies and the feelings locked in their muscles. In crisis situations, helpees are comforted to realize that the center of their being is a place where they can find peace and strength.

In this context, Corliss and Rabe (1969) speak of two modes of being, peripheral and central. The person existing at the peripheral level is concerned primarily with doing, with changing the physical world, whereas the centrally oriented person focuses more on internal personal states of feelings, dreams, wishes, and intuitions. The "center" exists more in fantasy; it is a place of quietude and receptivity. A key problem of living is maintaining an effective balance between these two modes of existence. The helping strategy involved in working through crises of life-style is to lead persons through an analysis of values associated with peripheral living and help them to center their existence. Then the helper facilitates helpee choices with decision skills cited in the next chapter and with communication skills described in the preceding chapter.

Strength analysis is also a method of centering, although it operates more as a descriptive device to build strength and confidence. It is applicable to nonstress situations as well and is a form of building strength to utilize future crises constructively. In this method the helper simply asks helpees to focus on their strong points and to list them out loud. It may be a matter of only three or four points, but they are usually sufficient to start helpees thinking of their positive qualities. In periods of stress the usual tendency is to focus on weak and negative personal qualities and to exaggerate them. Self-abnegation and criticism often accompany depressed moods. This method of strength analysis is *not* a method of reassuring the person, however, that she or he is strong and capable. Neither does it suggest that "every day in every way, you're getting better and better." The list of strengths, with specific examples, comes from the helpee's survey of his or her life experience.

Reviewing growth experiences is a method of asking the helpee to focus on pleasant or unpleasant experiences (the more recent, the better) that have had a profoundly positive effect on growth. This request is often interpreted to mean traumatic events that have had a frustrating or negative effect, but these may be dealt with productively at another time. The helpee's focus here must be on events that had positive outcomes. This process leads to reexperiencing feelings long outside of awareness. The effect is to strengthen helpees' images of themselves as capable persons with the strength to meet stress and crisis. They can point to specific instances where they have done so in the past.

Reviewing peak experiences has an effect similar to the analysis of growth experiences above. In Chapter 1, we defined Maslow's term *peak experience* to mean those life experiences, usually short and infrequent, when the person is aware of intense pleasure, exhilaration, joy, and fulfillment. Recalling and focusing on such experiences can be rewarding in terms of comfort and satisfaction.

You can practice this review yourself to know better how to assist your helpees. Put yourself in a relaxed state and make a broad sweep backward over the past decade or two. Focus on those experiences that made you feel happy about yourself, confident, competent, joyful, and satisfied. Scrupulously avoid focusing on the sad or unpleasant experiences. Relish those reexperienced pleasant events in a leisurely manner. What were your characteristics at that time that were associated with your pleasure? These are some personal strengths, so take careful note of them and bring them forward to present time. Come back to full awareness of the here and now; take a pencil and list these strengths garnered from this reexperience of former feelings of confidence and worth.

Developing Action Alternatives

One of the characteristics of people in crisis is a narrowing of perception—that is, they see very few solutions or alternatives. "Suicide is my only way out" is an example. One of the skill clusters to help such people is to encourage them to consider alternatives through suggesting some possibilities, as well as by drawing ideas from the helpee. The helping goals are to facilitate a realistic perception of the crisis event, provide support to reduce the tensions associated with the crisis or conflict, consider all the coping alternatives, and then make a commitment to action to achieve reasonable equilibrium, integration, and future growth.

The idea of equilibrium in crisis theory espoused by Aguilera and Messick (1994) and expanded through research cited by Slaiken (1990) states that people seek an emotional balance between their problems and possible solutions. When their coping skills are inadequate, or their action alternatives are too narrow, they experience inner tension or distress, which, when severe, creates the imbalance, or crisis. Part of the helper's task is to assist the person in avoiding abortive solutions to his or her problems during the crisis until the person's coping mechanisms are revitalized.

Another application of the equilibrium concept applies to families in crisis. A family, for example, that goes through a critical operation on a family member, or has a seriously ill child, suffers many stresses and fears of death, disability, or disfigurement. Epperson (1977) described six stages families typically go through to reach a state of equilibrium—anxiety, denial, anger, remorse, grief, and reconciliation. It is important for helpers in these critical situations to give family members essential information about what is happening, to explain the process of grieving and crisis resolution, and to apply the skills described previously to achieve the desired equilibrium and comfort level.

Referring Skills

At times even the most skilled and confident helpers admit frustration and defeat in dealing with persons in crisis. Referral is one approach where the helpee can have a fresh start. For the beginning helper, referral is a common method of managing crisis conditions in helpees. Although referral seems to be a simple skill, these specific methods can make it more effective:

1. Know the community's resources for different kinds of services.

2. Explore helpees' readiness for referral. Have they expressed interest in specialized help? Are they afraid of seeing a "shrink"? Do we frighten them with implications of the severity of their problems, such as through the connotation we give to "You had better see a psychiatrist!"?

3. Be direct and honest about your observations of their behavior that led to your suggested referral. Be honest also about your own limitations. If, after working with them for awhile, you feel that it would be in their best interest to receive more intensive help from a specialist, you might say something like "Let's explore what other possible resources would be available for help with this question." This illustrative statement does not imply they are too disturbed or confused for you to handle and therefore must be in *really* bad shape.

4. It is advisable to discuss the possibility of referral with the referral agency before the problem becomes urgent.

5. Determine what other persons have had contact with this helpee, and if you have permission from the helpee, confer with them before suggesting further steps.

6. If the helpee is a minor, it is wise to inform the parents of your recommendations and obtain their consent and cooperation.

7. Be fair in explaining the services of a referral agency by citing the possibilities and the limitations of that agency. Do not imply that miracles can be performed there.

8. Let the helpee or the helpee's parent make their own appointments for the new service, although supportive services such as transportation should sometimes be facilitated.

9. Do not release information to any referral source without permission from helpees or their parents in the form of a signed release.

10. If you have been having the primary helping relationship with the helpee, it is ethical to attempt to maintain that relationship until the referral is complete and a new relationship is begun.

Renewing or Building Support Systems

Mentioned earlier under steps in crisis intervention was the necessity to facilitate the person's linkage to a support system. Such a system provides the encouragement, love, and security so desired immediately by persons suffering loss. Later, a support system provides reality checks on expectations of others and honest feedback on one's behavior—so difficult to get from the larger community. Examples of support groups are families, clubs, close neighborhood groups, church organizations, and groups of friends specifically organized as a support group. This type of support goes beyond the friendly ear of a close associate or relative. A close-knit family group is probably the best source of such support when the self-destructive forces of loss impinge on a person. Persons in crisis desperately need refurbishing of their feelings of personal worth and an opportunity to check reality perceptions until they have mobilized their own resources to go on.

The principal problem with groups such as those described is that they often do not function for the person, either because the person in crisis has no connection with such a primary group or because the group extracts a price of conformity to its norms and values as a condition of offering support. Helpers need to know community resources for different helping situations. In many communities, groups such as widows' lifelines or divorce lifelines offer help to those without family support groups and also supplement the help of groups such as families and neighbors. The Suggestions for Further Readings at the end of this chapter offer further ideas on using support systems.

The specific steps suggested for renewing or building a support system are as follows:

1. *Identify* who is currently in the network. Make a diagram, putting names in circles and placing them at different distances from the helpee, to indicate social/emotional distance and the frequency of contact.

2. *List functions* the network serves for the helpee. The usual functions that go beyond basic nurturance are offering information, being available in crisis, feeling valued, giving challenging feedback, and sharing joy or humor.

3. *List the names* of the helpee's network members and the various supportive functions they perform in a column on a sheet of paper.

4. *Examine each support member critically* in terms of current contributions to the helpee, extent of reciprocal support, and gaps in the network where no person is performing essential functions.

5. *Decide where changes must be made* to strengthen relationships, renew old contacts, add new members with new functions, or delete members from the helpee's network.

6. *Determine skills* the helpee may need to carry out Steps 4 and 5, such as assertive and social skills.

Outcomes Self-Check

Now that you have studied this chapter you can (1) describe and illustrate the terms *transition, stress, crisis, coping, support, hope,* and *grief;* (2) describe and illustrate eight helping strategies for coping with stress and crisis; (3) list three skills from the chapter on understanding that have supportive effects also; (4) describe two arguments for and against using contacting, reassuring, and relaxing skills; (5) list ten principles for referral of helpees to other persons or agencies; and (6) list six steps for building or renewing a support system. The final test of this knowledge is your ability to apply these methods and principles such that helpees feel and act in ways that indicate confidence and comfort.

Suggestions for Further Study

Benson, A. *Relaxation Response.* New York: William Morrow, 1975.

Brammer, L. *How to Cope with Life Transitions.* Washington, DC: Hemisphere, 1991. (A practical approach to developing six clusters of coping skills for everyday life transitions.)

———, Abrego, P., and Shostrom, E. *Therapeutic Counseling and Psychotherapy.* 6th ed. Englewood Cliffs, NJ: Prentice Hall, 1993. (Ch. 7 on reducing stress, and on reassurance methods; Ch. 14 on human values.)

Bridges, W. *Transitions.* Reading, MA: Addison-Wesley, 1980.

Caplan, G., and Killilea, M., Eds. *Support Systems and Mutual Help.* New York: Grune & Stratton, 1976. (A collection of procedures and descriptions of exemplary programs of support for organizing support systems.)

Cautela, J., and Groden, J. *Relaxation: A Comprehensive Manual for Adults and Children with Special Needs.* Champaign, IL: Research Press, 1986. (Stress management ideas for all age groups.)

Dryden, W. *The Essential Albert Ellis: Seminal Writings on Psychotherapy.* New York: Institute of Rational-Emotive Therapy, 1991.

Ellis, A., and Dryden, W. *The Practice of RET.* New York: Institute of Rational-Emotive Therapy, 1990. (Recent research and sequenced steps for applying RET to individuals and groups.)

Farber, M. *A Theory of Suicide.* New York: Funk & Wagnalls, 1968. (An analysis of the experience of suicide prevention centers.)

Feifel, H. *The Meaning of Death.* New York: McGraw-Hill, 1959. (A psychological approach to death and dying.)

Figley, C. *Helping Traumatized Families.* San Francisco: Jossey-Bass, 1989. (Suggestions for helping families cope with crises.)

Galton, L. *Coping with Executive Stress.* New York: McGraw-Hill, 1983. (Signs of and solutions to stress in management.)

Gardner, J. *Self-Renewal.* New York: Harper & Row, 1963. (A short essay on the necessity for renewing individuals and changing institutions.)

Gottlieb, B. *Social Support Strategies: Guidelines for Mental Health Practice.* Beverly Hills, CA: Sage, 1983. (A summary of literature on social support with emphasis on prevention.)

Janosik, E. *Crisis Counseling: A Contemporary Approach.* Monterey, CA: Wadsworth, 2nd ed. 1994. (Steps to manage crises and follow-up counseling.)

Kirschenbaum, H., and Glaser, B. *Developing Support Groups: A Manual for Facilitators and Participants.* La Jolla, CA: University Associates, 1978. (A manual on how to establish and lead support groups.)

Kübler-Ross, E. *Death: The Final State of Growth.* Englewood Cliffs, NJ: Prentice Hall, 1975.

Lane, D. Counselling psychology in organisations. *European Review of Applied Psychology* 43 (1993): 41–46. (Special issue on the human factor in organizations. This article, for example, focuses on the use of helping skills in the banking industry.)

Lazarus, A. *In the Mind's Eye: The Power of Imagery for Personal Enrichment.* Champaign, IL: Research Press, 1985.

Lester, G., and Lester, D. *Suicide: The Gamble with Death*. Englewood Cliffs, NJ: Prentice Hall, 1971. (A broad behavioral science study of suicide.)

Lewis, J., and Lewis, M. *Community Counseling*. Pacific Grove, CA: Brooks/Cole, 1989. (A manual of community services for prevention and treatment.)

Lindemann, E. Symptomatology and management of acute grief. *American Journal of Psychiatry* 101 (1944):7–21. Reprinted in Parad, H., *Crisis Intervention: Selected Readings*. New York: Family Service Association of America. Ch. 1. (Practical suggestions for managing extreme loss reactions.)

Marin, P., and Cohen, A. *Understanding Drug Use*. New York: Harper & Row, 1971. (An adult's guide to drugs and the young.)

Michenbaum, D. *Stress Inoculation Training*. Boston: Allyn & Bacon, 1985. (A concise research-based manual on stress management and prevention.)

National Referral Network for Kids in Crisis. 1991. (A program of Wiley Krause, 1650 Broadway, Bethlehem, PA 18015-3998, a referral network for organizations serving children in crisis: 1-800-KID-SAVE.)

Parad, H. *Crisis Intervention: Selected Readings*. New York: Family Service Association of America, 1965. (A collection of reprints on grief, family crises, maternal reactions, school entry, relocation, illness, and psychiatric crises.)

Schlossberg, N. *Overwhelmed: Coping with Life's Ups and Downs*. Lexington, MA: Heath, 1989. (A practical approach to coping with stress and change.)

6

Helping Skills for Positive Action and Behavior Change

People come to helpers mainly because they are unhappy about some aspect of their behavior. Although they do not always state their goal as wanting to change a specific behavior, like shyness, they soon see that their actions must be the ultimate focus of their attention. Essentially, all helping is aimed toward action outcomes of some kind. If specific actions to change behavior through changing the environment are involved, the process is described usually as behavior modification. This process of changing behavior applies not only to observable actions but also to covert or internal behavior, such as how people think of themselves, how they feel about other people, or how they view their world. These internal states are determined from verbal self-reports, but we look for specific actions to verify them. For example, we look for positive self-descriptions if helpees feel good about themselves. By observing actions, such as the degree of assertive social behavior exhibited by helpees, we can infer how confident they feel about themselves when they are around others.

A positive action approach gives helpers specific evidence that they have been helpful to the extent that their helpees have reached their goals. There is much discussion about accountability in all helping agencies. Before proceeding, ask yourself what the term *accountability* means to you—accountability to whom and for what outcomes? Accountability means that you, as the helper, assume a large share of responsibility to meet specific behavioral outcomes of the helping process. It means also that you look for evidence that the helpee is achieving the goals determined in the early stages of the helping process. An action program in an accountability framework means that the helpee was involved extensively in both establishing and assessing the objectives.

Positive action refers to two types of processes that will form the remaining content of this chapter. One is a problem-solving and decision-making cluster of processes and skills. The other cluster of skills is aimed at changing specific kinds of behaviors, usually by acquiring a skill rather than removing a deficiency. Some examples of the kinds of concerns brought to helpers that have specific skill involvement are improving study skills, acquiring social skills, developing more assertive behaviors, and diminishing unnecessary fears. Essentially, the helper is in the position of a teacher of skills for solving problems, changing behavior, and achieving higher levels of functioning.

There are practically unlimited possibilities for improving human capacities. Numerous writers on the human potential estimate that we use about 10 percent of our potentialities. Records in sports, for example, are broken regularly. Studies underway on control of body functions, particularly brain powers, are opening vast reservoirs of energy and action potential. Various methods of monitoring our own behavior, controlling negative thoughts, improving self-images, and altering our consciousness are available now. Helpers skilled in teaching others how to manage their own behavior through knowledge of behavior-changing and problem-solving skills will have a powerful helping resource.

Outcomes You Can Expect

The purpose of this chapter is to examine the processes and skills that will accomplish the helping functions described above. The chapter focuses on problem solving and changing observable behavior, whereas the preceding two chapters emphasized more subtle changes in attitude, self-regard, and perception of life circumstances. As a result of studying this chapter you will be better able to (1) describe the steps in a problem-solving and decision-making model of helping; (2) apply relevant skills in appropriate sequences; and (3) describe and illustrate skills for changing behavior such as modeling, contracting, rewarding, extinguishing, desensitizing, and aversion controlling.

Although it is unrealistic to expect to apply these skills expertly after reading about them, it is reasonable for you to expect to try them out with understanding and to evaluate your success with them. Since you will have specific outcomes to observe, these skills should be easier to evaluate than those described in previous chapters. For example, the effects of a reward schedule on new behaviors such as weight control would be very obvious. A note of caution, though: These behavior change skills appear deceptively simple to apply, yet they require practice and feedback from those who are specialized in behavior modification methods. After you study the methods here and in the suggested readings, find a setting in which you can try these skills, preferably under the supervision of a behavioral change specialist.

The Action Approach to Helping

Characteristics and Models

The main focus in the action approach is on changing specific helpee behaviors. The action approach is characterized by specific objective methods to reach helpee goals and manage environmental change.

Two basic models describe the action approach. The first is problem solving, a self-directed action to find the answers to everyday questions. Problem-solving models include deciding and planning functions also. Examples are: Where should we go for our vacation? Should I change my job? Which college should I attend? The second model is a behavior-changing approach to specific behaviors I may want to acquire, such as how to make new friends. Behavior changing also includes modifying undesired behavior, such as overeating.

Helpers interested in behavior change look at the helpee's present behavior and the complex environment in which it takes place. Thus, the helper takes minimum notice of psychological traits and problems. Some behavioral helpers, especially in working with children, get a baseline count of the child's undesirable and desirable behaviors before doing anything else. This count gives them a basis for judging the effectiveness of the help in terms of decreases in undesirable and increases in desirable behavior.

Implications

Some implications of the action approach for the helping process are that helper and helpee try to establish goals, find solutions, and make plans together. As a helper, you will use a variety of methods to assist the helpee in achieving specific goals. You will be responsible for observing what is happening at all times so that you can define in concrete ways what progress, if any, the two of you are making toward the helpee's goals. While you will trust your judgment and feelings about what is going on, you will look for specific outcomes to check your impressions. By being very specific with the helpee about concrete outcomes, you keep vagueness and mysticism out of the helping process. You say, for example, "I agreed to work with you, but you need to do some work outside of our talk sessions because what you do out there is the important payoff of our work here. We will be talking about very concrete things you can do to help your situation out there, and we will want to look occasionally at the progress we are making."

This action approach is not an emotionally sterile and strictly rational procedure, as is often claimed. Action methods work very effectively in a relationship characterized by the facilitative conditions described in Chapter 2. Mickelson and Stevic (1971) found, for example, that behaviorally oriented counselors with high warmth, empathy, and genuineness were more effective in generating information-seeking responses in their helpees than behavioral counselors rated low on facilitative characteristics.

Problems and Goals

Problems Become Goals

Since action outcomes are our concern, it is very important to identify specific problems and translate those problems into precise goals. Helpees seldom come with neatly stated problems. They usually are expressed in vague feelings of confusion, dissatisfaction, or distress. Often complaints are focused on another person or institution. Thus, helpers begin, as in other styles of helping, with listening for understanding. They try to communicate this understanding, and often this is enough for the helpee to feel understood and comforted. But if the helper's listening reveals that the helpee needs to act differently, another strategy is needed. As helpers listen, they are gaining information about the specifics in helpees' lives—how they look at themselves and others, what they want, and what their environment is like. From these data about the helpee's initial complaints and feelings, the helper and helpee together describe how the helpee acts now and would like to act. Thus, goals are formulated toward which the person can work with some methods suggested by the helper.

Goals must meet three criteria: (1) they are desired by and tailored to the helpee; (2) the helper is willing to help the person work toward the goals; and (3) attainment of the goals is observable and assessable. General growth goals, such as "self-understanding" and "self-actualization," are accepted by almost everyone, but to be useful in an action approach they must be stated in the unique and specific language of the helpee. An example of such a specific action goal is "I want to avoid crying every time I am criticized." This goal implies that helpees will understand why they cry, but it goes beyond understanding and relief of distress to the action of changing one's crying behavior.

Goals of the helpee must fit the ethical, legal, and competency requirements of the helper. For example, it would not be appropriate for a helper to be a party to a helpee's scheme to cheat on an examination or take advantage of a weaker person, even though it was very important to the helpee to do so. Helpers should always have the option of refusing help if they feel the goals are questionable.

Difficulties in Stating Goals

Changing helpee problems into specific goals with observable outcomes is one of the principal difficulties in the action approach, according to research by Meichenbaum (1985) and Krumboltz and Thoreson (1976). Some guidelines follow:

1. It is important to *determine who the helpee is.* The following brief example will illustrate the problem in this special context. If a parent refers a child for counseling, it is easy to be confused about who needs help—the parent or the child. The helpee is defined as the one who brings the problem to the helper, since for the time being, at least, that person "owns" the problem. Although the helper may understand the plight of the person who is trying to bring another person in for help, sometimes it is necessary to say firmly, "Let's discuss how I might help you deal with this person so you can help him change his behavior." You, as a helper, may still want to see the other person, but at least you have established a helping partnership with the referring person and are not carrying the full responsibility for a most difficult helping situation.

2. Helpees *express their problems as feelings,* such as "I am miserable," "I am lonely," or "I am frustrated." After applying skills for understanding to clarify the feeling statements, the helpee is asked, "What could you *do* to make yourself wanted, attractive, or loved by other persons?" The assumption here is that helpees need to take action counter to the feeling expressed so that they may gain the response they want—love, respect, or money, for example. This step may mean acquiring a new competency.

Another problem faced by helpers is people with high aspirations who set unrealistic standards, continually comparing themselves to others of extraordinary competence. Furthermore, such people assume their feelings of incompetence or loneliness are unique because they seldom share these feelings and have little basis for judging the realism of their feelings. Help in this situation consists mainly of receiving accurate information about others' feelings, making realistic plans for achievement, and accepting the reality of the frustration and disillusionment.

3. *Lack of a goal* and not knowing their own desires can be a source of difficulty for helpees. Such helpees must come to realize that values and goals are not discovered but are created by people for themselves. Thus, the most helpful thing one can do with purposeless and alienated people is to encourage them to construct goals for *their* lives or to adopt goals of established groups—religious, political, social, service—to give purpose to their existence. Most people need some large purpose or cause to give meaning and zest to their lives. The general helping strategy is to engage them in an active, exploratory process where they try on different goals and organizational identities until they find some that match their vaguely defined desires.

4. Having *too many goals at one time* often leads to mental gridlock and great choice anxiety. The helping strategy for these people is to assist them in prioritizing and phasing their goals. Some people have great difficulty making choices when there are too many options. If underlying obsessiveness or indecision is suspected, referral to a specialist in these problems is indicated.

5. *Desired goals may be inappropriate or unclear.* Helpees may want to do something that, in your opinion, is against their best interests. If we really believe that they must make their own decisions, the most we can do is offer our opinions as additional information they can consider. It is best if our opinion is solicited. Sometimes helpees give helpers biased views, so helpers cannot get a clear idea of the helpees' problem. Helpees may not know why their behavior is disliked or unacceptable; an example is the young person who says others do not like her and she cannot tell why. The general helping strategy is to encourage her to note what she is doing to make herself unwanted and to set goals for trying new behaviors that make her more attractive to others.

6. *Choice conflict* also makes it difficult to set behavioral goals. A common condition brought to helpers is one in which all the choices are unacceptable or unattainable. An example is the couple who want separation to resolve their conflict, yet do not want the financial problems associated with a divorce. The general helping strategy is to decide whether the helpee needs to learn problem-solving skills or to explore the full range of alternatives. In any case, the helper must confront helpees with the necessity to pin down goals, such as exploring all the possible consequences of each choice facing them, and then to make the choice. In making this final choice helpees must be confident that they are making the best choice with the information they have now.

7. *Sometimes helpees have no real problem but just want to talk.* They do not want an action goal. Their goals appear to be social stimulation or support. Helpers then must decide if they want to spend their time socializing in this manner or suggest that their helpees find someone else to talk with. Sometimes what first appears to be a desire of the helpee to "just talk" is a test of trust before the true goals are shared.

Moving beyond Goals

We have been discussing some of the difficulties of translating problems into specific goal statements that make sense to the helpee. Once the goals have been agreed on, the skill of contracting is used to determine how, when, and by whom the goal-seeking efforts will be initiated and maintained. The process of comparing results with the goals is a continuous one, so helpers know when they are succeeding. If the helpee is not moving toward the mutually determined goals at a reasonable rate, a diagnostic inquiry must be started to answer the question, "Why not?" Then a corrective procedure can be instituted.

Finally the process is evaluated to see what can be learned that will make helping for action more successful. Evaluation of helpee outcomes against specific goals for action also makes accountability for performing the helping tasks much easier to demonstrate. Those helpers working in an agency context are finding this evaluative function a political necessity for survival as well as a continuing professional obligation.

The following is a summary of key characteristics of helping for action:

1. The helper uses listening and reflecting skills to *discover central problems* and assess the helpee's situation.

2. The helper assists the helpee in *stating problems in behavioral terms* as goals to be achieved.

3. The helper and helpee *agree on the priority of problems* to be solved at acceptable levels of success.

4. The helper *chooses a problem-solving or behavior-changing model* and then utilizes his or her full range of skills to work toward helpee goals.

5. Helpees show that they are *aware of the consequences and ethics* of each action alternative.

6. The action process is *monitored* continuously. The helper and helpee agree on evaluation of progress and any changes in strategy to be instituted.

7. The helper and helpee *plan the transition* from learning coping skills to maintaining new behaviors in their natural setting without the helping relationship.

8. The helper and helpee decide if the *primary goal* and subgoals have been reached.

9. The entire helping *process is evaluated* and *examined for knowledge* to be applied in future helping relationships. For example, has the helpee learned the principles and steps of the personal problem-solving or behavior-changing process?

First, we will consider a decision-making and problem-solving model with related skills. Then, we will look at skills helpful in changing specific behaviors.

Problem Solving, Decision Making, and Planning

A significant number of helpee concerns can be translated into problems to be solved or decisions to be made among two or more alternatives. There is sufficient research available to indicate the most efficient and effective ways to solve personal problems (Heppner & Krauskopf, 1987; Heppner, 1990; Dixon & Glover, 1984). Common life decisions such as "What career should I plan for?" "What changes should I make in my life?" "Should I marry this person?" "Should I stay here or take this new job offer?" are suited to this problem-solving strategy of helping.

A second important helper consideration is how to teach helpees to solve their own problems. We are not helping them very much if we provide a temporary process for helpees to solve immediate problems, and then they continue to seek out helpers every time they face a new problem. One strategy for learning this process is direct instruction in the problem-solving procedure. Another strategy is simulation—an artificial or game approach similar to the real-life situation. The helpee can make choices and experience consequences vicariously without dire results. An example is the Career Game by Varenhorst (1976), which provides simulated decision-making conditions for helpees planning a career. A fictitious person making career choices is presented, and helpees work in teams deciding how that person will spend his or her time over eight years. Decisions are interdependent, and scoring is based on probability tables that reflect job, education, and marriage opportunities in U.S. culture. Many decisions are involved, and the consequences are known immediately to the teams, so the helpee players can learn the problem-solving process from early feedback. Computer software programs have simulations to try various problem solutions.

Taking risks is part of the problem-solving process. It is comfortable to stay in one's present condition, even though distasteful, compared to the discomfort of reaching out toward solutions. To solve problems, then, involves some risk not only of the discomfort of change but also the pain of failing to find a satisfactory solution. Taking risks does not mean impulsively grasping at solutions that may have danger to self and others, but risking is a creative confrontation with the pain of change.

An important growth goal is to achieve competence and flexibility in problem solving. This means having several models of problem solving to meet different problem demands (Meichenbaum, 1977; Bents & Bents, 1986; Brammer, 1990). For example, some problems, such as which house to buy, demand factual knowledge and comparative analyses, but there is also a point when it "feels right" to buy a certain house. Some problems thus demand an intuitive approach where the answers come from within—from feelings and tastes rather than rational analyses. Part of problem solving is to know when to trust those intuitive messages.

Some problems, such as puzzles, also require a discovery process, where the solution suddenly falls into place with an "aha" experience. Then, there is the ever-present trial-and-error approach to solving problems where we try blindly or impulsively to solve the problem until we stumble into a solution. For example, we find the handle of the door in the dark by fumbling around for it, or we pound the balky engine here and there in the hope that it will start. Since most problems require, at least in part, a rational, systematic approach, this is the type of problem solving that will be emphasized in the next section. Since most of us depend on an intuitive approach to some problems, a brief description is presented also. What style of solving problems do you use? How effective is it?

Problem-solving steps appear so simple and compelling that perhaps you wonder why we do not think more rationally about our problems. From the viewpoint of the helper with wide experience, it is no surprise that problems are so difficult to solve and behaviors so resistant to change. In part, it is the incredible complexity of most human problems, but more importantly these maladaptive behaviors are so deeply ingrained from years of practice that a few hours discussion with a helper seems to make hardly a dent. In addition, these maladaptive behaviors serve some important functions for the person that make them hard to give up. For example, these behaviors may help the person to control his or her anxiety, and in that sense, they serve an adaptive function. Some behaviors, such as smoking, also have physical as well as psychologically addictive qualities.

It is important to recognize that people are usually doing the best they can to solve their problems, but often they are using inefficient or nonproductive problem-solving skills. A question to be asked in a helping relationship is "What have you already done to try to solve the problem?" Often helpees have tried one or two solutions, and when those did not work, tried the same ones again, often repeating this pattern multiple times, with increasing intensity. No wonder they are frustrated by the time they seek help from someone else. The helper's job then becomes one of looking at the goal and what strategies have or have not worked. Then the helper and helpee together can explore other untried or unimagined options.

The next two sections will emphasize that it is possible to identify the basic skills in rational and intuitive problem solving and teach them to helpees. A significant part of this process is developing helpees' confidence in their problem-solving capacities.

The Rational Problem-Solving Process

The steps on the next page follow rational problem-solving sequences and are applied to many problems, but most of the illustrations are in the area of life planning, as exemplified by Brammer, Abrego, and Shostrom (1993) and Krumboltz and Sheppard (1976). To make the following procedures meaning-ful, relate them to a present problem in your life. Record the steps you are taking and comments on how each step contributed to your action plan.

These general steps in rational problem solving are:

1. *Establish a relationship and get the helpee involved.* Helpees must be inter-ested in the process and believe that they have the power to make decisions that will influence their lives. Helpees must also have the mental set that prob-lems are a normal part of living and that they can cope. Good problem solvers also do not act impulsively but go systematically through a set of behaviors described below. Good problem solvers, however, do not avoid the problem or procrastinate either.

2. *State and clarify the problem and then translate the problem into a goal statement.* For example, the problem may be an aching loneliness; the goal becomes making two new friends in the next week.

3. *Determine and explore alternatives* to the more apparent solutions. For example, making new friends may require broadening one's interests or acquiring additional social skills.

4. *Gather relevant information.* This step may take the form of active seek-ing and reading by the helpee, resources offered by the helper, simulation games, films, or tests. The helpee, for example, should be encouraged to sam-ple likely locations where new friends could be found.

5. *Explore the implications of the information and the consequences of the alternatives.* For example, a consequence of deciding to make new friends may be learning new social skills or risking rejections.

6. *Clarify values that underlie personal choices.* Helpees must know what they need and desire and their priority order. Lead helpees to explore their interests, competencies, family circumstances, social expectations, and realities.

7. *Reexamine the goals, alternative choices, risks, and consequences.* A final check on understanding the information and implications is made before the final decision.

8. *Decide on one of the alternatives and formulate an implementing plan* for that decision. For example, the helpee may decide on a cruise as the alterna-tive action step. The plan should include a timetable for doing the sequential tasks leading to the cruise, for example. A plan should include a list of resources already possessed and whatever personal, skill-related, or informa-tional resources are still needed.

9. *Try out the plan for implementing the decision with periodic reevaluations* in the light of new information and changing circumstances.

10. *Generalize the process* to new life problems.

Most people, particularly young ones, have limited life experiences in making decisions and are generally unfamiliar with this rational process. Therefore, many helpees must be taught this process through problem-solving interviews, direct trial-and-error experiences, and simulations, such as career or marriage games. Young helpees often ask outright, "What shall I do?" "What course should I take?" "Should I try drugs?" "What career should I choose?" "What college should I apply to?" Instead of giving advice or opinions, it is preferable to say, "I can't tell you, because I don't know what is best for you; but I can help you decide for yourself what to do. Would you like to learn how?" Abundant evidence in guidance studies shows that school-aged youths make poor decisions about many areas of their lives. An illustrative decision-making program designed for students from grades seven through nine is described by Gelatt and Brew (1980). They have constructed a program that includes helping young students to (1) identify critical decision points; (2) recognize and clarify personal values; (3) identify alternatives and create new ones; (4) seek, evaluate, and utilize information; (5) take risks; and (6) develop strategies for decision making.

Decisions in the area of interpersonal problems, such as sexual behavior involving previously learned response patterns, are more complicated. Solutions to these problems involve relearning methods as well as applying rational problem solving described previously. Adult helpees who face difficult choices, such as what to do with rebellious children, dependent relatives, errant spouses, or changes of work locale, must be taught this same problem-solving process as a substitute for acting on impulses, stereotypes, or advice. A successful approach to depression using a problem-solving framework is described by Nezu, Nezu, and Perri (1990). They taught depressed people skills in problem orientation (identifying life stressors), problem definition, generation of alternatives, decision making, and implementation of solutions similar to the model described next.

Skills Required in Rational Problem Solving

Most problem-solving skills are combinations of those described in the previous section: problem identification, goal setting, informing, interpreting, diagnosing, and evaluating feedback. Problem identification in Step 2 involves a clear answer to the question, "What is the problem?" Usually, this question provokes an analysis of the discrepancy between personal conditions as they are now and what we would like them to be. Narrowing this gap between reality and aspiration constitutes the goal for helpful problem solving. Once this basic skill is learned the other skills and steps fall naturally into place.

A skill called *force field analysis* (Lewin, 1969) can be applied to Step 3, generating and weighing alternatives. This skill utilizes physics concepts of fields of force and polarized valences, and is a method of comparing personal

---

PROBLEM: OVERWEIGHT, CAUSING HEALTH PROBLEMS AND DISCOMFORT.

GOAL: REDUCING WEIGHT BY THREE POUNDS A WEEK FOR SIX WEEKS. →

+	Rank	−	Rank
Spouse likes me thinner	1	Like rich foods	3
Better for my health	2	Dislike diets and diet foods	1
Live longer	3	Lack knowledge of low calorie foods	2
Clothes will fit better	1		
Less fatigue	3	Will smoke instead of eat	2
		Three pounds seems too much in a week	1

Balance
point for
forces

FIGURE 6–1 Illustration of Force Field Analysis

and social forces that are, at the same time, propelling and distracting helpees from their goals. Force field skills apply to many decision-making situations. The helpee's problem and goal are stated briefly at the top of Figure 6-1, and the direction of solution is indicated by an arrow. The forces pushing him toward his alternative goal (in this simple illustration, to reduce weight by three pounds a week for six weeks) are indicated by a + sign, and those working against him by a − sign. After listing the + and − forces, a helpee can see more clearly where he is in relation to the feasibility of his goal. He then can rank the forces on their strength by rating each from 1 to 3, with 1 as the strongest rating. Now the helpee can decide on a strategy of strengthening the + forces or weakening the − forces. If it is a conflict-of-choice problem, each alternative goal can be analyzed and then compared. Drug counselors, for example, would find such a model useful when helping youths to decide whether to experiment with hard drugs. Retirement counselors can use this skill for people facing retirement choices also.

The following list is a summary of problem-solving steps:

1. Involve the helpee and explore her or his current life situation.
2. State the problem, assess the setting, and determine the goal.
3. State and explore alternatives.
4. Gather information.
5. Explore implications of alternatives and the new information.
6. Clarify values.
7. Reexamine goals, alternative choices, risks, and consequences.

8. Decide from alternatives and plan for implementation.

9. Evaluate the process and outcomes.

10. Generalize to other situations.

Skills in Intuitive Problem Solving

Many everyday problems do not fit the linear rational model described above; so people must depend on their intuitions. Intuitions are expressed as vague bodily sensations, illogical hunches, or an awareness of feelings of rightness or wrongness about a solution to a problem. Some people distrust their intuitions because they are "soft" and "mushy" compared to "hard" logic and cognitive data. Intuition appears to many people to have a formal religious connection, but intuitive methods of knowing and solving human problems are as old as human history.

The question is not whether to use rational or intuitive styles, but under what conditions is either one the more appropriate method. Often both are needed, such as when buying a home. The decision must "feel right," but it is important to know if there are termites in the basement. Intuition often expands from information and logic. It leads from the struggle with data to the "aha" experience when all the pieces fall into place. Research done by Lawrence (1983) and reported in Heppner (1990), for example, found that judges' decisions often are made on an intuitive basis. Similar studies in the health care field indicate that diagnostic and treatment decisions often are made after the information gathering process is exhausted. So, intuition for many helpers is a way of knowing without really knowing how you know. They risk the "intuitive leap."

A practical consideration in using the intuitive problem-solving approach is the *problem set.* This means that the helpees must believe that their past experience is an important source of intuitive insights. In addition, they must learn to trust their present experience, especially messages from their bodies. An open attitude toward experience will help to prevent the use of past experience as an obstacle to creative thought and change. Intuition is often born out of the accumulation of past experiences, activities done so many times they now feel natural and obvious. If they have been functional in the past, it is reasonable to trust these types of natural responses.

Viewing problems as challenges rather than catastrophes is another aspect of the problem set. Problems need to be accepted as a normal part of living as does belief that we have the solutions within our reach. Some problems need redefining. For example, after a disabling accident the person says, "Isn't this terrible, why did this happen to me?" The helpee may need to do some cognitive restructuring as described in Chapter 4. To prepare for intuitive problem solving the helpee needs to restructure the reaction above to something like "Here I go again, I wouldn't choose this condition, but it is a big challenge for me. I need to trust myself more to work out of this difficulty. I know I can lick this problem."

The second step is to *saturate* one's self in all aspects of the problem. This is not a focused aggressive search for a solution, but it is a process of steeping one's self in information, recalling past experience, and soliciting advice. This is a time of asking many questions.

The third needed skill is *relaxation*. This state leads to receptiveness and openness to ideas, hunches, and insights. A relaxed state also allows more awareness of feelings and body states. The skills described under relaxation and meditation in Chapter 5 apply here.

Incubation time is a requirement for intuitive problem solving. It is neither an active search nor a passive state, but much is going on in the process of formulating hunches, emerging ideas, and exploring new perceptions. The helpee is seeing, hearing, and feeling data continuously. Pirsig's classic book on *Zen and The Art of Motorcycle Maintenance* (1974) stresses a contemplative stance when looking at the broken machine. This stance helps to get rid of old opinions about what might be wrong and prevents impulsive solutions. Incubation time allows the helpee to be open to new information or approaches, redefinitions of the problem, and assurances that the right questions are being asked.

Focusing on felt body experiences often helps the intuitive process. The first stage is awareness of body state—tense or relaxed, for example. Then one describes emotions experienced—fear, uneasiness, or anger, for example. A third step is to focus on these body sensations to get a clear "felt sense" of what is going on. Gently asking oneself what these feelings are about often results in a "come-about" experience which is expressed as vague images or ideas. Continued receptiveness and focusing, or "listening" to one's body, results frequently in awareness of a solution. Using the home-buying example cited previously, one might experience feelings of intense uneasiness, expressed as body tension, about the venture. The buyer says, "It doesn't feel right." Carrying this example a step further, the person would be wise to reconsider the purchase, or at least postpone it, until the "come about" experience takes place—that awareness of relief and relaxation about the problem. More information about this focusing method, especially what to do when "stuck" in a decision, can be obtained from Gendlin (1978).

Imagery is an important aid to intuitive problem solving. The underlying assumption here is that people have potential solutions to their problems within themselves. The task is to access these solutions. The experiential focusing method just described is one. Imagery, or visualized solutions to problems, is another. Symbols and rituals are a rich source of such wisdom. For example, imaging an old person giving you a piece of paper on which a message is written. Even though usually cryptic and symbolic, these messages frequently are indications of appropriate action. One must trust that these messages emerge from the wisdom of one's whole being. Often, much incubation time is needed to discern the full import of these messages.

Finally, the task of all problem solvers must be faced—*action*. The point arrives when awareness must move to intention to act, and finally commitment to act, or not to act. Hopefully under the helper's facilitative tutoring, helpees can draw upon a combination of logical problem solving and intuitive methods to arrive at the most appropriate solutions for themselves.

The basic guidelines for intuitive problem solving are:

1. Acquire an effective problem set—readiness, confidence, trust, challenge, and openness.
2. Saturate oneself in all aspects of the problem.
3. Relax to facilitate receptivity to new ideas.
4. Plan on incubation time for new ideas, problem redefinition, and asking the right questions.
5. Focus on body experiences—sensations, feelings—for emergent wisdom.
6. Utilize imagery to facilitate awareness of possible solutions.
7. Move from awareness to intention, to commitment, to action.

Behavior Changing

Assumptions of Behavior-Changing Methods

Behavior is the result of external environmental forces interacting with internal heredity forces. Continued responses are the result of learning by imitation and reward. Behavior is mediated somewhat by thinking processes also and is not only an automatic response to a rewarding environment. Social learning is a function of the interaction between the person's early behavior patterns and controlling environmental social conditions. The basic framework for action-helping methods is the social learning approach described by Bandura (1969) and elaborated by Meichenbaum (1977). Although the environment has profound impact on people's behavior, sometimes their behavior also alters the social environment considerably. The basic assumption, however, is that environmental conditions mold our behavior.

The use of behavior change methods assumes that helpees come for expert help in changing a specific behavior and are not seeking supportive friendly relationships or an examination of their value commitments. Such help, covered in previous chapters, is not suited to the behavior technology approaches described below. It is assumed here that helpers will use behavior changing methods only for the benefit of the helpee. It is prudent and ethical also to explain to helpees why certain methods, such as controlling rewards, are being utilized by the helper. It is important for maintaining trust that the helpee not feel manipulated or controlled.

Behavior Change Strategy

Action approaches come under the helping strategy called behavioral counseling. The principal characteristics of this strategy are (1) careful assessment of the helpee's problem behavior and conditions that maintain that behavior; (2) agreement on precise goals for new behaviors; (3) application mainly of change skills described below but utilization of all helping skills; (4) evaluation of outcomes in relation to goals; and (5) feedback information to improve the process and prevent relapse.

To make the steps listed above clearer, a model for taking a problem or complaint through behavior change steps to outcomes is presented. This is also a model for applying behavior change technology in a helping relationship. The major steps in this model are listed and illustrated in Figure 6-2. The first task is to make a clear statement of the problem and who "owns" it. For example, a helpee says that her problem is "My husband's drinking—I get so depressed over it." The second task is to help her realize that while she may not be able to change her husband's behavior, she can change herself, especially her depressive reactions to her husband's drinking.

Using helping skills cited in earlier chapters, the helper clarifies the nature of the problem so that it comes out as "I must learn to cope with my husband's drinking and manage my depressed feelings more constructively." This

PROBLEM	TARGET BEHAVIORS		RECORD PRESENT BEHAVIOR	SELF-HELP PLAN	EVALUATION
	DECREASE	INCREASE			
Depressed over husband's drinking	Daytime sleep Daytime snacks by 50%	Walking by 50% Pleasurable activities to 2 each day	Sleep 2 hours a day Snack 5 times a day Walk 2 hours a week Have no pleasant events on some days Mood rating —first day: ————	Keep log of sleeping and eating habits Reward self with treat when goal is reached each day Walk one hour each day briskly Shop for new clothes on Saturday Record daily mood ratings on 5-point scale	25% successful on sleep 100% successful in eating restraint Walked one hour most days One pleasant event each day; some days, two Felt better at end of first week Set goals for second week

FIGURE 6–2   A Behavior Change Format

is still a very large problem, and one task at this early stage is to break the problem into smaller pieces. She elects to work on the depressed feelings that so distress her first. Therefore, in column 1 of Figure 6-2 is placed "Problem: Depressed over husband's drinking." The "target behaviors" are goals to work toward. These behaviors may be things the helpee wishes either to increase or to decrease. By focusing on what they want to do or want to be, helpees avoid thinking in terms of the unproductive question "What's wrong with me?" In this instance the helpee decided that she would work on decreasing her daytime sleeping totally (she takes two-hour naps and wakes up early in the morning). She also plans to decrease her snacks during the day by 50 percent. It is desirable to attach a time frame to the goal, such as reducing snacks 50 percent in the first week.

You will note also in the "increase" column that the helpee wants to walk more and experience more pleasure. These specific targets, of course, are worked out in discussions with the helpees, since they must "own" these goals and work toward them on their own initiative. All we are doing as consultant-helpers is providing the technology and a temporary relationship.

In the "record" column the helpee gets a baseline estimate of where she is now on the behaviors she agrees to change. This recording process is helpful in itself. Then she lists the things she will do to reach her targets, again keeping records of what she did and what her daily mood ratings were. Seeing moods change from day to day, even though marginally, is helpful also. Finally, she makes an assessment at the end of the week (her first trial period) to see how she is doing. Usually adjustments need to be made on the activities, the targets, or her persistence. Behavior change comes slowly, and sometimes painfully, so helpees need much encouragement and the reinforcement that comes from perceiving progress. Targets need to be small and achievable, as well as time-limited. Adjustments can always be made so that the motivation for continued work toward new goals is strong.

It must be emphasized in this example that the issue is not coping with the depression per se, but an effort to change the behaviors that lead to the symptoms of depression. Of course, if depressed feelings are severe and of long duration, specialists should be involved since monitoring care and medication may be helpful. This illustration was of a typical "blue" state related to a specific event she felt helpless to influence—her husband's drinking. She realized that she could control her own behavior. She may want to continue trying to change her husband's drinking behavior, but this is another problem requiring different strategies for solution.

The self-help plan is worked out jointly between the helper and helpee with the primary responsibility put on the helpee. It is highly specific regarding who, what, where, and when kinds of questions. The plan also includes a commitment to record the accomplishments. Finally, the evaluation step includes a careful look at the extent to which the goals for change were achieved.

The problem of relapse into old habits of thinking and acting is continuous. *Relapse prevention* consists of steps to keep the planned behavior change going when the helping process ends. The idea of relapse is most commonly associated with lapses in eating, drinking, smoking, and drug abuse, but the principles of relapse prevention discussed here apply to any attempt at behavior change. Marlatt and Gordon (1985) have reported their extensive research on relapse, especially in regard to addictive behavior. During the helping process the addicted helpees maintain a high rate of abstinence, but when the helping relationship ceases, three-fourths return to their addictive behaviors.

The basic helping strategy to prevent relapse is teaching self-management, since often the environment provides little support. Friends who drink and smoke are everywhere, for example, and the constant message is "It's okay and fun to drink all you want!" The following *self-control strategies* are based on Marx's (1984) work and are central to his programs of relapse prevention.

1. Become familiar with the *principles of addiction and the environment* that supports addiction. Thus, helpees can predict the places and people who will threaten their resolution to change. High-risk situations need to be identified and avoided. Warning signals must be heeded when helpees are about to be sabotaged by a vulnerable situation or an uncooperative person.

2. Helpees must observe and *control emotions* that tend to get out of control or lead them to conclude that they cannot manage their behavior, are incompetent, or are irrational. Helpees must expect that they will react to vulnerable situations or intense feelings and cravings with rational controlled responses. Helpees must give themselves messages that indicate they have the strength to control their cravings, feelings, and behavior, and that they can learn from their mistakes.

3. The helpee's *support system* needs careful attention. Helpees should associate with people who do not drink alcohol or overeat, and who exercise regularly. Obtaining the cooperation of "significant others," such as spouses, in the relapse prevention program helps also.

4. Assist the helpee to create a *self-management system* of internal rewards. When he or she reaches for the glass when others are not around to say, "Hey, don't," the helpee must provide the satisfaction for not giving in to the impulse. Having a program with a system of recording weight loss or abstinence, for example, is useful. It helps to document on paper that the self-management system is working and, if it is not working, to reassess the strategy and reward system. Helpees need to realize that such a system takes patience and practice, but they should be reassured also that it works.

Modeling

Modeling is a method of learning by vicarious experience or imitation, such as watching the performance of others. The accumulating research evidence (Bandura, 1969, 1986; Krumboltz & Thoreson, 1976; Meichenbaum, 1985) suggests that a wide variety of behavior can be changed through modeling, and commonsense experience attests to the power of examples also. Helpees tend to do what the helper does. If helpers use colorful street language to express themselves, so will the helpee; if helpers disclose personal data about themselves, the helpee will be more inclined to do so. One of the problems in helping interviews is that helpees do not know what to do, and verbal explanations often do not help. A helper who models expression of feeling gives the helpee a clearer picture of what behavior is expected. Another requirement is that the helper's behavior be at a higher level of functioning than the helpee's performance so the helpee has a behavioral standard to strive for.

Role playing is another example of vicarious behavior where the helpee can see, through roles performed by others, what is expected. If the helpee is afraid of approaching an employer about a job, for example, the helper can perform the role of an applicant (the helpee), as the helpee acts as the employer. The two then continue until the helpee sees other ways of acting in an employment interview. Then helpees try on the new behavior themselves through reversing roles and having them critiqued repeatedly until they learn the new behaviors to their satisfaction.

A third example of modeling effectiveness is the removal of fears by observing fearless behavior in a model, acquiring information about the feared object, and, finally, having a direct experience with the threatening object with no ill effects. This approach would be effective with fears of snakes or of making speeches, for example.

Modeling seems to be most effective when the model has characteristics of status, competence, knowledge, and power. If the models possess qualities similar to helpers, they are effective. Advertising methods take advantage of these facts. Helpers thus need to discover which qualities are most attractive to helpees and then use them as guidelines for selecting models.

Modeling can be done by live, filmed, or taped methods. Although live methods have some advantages, such as maintenance of interest, filmed versions allow for more careful emphasis on the behaviors that one wants to model. An example of a helping situation with delinquent boys, which utilized live college-age models, is the work of Sarason (1968). Adolescent boys observed special modeling of the following situations: (1) vocational planning; (2) motivation and interests; (3) attitudes toward work and education; and (4) utility of socially appropriate behavior. When the boys observed socially acceptable models, they improved their own planning skills and ability to think in socially positive terms. The models were attractive to the boys, and the role-playing methods sustained their interest.

Filmed models have been used with effectiveness also. Hosford and Sorenson (1969) used audio tape and filmed models successfully with fourth to sixth graders who wanted to speak up more in class. Motivating teenaged students to do the investigational work necessary to career planning is a problem also. Stewart (1969), using group models on audio tape, found that students improved their interest in career information and more actively explored sources of information after listening to the tapes.

General principles of using modeling are:

1. Determine which features of a model would be most attractive to the helpee.
2. Decide on the objectives of the modeling.
3. Choose believable models similar to the helpees in age, sex, and race.
4. Decide if live or simulated modeling would be more appropriate and practical.
5. Design a modeling format, script, or role-playing sequence.
6. Conduct the modeling exercise.
7. Discuss the helpee's reactions in terms of feelings, learnings, and suggestions.
8. Recognize that informally we are modeling behaviors constantly for helpees.

Rewarding Skills

At several points in this book we have described the reinforcing, or rewarding, effect of various helping procedures. This section will develop this idea as a consciously applied skill. The basic idea is that rewarded behavior tends to be repeated and that a wide variety of events can have reinforcing functions. We can use reinforcement to (1) overcome behavior deficiencies (as in encouraging a helpee to plan ahead); (2) change undesirable behavior (as in eliminating chronic stealing); and (3) maintain present responses (as in encouraging statements of feeling).

Although the idea of using rewards to shape behavior is a simple one, there are some pitfalls. Most of the principles of reinforcement have come from learning studies in which animals were deprived of food and water, which then became the reinforcers. Since human responses are so much more complex, rewards have varied meanings. In helping situations we depend mainly on words, which have different effects depending on the cultural background of the helpee. Praise words, such as "good job," are used commonly, but soon lose their effect because of overuse and because they have differing levels of potency for different people. Verbal rewards are most effective when the helper and helpee are working toward common goals. They are resented as blatant manipulation when used to influence helpees in ways that are not in their apparent best interests.

Some general principles in using reinforcement as a skill are that the reward, or incentive system, must be capable of maintaining a high level of action over a long period. In other words, the learning should be lasting. Secondly, the reward should depend on the presence of the behavior we want. But it is difficult to have the desired behavior rewarded consistently, because in ordinary life situations the reward is often badly timed or is given haphazardly. As a result, sometimes the undesired behavior is rewarded. Finally, the reward must be strong enough and given often enough for the desired behavior to be repeated. We also want the behavior to generalize to similar situations when the rewards are not present; for example, the helpee should be able to solve problems in other contexts. This reinforcement process is aided by using natural settings, varying the reward, and rewarding certain conditions systematically.

The general strategy for using rewards is to plan them selectively in a pattern so that the desired behavior is emitted in the form and sequence desired. This is a *reinforcement schedule* or *contingency*. We apply these stimuli (such as praise) in the appropriate strength and frequency until the appearance of the desired behavior is as strong and as frequent as required. With children, tangible reinforcers such as toys and candy are used. Adults usually respond to praise and money. The strategy begins with finding the appropriate type and strength of reinforcing agent. In the example given earlier of the lonely person, a reinforcement schedule based upon pleasure from close relationships must be built. The anticipated reward for making friends overcomes the initial fears that make us avoid people.

Using tangible reinforcers is very controversial since some claim it to be similar to bribing. Bribery, however, is "pay" before the act whereas reinforcers are given after the act is performed. Nevertheless, it is generally conceded by writers on the subject (for example, O'Leary, Poulos, and Devine, 1972) that social reinforcers, such as praise, are more desirable. Tangible reinforcers have a place if they are *not* used (1) to control others; (2) to reward an act required in daily living; (3) to stop undesirable behavior (such as giving ice cream to stop crying); (4) to replace intrinsic rewards (such as self-satisfaction); or (5) to affect others adversely (such as favoritism with rewards). Tangible reinforcers may be used to establish desired behavior, but they should be reduced as soon as possible. It is hoped that more intrinsic personal rewards will take their place and that people of all ages will outgrow their dependence on "gold stars." We must recognize, however, that people seemingly never outgrow their need for praise and affection, which usually remain through life as powerful reinforcers in the helping process.

Generally, it is desirable not to use "if–then" statements, because they imply doubt about the person's willingness or ability to do the task. Instead of saying, "If you learn this vocabulary list, then you may eat lunch," use a "when–then" statement, "When you have learned this list, then you may eat lunch."

A final word on the strategy of reward is to *praise the action, not the person.* An example is "I liked the way you helped Bob this morning, Jim," rather than "You are a good boy, Jim, because of the way you help others." To get the feel of this influential skill think of a person you know who is not apparently aware of his or her strengths. When you see such a person engaging in the strong behavior, give an appropriate reinforcement, such as a smile, nod, comment, or touch. Then note the response and whether or not the strong behavior you wanted to reinforce increases in frequency.

This process may sound very mechanical and manipulative, but remember that we are describing a behavior change technique used in an ethical context where these methods are used with the helpee's knowledge and consent. If we are interested in the effects of these methods on the group, we can use these same principles at a social system level. Individual performance can be made contingent on the group performance and vice versa. We may design double reinforcement contingencies for the person and the group. For example, we can influence the degree of support, cohesiveness, productivity, and level of responsible behavior in individuals and groups by planning a suitable system of rewards.

Helping interviews or groups offer many opportunities to use rewards. If we want the helpee, for example, to focus on feeling expression, our attention to these expressions, as well as overt praise, will tend to increase this behavior. If initiative in seeking information to solve his problems is important, there are many ways to show approval in a reinforcing manner. This discussion of reward should make us more aware of all aspects of our helper behavior that have a reinforcing effect on the helpee's behavior.

Reinforcement has a decided effect on the helpee interview behavior, as demonstrated by Ryan and Krumboltz (1964). In decision-making interviews, they used verbal reinforcers such as "good" and "fine" and nonverbal reinforcers such as approval nods and were able to effect significant increases in helpee deliberation and decision responses. Similarly, a study of rural youth in group settings done by Meyer, Strowig, and Hosford (1970) revealed that information-seeking behavior can be increased considerably in eleventh graders by reinforcement methods. They found also that counselors could be taught to use these skills very quickly.

A method used in some forms of counseling called *anchoring* has a reinforcing effect (Bandler & Grinder, 1982). When helpees act in ways that are in harmony with their goals or their relationships with the helper, then the helper recognizes that behavior with a smile, a comment of "good," or a handclap. Sometimes reaching out and lightly and unobtrusively touching the helpee on the shoulder has an anchoring effect. For example, a helpee relates a story of how he acted in a confident, affirming manner. The helper moves, reaches over and touches the helpee lightly, and says "great," all at the same time. The anchoring thus takes place visually, aurally, and tactilely.

A summary of rewarding principles in the helping process follows:

1. Reward performance, not the person.

2. Determine the reward most appropriate to the helpee, considering unique interests, age, and setting.

3. Utilize social rather than tangible reinforcers.

4. Use anchoring methods for desired behaviors in the helping interview.

5. Apply the reinforcer as soon after appearance of the desired behavior as possible.

6. As an ethical matter, obtain the understanding and permission of the helpee when using rewarding methods.

Extinguishing Skills

To extinguish a behavior means to stop doing it. Extinguishing skills are closely related to reinforcing methods, since behavior gradually subsides and eventually disappears when rewards are discontinued. Thus, the skill element for the helper is applying extinction in systematic ways. If helpees want to change undesirable behaviors, for example, helpers assist them in identifying the conditions that are reinforcing them and then in removing or weakening them.

Characteristics of extinction are that (1) rates of extinction are variable and depend on the regularity of reinforcement, the effort required to perform, the perceived changes in the reinforcement pattern, and the availability of alternative responses; (2) avoidance behaviors can be extinguished by prevention of punishing consequences; (3) behavior is displaced rather than lost, since it can be reinstated quickly through reestablishing the reward schedule; (4) using extinction does not guarantee that more desirable behavior patterns will emerge; and (5) extinction strategy is slower than reinforcement strategy in producing results.

Usually, after extinction of the undesirable behavior, efforts to elicit and reward desired behavior need to be undertaken. Behavior changes can be brought about most effectively by a combination strategy of extinguishing undesirable behavior while modeling and reinforcing desirable behavior. This is important because if a helpee eliminates an undesirable but adaptive behavior, a vacuum will result. The filling of this vacuum is the key goal of reinforcement of desirable behavior. Removing a behavior that played a function in the person's life (even if it was harmful) without giving a positive alternative will result in early relapse to that negative behavior. An example is working with gang "wanna-be" adolescents. It is not enough to provide education and positive role models. The kids need positive alternatives, such as basketball courts open for supervised, late night games.

Methods of extinction include (1) simple removal of reinforcing conditions (as in not attending to an overly talkative helpee); and (2) gradually changing the external stimulus for an undesirable behavior, for example, by exposing the person in small increments to a fearsome situation, where the fear is minimally elicited and the fear response is blocked. Gradually, the fear will be neutralized. One method for doing this is through "behavior rehearsal," a kind of role playing (Lazarus 1966, 1976) in which helper and helpee role play scenes from actual problem situations. The method works well with helpees who want to be more assertive. In this case, the helper poses problems for the helpee around asking favors, making complaints, or refusing a request, in a gradual manner until the most difficult situations are encountered. The experience is critiqued, and occasionally the helper models the role of the helpee. The helpee is urged to try the new techniques under conditions where anxiety arousal is least probable. The advantage of this behavior-rehearsal method is that the helpee actively solves a close-to-life problem and then generalizes to real problems.

The main implication of extinction phenomena for helpers is to know how to change undesirable helpee behavior by removing the rewarding conditions. Does our intense attending behavior, for example, always reward the desired helpee behavior? Are there some behaviors, such as tendencies to overintellectualize, or to talk to the floor, that we would like to extinguish by altering the reinforcing stimuli? In summary, then, helpers can use extinction by showing helpees how they can remove rewarding conditions for unwanted behavior. They can help also by neutralizing undesirable emotional behaviors, such as fear of crowds, by gradually exposing helpees to fearsome situations or by helping them to avoid punishing consequences.

A summary of principles for using extinction is:

1. Examine the situation to *determine what is reinforcing the unwanted behavior,* noting especially the events just before and after the reinforced event.
2. *Withhold reinforcers.*
3. *Reinforce the opposite,* or competing, behaviors when they occur.

Contracting Skills

Contracting is a method for systematically arranging the rewards so that the probability of a response is increased. A contract is an agreement with the helpee that identifies the specific tasks both helper and helpee will perform in return for a specific reward. An example with a child helpee would be an agreement to get homework in regularly for one week in return for a special privilege. With an adult helpee an example would be the helpee's agreement to do some "homework" on a problem in return for helper talk time. Helping relationships with mature helpees have informal contracts that run something like, "I do [something specific] for you and in return you do [something specific] for me so we can achieve our mutual goals." Formal helping relationships, particularly forms labeled counseling and psychotherapy, are judged to be successful in terms of the extent to which both helper and helpee carry out their parts of the implied contract to reach certain goals.

Characteristics of contracts are: (1) *Specificity*—helpees know what is expected of them and the consequences for doing or not doing the agreed tasks. They make the choices, so they learn to make decisions and to take responsibility for their own behavior. (2) *Impersonality*—the helpee is not emotionally obligated to do the agreed task, nor is the helper emotionally involved in the doing of the task. Both parties understand the consequences of not fulfilling the contract, so the whole issue of achievement is put on an impartial and impersonal basis. (3) *Feasibility*—the specified task must be in the behavioral repertoire of the helpee. If a helper expects the helpee to listen more accurately, the helpee must be able to attend for a sufficient time.

Although all formal helping relationships have implied contracts—understandings that both will have responsibilities to carry out—they usually are not formalized to the extent of writing down the conditions. Written contracts are constructed only when there is some doubt, as in the case of children, that they understand the nature of a contract, or that they will respond with expected responsible behavior.

Formal contracts usually include statements of (1) privileges extended; (2) responsibilities incurred; (3) bonuses and sanctions for completing or not completing agreed-upon responsibilities; and (4) how and by whom the contract is to be monitored. Contracts are commonly made between parents or teachers and children whose behavior has resulted in a breakdown of communication or confidence. Since these contracts are often negotiated with the help of an outside person, helpers should understand the principles and skills in behavior change contracting.

Some of the conditions to be determined before constructing the contract include (1) identify the specific behavior that is inappropriate; (2) identify the specific desired behavior; (3) identify the conditions that arouse and maintain the inappropriate behavior (what sets off the behavior—what is the person doing at the time, and what are the rewards for doing it?); (4) collect baseline data about when the inappropriate behavior occurs (how often? who are significant persons to the helpee? their influence?); (5) identify the conditions that arouse the appropriate behavior (what do the other persons do, or could they do, to arouse and reinforce this behavior?); (6) determine reinforcers and establish a schedule of reinforcement; and (7) negotiate a contract with all persons concerned and secure commitment to it for a specified time. A simple contract with a young person who was consistently truant from school, a parent, and a school official is presented in Figure 6.3.

---

1. Name of student.
2. Complaint: Excessive absence from school (three full days and four tardy slips in past month).
3. Desired behavior: Arrive on time for all classes and maintain consistent school attendance.
4. Student will perform the following:
   a. Attend every scheduled class on time.
   b. Obtain teachers' initials on attendance card for each period for one week.
   c. Keep a personal record of daily attendance and on-time arrival for each week.
   d. Turn in attendance card to the principal's office at the end of each of the first three weeks.
   e. Attend a group counseling session once each week for the remainder of the semester.
5. Upon successful completion of above requirements:
   a. At the end of the first week Mother will remove restrictions for four hours Friday night (times to be negotiated).
   b. At the end of the second week Mother will remove restrictions for six hours Saturday (times to be negotiated).
   c. At the end of the third week all restrictions for Friday and Saturday will be removed.
6. Following the third week a conference will be held with all three parties to determine if a new contract or a new reinforcement schedule is needed.
7. Agreements:

Student   Mother

I agree to monitor this contract and to make verbal or written progress reports to Student and Mother at the end of each week.

Vice Principal

FIGURE 6–3   A Sample Contract

Both informal and written contracts are used commonly in educational settings where specific tasks are to be performed. Homme's (1971) manual is a practical guide to writing contracts in a classroom, but it applies equally well to family situations in which helpers often develop contingency contracts between parents and children and between husbands and wives. Conditions usually included in contracts are as follows: (1) *Rewards* should be given liberally, even for small approximations of the desired behavior. (2) Rewards should be given *soon* after the performances. (3) Contracts should be *understood* clearly by all parties and be considered *fair* and reasonable. (4) The contract should be expressed in *positive* "when-then" terms, such as "When you finish your homework; then you can swim," rather than negatively, "Finish your homework or you will not get to swim."

A summary of principles for using contracting skills is:

1. Recognize a contract as an agreement between you and the helpee about the nature and conduct of your responsibilities.

2. Decide if a formal contract would facilitate the use of reinforcing conditions in a behavior change problem, or if an informal agreement would suffice.

3. Formulate the contract for the specified time.

4. Ascertain that all parties understand and agree to the contract.

5. Provide for monitoring the contract and deciding when the contract is to be terminated.

Aversive Control Skill

This skill, related to reinforcement and extinction, involves a process of removing undesired behaviors through use of "punishing" or "aversive" stimuli. The principal theory of aversive control is that the punishing effect results in a conditioned fear that has an inhibiting or suppressing effect. Aversive control is used to reduce undesirable and persistent responses that are self-reinforcing. Examples are self-punishing activities in children and unwanted smoking, overeating, and drinking in adults. To be used successfully, however, aversive methods should be paired with a positive reinforcement program for desired behaviors. Usually, other forms of help are needed, since aversive control methods deprive helpees of much pleasure. Helpees must be unusually cooperative and desire behavior change intensely. This method must be used cautiously and after some supervised practice.

Elements of aversive control are as follows: (1) *Introduce an aversive stimulus at the time the person is engaging in the unwanted behavior.* Standard efforts for problem drinkers, for example, have been to put an emetic with their drinks so they get nauseous and vomit when they drink. Dire warnings of impending cancer are given to smokers when they light up. Temporary banishment from the group is effected for stealing property. (2) *Develop a positive reinforcing schedule for new behaviors* when the noxious behavior has ceased. (3) *Be alert to undesirable side effects* such as excessive fear arousal or unwanted negative attitudes toward the helper who suggested or administered the aversive stimulus.

Sometimes aversive consequences can be imagined with desirable effects. Helpees may be asked to fantasize situations like the ones they face. For example, a helpee may be having great trouble fighting with a demanding mother. He wants to avoid his strong responses, so with the aid of the helper, he imagines his demanding mother and works out alternative responses to her.

A summary of aversive control skills is:

1. Use aversive methods when the person is engaging in the unwanted behavior.

2. Initiate reinforcement for desired behaviors.

3. Watch for unwanted side effects and adjust the aversive program.

Desensitizing Skill

Desensitization is a method of reducing the emotional responsiveness to threatening or unpleasant stimuli by introducing an activity incompatible with the threat response. Sometimes this process is known as *counterconditioning*. For example, the helpee learns to associate fear of speaking up in class with an incompatible pleasant and relaxed feeling. The unpleasant response (fear) cannot be experienced when the pleasant response (relaxation) is present. Most desensitization activities are concerned with introducing relaxation in the imaginary presence of anxiety, although it has been used with feelings of anger and guilt also. Occasionally, desensitization is used in combination with modeling and reinforcement.

There are two types of desensitization, in-life and systematic. Helpers will find the de vivo or in-life method most applicable because of its simplicity and closeness to concrete life situations. Systematic desensitization, as will be described in the next section, is more complex and symbolic. Hence, it is utilized mainly by professional helpers. *In-life desensitization* is a process of replacing fear with confidence and ease. For example, a helpee may have a mild fear of driving on freeways, but the fear is strong enough to cause considerable discomfort and leads to the inconvenience of driving exclusively on side roads. The helping process consists of gradually moving toward the goal of confident freeway driving. The helper goes with the driver, encouraging a relaxed but alert driving behavior on side streets. They gradually approach the freeway, stopping for deep breathing and other relaxation routines, before entering the freeway. It may be more effective for the helper to take the wheel first, modeling a relaxed and confident manner. In any case, the basic principle is to approach the freeway driving gradually in short steps, mastering relaxation along the way so that the relaxation response substitutes for the fear response. A similar example is a young child who is afraid of furry objects, including his animal toys. The helper gradually reintroduces the furry toys with verbal assurances and relaxation responses to reassociate pleasure with the objects of fear.

A summary of in-life desensitization principles are:

1. Explain the rationale of desensitization to the helpee.
2. Practice relaxation routines.
3. Introduce the helpee to the feared task or object gradually in a relaxed state.
4. Continue the process until the helpee achieves the desired ease and confidence.

Systematic desensitization methods were developed initially by Wolpe (1952) and were refined by him and numerous other behavioral scientists for coping with strong fears. There are several steps in the systematic desensitization procedure: (1) discussing conditions under which the problem occurs; (2) explaining the method and its rationale, as a learning process, to the helpee; (3) relaxation training; (4) constructing an anxiety hierarchy; and (5) working through that hierarchy. This process requires supervised practice to master the subskills sufficiently to be effective.

Skills for Steps 1 through 3 on defining problems and inducing relaxation were described in previous chapters. Step 4, hierarchy construction, is conducted at the same time that the relaxation training takes place. Essentially, the hierarchy is a list of 12 to 14 anxiety-producing situations organized around the same theme, such as taking tests. These situations are ranked in the helpee's imagination from lowest anxiety at the top to highest anxiety at the bottom. It is desirable to go over the list with the helpee to determine the strength of each and the equality of intervals between items. They should be evenly spaced as to their potency in arousing anxiety. In the fear of testing example, items would include initial events such as "waking up the morning of the test" all the way to the test itself—"opening the cover page of the test booklet."

The items in the hierarchy should be similar to, or represent, the person's real-life experiences. They should be sufficiently detailed to elicit a clear image of the incident. Items should include a broad sample of situations where the incident might take place. Helpees should be able to see themselves as actively involved rather than passively observing.

After the hierarchy is constructed and checked, the working-through process (Step 5) is begun. In the relaxed state with eyes closed, helpees are asked to imagine a few neutral scenes, such as a path in the forest. Then they are asked to project themselves into the real problem and are given the top item in the hierarchy (lowest in anxiety). They are asked to indicate with a signal, such as raising an index finger, if they feel any anxiety. If so, relaxation exercises are undertaken again briefly. Then the helper returns to the hierarchy, reading the same item, and proceeding in the same manner through the hierarchy. If successful, helpees should still feel generally relaxed even after imagining the most potent anxiety-provoking situation on their lists.

There are numerous nuances to the desensitization skill cluster. It is a sufficiently complex method to justify that you read more about it in the specialized readings at the end of this chapter and experience it yourself under an expert in the method. You can then try it yourself with a helpee under supervision until you master the steps.

The following list is a summary of systematic desensitizing skill utilization:

1. Discuss the problem with the helpee.

2. Decide if systematic desensitization is applicable. (Desensitization might be indicated when a strong isolated fear situation needs to be faced.)

3. Teach relaxation routines.

4. Construct a hierarchy with the helpee.

5. Test the hierarchy for rank order of potency and evenness of intervals between items by asking helpee, "Which is more anxiety-provoking, A or B?"

6. Conduct desensitization by reading from the list, the least potent first, in about 30-minute sessions.

7. Check for relaxation and repeat items from the hierarchy until relaxed—stop and go back to relaxation methods if you cannot go on without anxiety.

8. Complete the entire hierarchy (usually twelve to twenty items).

Outcomes Self-Check

You now have competencies to (1) describe the behavioral approach to changing specific performance; (2) identify the principal steps in problem solving; (3) demonstrate that you can help a person through the steps in problem solving; (4) describe and illustrate the behavior-changing skills of modeling, rewarding, contracting, extinguishing, aversion controlling, and desensitizing. Since the criteria of success with action skills are more apparent than with understanding and support skills, clearer outcomes can be observed. You can determine if your helpees did what they said they were going to do and at what level of proficiency.

Suggestions for Further Study

Bandura, A. *Principles of Behavior Modification.* New York: Holt, Rinehart & Winston, 1969. (General principles on which behavior-changing methods can be built.)

————. Psychotherapy and the learning process. *Psychological Bulletin* 58 (1961):143–157. (Basic article on applications of learning principles to the helping function of psychotherapy.)

Brammer, L., Abrego, P., and Shostrom, E. *Therapeutic Counseling and Psychotherapy.* 6th ed. Englewood Cliffs, NJ: Prentice Hall, 1993. (Ch. 10, Counseling with Couples and Families; Ch. 11, Counseling for Career Transitions; Ch. 13, Counseling and Human Values.)

Buckley, N., and Walker, H. *Modifying Classroom Behavior.* Champaign, IL: Research Press, 1970. (A simplified approach to changing behavior in classroom settings.)

Carkhuff, R. *Helping and Human Relations.* New York: Holt, Rinehart & Winston, 1969. (The appendix of vol. 2 contains a clear account of the process of desensitization.)

Gendlin, E. *Focusing.* New York: Everett House, 1978. (A detailed description of experiential focusing as an aid to intuitive problem solving.)

Grossberg, J. Behavioral therapy: A review. *Psychological Bulletin* 62 (1964):73–88. (Overview of limitations and possibilities of behavior modification methods.)

Krumboltz, J., and Thoreson, C. *Counseling.* New York: Holt, Rinehart & Winston, 1976. (Papers on behavior modification principles and techniques.)

————, and Krumboltz, H. *Changing Children's Behavior.* Englewood Cliffs, NJ: Prentice Hall, 1972. (A manual of helping methods with children from a behavioral viewpoint.)

Meichenbaum, D. *Cognitive Behavior Modification.* New York: Plenum, 1977. (A research-based review of methods of behavior change using cognitive skills.)

————. *Stress Inoculation Training.* Boston: Allyn & Bacon, 1985. (A manual on controlling anxiety using a variety of behavior change strategies.)

Osipow, S. *Strategies in Counseling for Behavior Change.* New York: Appleton-Century-Crofts, 1970. (A theoretical and practical approach to behavior analysis and counseling strategy.)

————, and Walsh, B. *Behavior Change in Counseling: Readings and Cases.* New York: Appleton-Century-Crofts, 1970. (A collection of papers on issues and cases in behavior change.)

Rhodes, W. Psychological techniques and theory applied to behavior modification. *Exceptional Child* 28 (1962):330–333. (Principles underlying behavior modification in clear practical terms.)

Tyler, L. *The Work of the Counselor.* 2nd ed. New York: Appleton-Century-Crofts, 1961. (An overview of planning and decision-making counseling.)

Wolpe, J. *The Practice of Behavior Therapy.* New York: Pergamon, 1969. (Detailed account of desensitization with illustrative cases.)

Woody, R. Behavior therapy and school psychology. *Journal of School Psychology* 4 (1966):1–14. (Overview of behavior modification methods for school settings.)

Zifferblatt, S. *You Can Help Your Child Improve Study and Homework Behaviors.* Champaign, IL.: Research Press, 1970. (A practical guide for improving school performance.)

7

Ethical Issues in
Helping Relationships

This book was written especially for the paraprofessional helper, who perhaps technically might not be held responsible for upholding the same ethical behavior as the professional counselor or psychologist. A wise helper, nevertheless, is knowledgeable and mindful of these guidelines. This chapter will discuss briefly some of the ethical issues and expectations of helping.

Outcomes You Can Expect

By studying this chapter you should be able to (1) define the term *ethics* and explain how ethics differ from the law; (2) discuss some critical elements of self-care needed for helpers; (3) identify issues in interpersonal relationships be-tween helpers and helpees that can be problematic; (4) address issues of help-er competence and the limits in helping relationships; and (5) increase your awareness of how to respond ethically in some emergency situations.

What Are Ethics?

Ethics are moral principles adopted by an individual or group to provide rules for appropriate conduct (Corey, Corey, & Callanan, 1993). This is somewhat different from the definition of values. *Values* consider what is good and desir-able, whereas *ethics* consider what is right and correct behavior in given sit-uations (Loewenberg & Dolgoff, 1988). Other forces help determine appropriate behavior as well. Community standards and practices, moral expectations based on cultural patterns or religious beliefs, and local, state, and federal laws all guide helper behavior.

In the professional field of helping, national professional organizations develop these rules for their respective memberships (e.g., American Counseling Association, American Psychological Association, National Association of Social Workers, American Association for Marriage and Family Therapy). While ethics remain fairly constant, they do change over time and are officially changed every few years, so helpers must continually pay attention to what is the accepted code of conduct in their professional arena.

Difference between Law and Ethics

Laws are rules of behavior established by the courts or legislature for defining minimum standards that help society operate in an orderly fashion. Ethical codes represent the ideal standards set by a professional organization (Corey et al., 1993). The key importance of these ethical codes to helpers is to provide some frame of reference for judgments about helpee welfare and social responsibility. For example, while helpers' ultimate allegiance generally is to the society they serve, their primary responsibility is to their helpees. Information must not be revealed unless there is clear and imminent danger to the helpee or other people. Helpers are left with the real-world challenge of deciding when the legal and ethical guidelines pertain to their specific situation. This is not always easy. In fact, knowing and choosing ethical behavior that is in the helpee's best interest, and yet protects the helper from liability and the public from harm, is often quite difficult to balance. The main point here is that helpers must become committed to a set of ethical behaviors that are reflections of their own moral standards, society's codes, and the norms of the helping profession. This chapter intends to provide some guidance in this regard.

Helper Self-Care

When we begin to discuss ethical behavior on the part of helpers, we turn first to the helper's personal life. Across all of the helping professions, there is a dictum that could be summarized as "Do your best to promote the well-being of your helpee." As discussed in chapter 2, the life-style of a helper can be demanding and, at times, exhausting. Working with people who have significant emotional needs is both rewarding and draining. In order to truly help others, helpers must take care of their own emotional, physical, intellectual, and spiritual health needs. When we do not find balance in our lives in these areas, we may experience distress in our ability to help others, commonly called *burnout*. Workers in many "people professions" experience burnout. Teachers, for example, are vulnerable to the burnout effect unless they plan systematically for renewal experiences to regain their enthusiasm, energy, and effectiveness.

In helping relationships, some specific patterns cause frustration among helpers (Farber & Heifetz ,1982). The most significant is that often those persons we spend so much time helping do not improve in the way we think best, so we feel unsuccessful. Often, we will spend time giving attention and energy to an individual in need, but at some level resent that the helping relationship is a one-way street and that the person does not reciprocate, or even express gratitude. Helping others can be very time consuming, and when it comes on top of the normal work-week can be too demanding. Also, helpee issues may stir up the helper's own past issues. Another significant cause of burnout is when the need for helping others comes at the same time as stressful events in the helper's own life, so the helper feels the weight of two heavy burdens.

Some of the indicators of needed renewal are increasing irritability, low energy level, cynicism about people, indifference to the suffering of others, loss of self-confidence, and general malaise. While the helping process has some built-in renewal potential, most helpers find that they must seek their renewal outside their helping relationships.

The best way for helpers to deal with burnout is to recognize their own weak spots and work on prevention. For example, are you one who is always listening to others, yet no one seems to listen to you? You need to find someone with whom you have a more reciprocal relationship, so your needs will be heard also. Are you one who cannot say "no" to anyone in need? You are setting yourself up for tiredness burnout unless you set some limits on the amount of time you can spend or the number of helping projects you can undertake at once. Ask yourself, "What is the most stressful aspect about my helping relationships, and what could I do to make them more manageable?" Over the long term, planning ahead like this will allow you to be a more effective helper than if you burn out and are not able to help others in the future.

For occupations in which helping is the prime function, preventative measures are critical to helpful responding. For example, fire and police departments, rescue workers, or Red Cross volunteer squads know now that first-line disaster workers must have ways to work through *their* grief just as the victims do. These institutions must have relief measures in place prior to dispatching workers so that they may be most helpful to victims of the disaster (Duckworth, 1991).

Changes in the working environment often help resolve institutional burnout. Since noxious work settings often contribute to personal strain and burnout, a thorough assessment of the influence of the environment versus helpers' own contributions is necessary. If possible, a program of organizational change may provide an alternative to a helper's leaving the organization. In any case, helpers need to look for environmental stressors that interfere with their helping relationships. Other, more individual solutions were discussed in Chapter 3 under transference and countertransference feelings.

Ethics and Interpersonal Relationships

Most ethical issues in helping relationships involve interactions with others. We will consider two broad categories, *dual relationships* and *physical relationships.*

Dual Relationships

A dual relationship is one in which the helper has two (or more) overlapping roles with the helpee. For example, a nurse floor supervisor may have a nurse employee who is experiencing personal problems at home. They develop a helping relationship, where the supervisor is listening and providing counsel about the home situation. This is a dual relationship, because the supervisor is also responsible for evaluation of this nurse's hospital work performance, and the two relationships are not always compatible. Virtually all helpers encounter dual (or multiple) relationships in their daily lives and work. Recognizing them and managing them is the ethical issue.

All of the professional ethical codes urge caution about dual relationships. Ethical difficulty arises when helpers fail to recognize or effectively respond to blurred boundaries in their helping relationships. Prior to entering into a helping relationship, there are several questions a helper should ask.

Is There a Power Difference between Us?

If there already exists a difference in power or prestige, the helpee may feel less free to make independent choices. For example, abuses of power in relationships are more common with adults helping adolescents than helping adults, or more likely with adult male helping adult female alone than helping male alone. A college professor who has a heart for students and a good listening ear, yet also must give grades at the end of the quarter, has an ethical dilemma to face based on the imbalance of power in the relationship.

What Other Role Obligations Do I Have in This Situation?

Normally, a helper's primary obligation is to the helpee. This becomes complicated when other competing obligations exist. For example, a school social worker is requested to help a student in need. An important question to ask regarding dual relationships is, "Who is the client here?" Is it the student, the parents who want to help, the school who cannot deal with the student, or the district who is liable for the student's education? Depending on how the social worker answers the question, the nature of the help will be different.

How Will My Knowledge about You Change Our Relationships?

This discussion is about *role* limits and how sometimes knowledge interferes with the helping relationship. Sometimes the helpee may know the helper in two different roles, which, while actually working together, appear contradictory. As a helper, one may offer support unconditionally, yet in another role, may exercise authority or pass judgment on the helpee. This works two ways. Knowledge shared in a helping relationship can influence future or current outside relationships. For example, suppose a helper works with someone around issues of stress and lack of commitment to family. By chance, they both go to the same church and in a church board meeting the helper must vote on appointing the helpee as chair of the board, which would demand much time and many evenings away from home. Knowledge gleaned solely from the privacy of the helping relationship makes this vote more difficult.

It can work the other way as well, where knowledge prior to or outside the helping relationship, such as observing the individual using offensive interpersonal skills with subordinates, makes listening in the helping relationship less objective. For another example, a nutritionist may work with a client with eating disorders and then see the person in the grocery store buying forbidden food items. It is also important to be aware that, even when the helper is maintaining objectivity and separating out information from two places and roles, the helpee may perceive bias, and this perception may alter the current or future relationship.

In order to be an ethical helper, one must monitor the dual nature of helping relationships and constantly review personal motivations for action. These relationships can be tricky and, without vigilance, can be harmful to the helpee. Helpers should seek supervision regarding potential pitfalls in these dual relationship. Often the helper is too close to the situation to see these independently. Where risks exist for harm to the helpee, the helper must identify this risk, and seek to reduce it. Often this involves an open discussion with the helpee about such risk.

Physical Contact with Helpees

Sexual relationships of any kind are unethical in the helping setting. All professional organizations are very clear about prohibition of sexual intimacy between helper and helpee. While the wording is slightly different in each code, the principles are the same. Helpers do not engage in *sexual harass-*

ment. This includes sexual solicitation, physical advances or verbal or non-verbal conduct that is sexual in nature. It can be defined by a single act or a series of acts. A helping relationship is so unique and unbalanced in power and dependency issues, that the reciprocal nature of a healthy intimate relationship is not possible. Most professional ethical codes also speak to the restriction of sexual behavior between helper and helpee *after* the helping relationship has ended. Some say at least two years must pass before a personal relationship may be entered into (APA, 1992). Some say that a helping relationship in a sense never ends, so sexual intimacies may never occur between helper and helpee (Gutheil, 1989; Sell, Gottlieb, & Schoenfeld, 1986). Paraprofessional helpers will need to make their own determination about these issues, but should take great caution from the professional codes.

A more complex ethical dilemma concerns the question of touching clients for support, out of compassion, or to express care. This is an increasingly controversial issue. We know, for example, that a hug can be very comforting in a time of despair. Yet even the most innocent hug can be interpreted by the helpee as representing a sexual gesture, especially if the helpee's issue relates to inappropriate touch from others. Holding a helpee's hand or putting a firm hand on the person's arm or shoulder while he or she is struggling with a painful feeling can be most helpful to comfort or to facilitate further exploration. On the other hand, embracing or sitting on laps could be considered high-risk behavior in today's culture. Teachers and school personnel are now often instructed to only give side hugs, or no hugs at all. Touch should be used with discretion, after consideration of agency policy and the age, sex, and cultural background of the helpee. It also is respectful to ask the helpee, "Is it all right if I touch your arm?" or "May I hold your hand?" prior to assuming it would be appreciated.

Because helping relationships often involve feelings and discussion of personal issues, both helpers and helpees are vulnerable to sexual fantasies and sensitive to sexual innuendoes. Since this is a continual risk in intimate helping relationships, helpers need to be especially alert to their own feelings and behaviors and to deal ethically and humanely with any sex-related issues that emerge.

When helpers use physical contact or discuss sexually intimate issues, it is important that they have a high degree of awareness of their own needs for contact and are sufficiently aware of their own feelings that they can be perceptive about the helpees' needs and reactions to their contacting skills. In other words, the foremost question to be answered is, "Whose needs are being served?" We should be alert, for example, to helpees whose sexual experiences and close human relationships generally have been so restricted that they react with intense anxiety to any kind of physical contact. From your experience as both helpee and helper, what is your stand on the issue of physical contact? Under what conditions are you more or less comfortable with it?

In summary, this contact issue must be decided on the bases of:

1. The good judgment of the helper about the needs of this helpee.
2. The helper's awareness of his or her own needs and ethics.
3. What is likely to be most helpful within the helper's rationale of helping.
4. What risks the helper is willing to take, having considered agency policy, local custom, professional ethics, and the age, sex, culture, and attitude of the helpee.

Helper Competence and Limitations

Helpers of all levels of training must recognize their boundaries of competence and provide services only in their areas of training and expertise. The helper must never claim nor imply professional qualifications exceeding those possessed and is responsible to correct misrepresentations that others may have. Some states legally protect the title *psychologist* or *counselor* for individuals with specific types of education, so these titles should be used only if appropriate.

A key ethical focus for the discussion on competence, as in most other issues in this chapter, is how the helper can provide the most help, without harming the helpee or others affected by their relationship. Helpers must define their relationships to helpees in a manner clear to the helpees and others. Standards of professional helpers should apply to all types of helpers; namely that once a helping relationship is agreed on, the helper will do all in her or his power to make it productive until such time as a transfer of responsibility is made to another helper, or until either person voluntarily and formally terminates the relationship. In their first contact, the helper says, for example, "I see my task as helping to clarify the ways you see this problem and to look at some alternatives. You must then make the commitment to action and do something about it. If we can't work this out together, then we can explore possibilities of other people with whom you might work more effectively." The helpee makes this responsible choice.

Informed Consent

In professional helping, the helper has legal and ethical responsibilities for informing the helpee about the limitations of the helping relationship. It is logical that even in less formal situations, the helpee be informed of what to expect. The structure of this discussion is delineated in the professional literature and several sources are mentioned at the end of this chapter. Details are determined by the nature of the helper's training, experience, policy of the institution, and areas of specialization. For our purposes, here are some guidelines that should be included in an oral discussion or written statement about the nature and limitations of the helping relationship:

1. *General expectations.* It is anxiety reducing for helpees to have some idea of what the process of the relationship will be like. How often will you meet and for how long? Can helpees choose what to talk about, or do they have to "spill their guts" at your demand? What are the possibilities of change? What are your goals for the helping relationship and how do these mesh or conflict with the helpees' goals?

2. *Background of the helper.* Helpees like to know if their potential helper has any training or background in their issues. This discussion must be clear and honest, especially so the helpee is not misled to believe the helper has greater expertise than is the case.

3. *Costs.* If any fees are involved (formal or otherwise), this must be discussed openly and in the first meeting. Some states have regulations about charging fees for helping relationships whether or not they are actually called "counseling," so helpers should become cognizant of their state requirements.

4. *Confidentiality.* This is a very complicated issue in helping relationships. Legally, *paraprofessional helpers do not have any rights of legal privilege or confidentiality.* That means should you be subpoenaed by the court to tell anything you know, including any personal notes you have made about the helpee, you would have to do so. Ethically, however, all types of helpers have a responsibility to maintain confidentiality. This means the helper provides protection from unauthorized access to information about the helping relationship. An example will help make this distinction clearer.

An employee in a factory is under a great deal of personal stress and lately has been drinking too much. He is aware of this and goes to the company-appointed human resource director for help. Later his supervisor calls the helper to ask how the employee is doing in their sessions. The helper ethically will maintain confidentiality and not disclose anything to the supervisor. However, should the employee later be drinking on the job, cause an accident, and be named in an ensuing lawsuit, the helper could be subpoenaed and, because the helper does not have privileged communication, may have to disclose to the judge information about the sessions.

The important issue here is that helpees must be told in advance about the limits of confidentiality. In the professional domain, these limits are usually summarized to the helpee as follows: "Because trust is so important to our working relationship, I will keep everything you tell me confidential, with a few rare, but important exceptions. These are (1) if I believe you are a danger to yourself or another person; (2) if I suspect that a child or dependent adult is in danger or has been harmed; (3) if you request your records be released to someone; or (4) if a court orders me to disclose information. In any event, should I need to break our confidentiality, I will tell you."

This informed consent allows the helpee to make responsible choices about what to tell the helper, and then also makes it easier on the helper to report those things that must be reported. For this reason, it is important to inform the helpee of these conditions early in the helping relationship.

Emergency/Crisis Response

People who attempt to be helpful, even in casual and informal situations, need to be reasonably cautious and alert to conditions that may lead them into legal difficulties. While we do not want to be alarmist, there are four situations about which all helpers need to be watchful, and if they happen, supervision should be sought immediately and appropriate authorities notified. These four conditions are (1) threat of suicide, (2) threats of danger to others (such as homicidal indications), (3) evidence of abuse, and (4) sexual harassment accusations. Many states make it mandatory to report even suspected child abuse within short time limits (e.g., 48 hours). Professional helpers are under special ethical and legal constraints to report these conditions, but personal ethics, concern for others, and potential legal action should prompt prudent action if informal helpers encounter these conditions.

In the four conditions stated above, there are three keys for the nonprofessional helper:

1. Take all indications or suspicions of these conditions seriously. Your job is *not* to determine if the helpee is truly suicidal or homicidal or if the allegations of abuse or harassment are warranted. This may seem counter-intuitive if you think you know the person or the situation better than an outsider. Especially in the first three cases, there is a great deal of professional judgment and complexity surrounding these potentially life-threatening issues. The correct, ethical (and sometimes legal) behavior, for all helpers, is to get help immediately. Do not attempt to work this out on your own.

2. Do not bear too much personal responsibility for outcomes once you have made the appropriate referrals. This is a difficult principle, because when we are helping persons in grave distress, we become very personally involved. However, helpees maintain their free will, and in spite of helper intentions, helpees sometimes make destructive choices. This does not mean that the helper was ineffective, should have done something differently, or bears fault in the situation. One reason that supervision is so important here is the maintenance of this more objective perspective.

3. Develop an emergency support network before you need it. If you are a person who is involved in helping, you should have a list of phone numbers easily accessible, perhaps a few even carried on a card in your wallet. For example, depending on the type of helping you provide, you need numbers for the local crisis line, police department, women's shelter, child protective services, sexual assault center, drug/alcohol helpline, and a trusted psychiatrist or psychologist for supervision.

Outcomes Self-Check

After reading this chapter you should be able to (1) explain what is meant by *ethics* and explain how ethics differ from the law; (2) be able to describe some critical elements of self-care you might need in your role as a helper; (3) identify issues in interpersonal relationships between helpers and helpees that can be difficult and have thought through some possible precautions; (4) address issues of helper personal competence, and know some of the limits in helping relationships; and (5) demonstrate awareness of how to respond ethically in some emergency situations.

Suggestions for Further Study

American Association for Marriage and Family Therapy. *AAMFT code of ethics*. Washington, DC: American Association for Marriage and Family Therapy, 1991.

American Counseling Association. *Ethical standards*. Alexandria, VA: American Counseling Association, 1995.

American Psychological Association. Ethical principles of psychologists and code of conduct. *American Psychologist* 47 (1992):1597–1611.

American School Counselor Association. *Ethical standards for school counse-*

lors. Alexandria, VA: American School Counselor Association, 1992.

Corey, G., Corey, M. S., and Callanan, P. *Issues and ethics in the helping professions*. 3rd ed. Pacific Grove, CA: Brooks/Cole, 1993.

National Association of Social Workers. *Code of Ethics*. (1993).

Salo, M. M. and Shumate, S. G. *Counseling Minor Clients*. Alexandria, VA: American Counseling Association, 1993.

8

Thinking about the Helping Process

The purpose of this chapter is to describe some ways of thinking about the helping process that will lead to more effective helping outcomes. The helper functions as a whole person, not only as a skilled technician, while in contact with the helpee. Thinking is part of the helper's personhood. At times helpers evaluate the helping process while they conduct it, but generally they think about and evaluate themselves, their helpees, and the helping process in private after the helping event. This chapter, therefore, focuses on questions that helpers tend to ask when they are alone.

Theory as a Guide

A frequent question is why does a particular method or strategy work or not work? We call this mental activity theorizing. Theorizing refers to a rational rather than a feeling function. Helpers need a guiding theory to help them make sense of the complex helping process. Of course, people can help others in ways described in Chapter 1 without a thought about theory, but if they are going to work systematically in a helping function, they need some "hooks" on which to hang their experiences and some frame of reference for gaining perspectives on their work and improving their services. The main value of theory, in our opinion, is to give direction to the action phase of helping. Theory is not necessary to establish a relationship, but it becomes crucial when deciding to assist helpees in behavior change. Helpers must have clear assumptions about how behavior changes.

For example, the helpee's statement "I have a problem and I want help" usually translates into "I am unhappy with the way things are; I want to change...," or "I want to decide...." Our theory of helping explains how one sees this process of change and where the focus of effort needs to take place. As one's helping theory develops, one experiences increased awareness of the process and increased ability to explain one's views to others. Hence, helpers need a language of description for their work.

Each helper has an implicit theory of helping. This means we all have some ideas that guide our actions, although we usually are not aware of them. For example, you may hold an assumption that all people are basically social and humane. You may also believe that antisocial behavior is learned. You will then expect people to act in a humane way. If they do not, you conclude that they have learned their antisocial behavior.

Outcomes You Can Expect

This chapter describes the need for a systematic way of thinking about helping and the principal ways other helpers have described their work. The outcomes you can expect from studying this chapter are to (1) identify guidelines for thinking about your own theory of helping; (2) describe contributions of the major categories of current helping theory; and (3) list twenty theoretical concepts and vocabulary terms related to theories used to describe helping skills.

A Personal Theory of Helpfulness

Each helper must develop his or her own style and theory about helping, because each person has had different life experiences and has different ways of looking at people. We may find others' assumptions similar to our own, but each helper must take responsibility for revamping them into his or her unique ideas and beliefs. Freud was not a Freudian, and Rogers was not a Rogerian; each was himself, and each built on the wisdom of the past. Admiring disciples of these men often gave their own explanations of the helping process, even though they retained a Freudian or Rogerian label.

Helpers build theory through three overlapping stages. First, they reflect on their own experiences. They become aware of their values, needs, communication style, and impact on others. The helper strives for a clear perception of his or her personal myth. A personal myth is a story about what you cherish in yourself and your culture, how you got here, and how you see your life developing in the future. At one time in history individuals were primarily reflections of their familial or ethnic cultures, but now the emphasis on individual development makes us very different from one another.

Second, they read widely about the experience of other practitioners who have tried to construct a systematic theory based on their clinical observations, and research findings. In this sense theories are a sophisticated form of common sense. Finally, the helper forges his or her own experiences and those of others together into a unique theory. If the theory is written down in a systematic manner, given a label, and attracts followers, the helper may even become the founder of another theory of helping!

There is no one preferred helping theory. Each approach to more formal counseling, psychotherapy, or caregiving has limitations and strengths in terms of explaining the events in the helping process. We are a long way from a generally applicable theory of helpfulness. The data from research studies and observations of students in practice reveal the impressive effectiveness of numerous styles and approaches. Although helpees generally are fair judges of what is effective with them, their judgments are not the final answer either. Some helpees profess to be helped by tea leaf and card readers, magicians, and other "helpers" with mystical and extravagant claims.

Constructing a Theory

Basically, a theory should be a rationale for what one does in the name of helping. It should include basic assumptions of how people learn and change their behavior. It should have some element of how personality is put together (structure), how it develops (growth), its cultural context, and how activity is generated (motivation). One's theory is also a reflection of one's personal myth as described previously.

A theory of helpfulness should contain a *philosophical* dimension that includes one's values and expected outcomes (Brammer, Abrego, & Shostrom, 1993). It is a statement of the kind of person who should emerge from the helping process—an ideal growth model. Theory has a *structural* dimension that provides a cognitive map for looking at the whole person, and specifically at his or her current stage of growth. It is a scheme for helping to picture how the helpee's personality is organized. A *developmental* dimension is important to help differentiate the helpee's various normal and deviant growth stages as he or she moves from dependence to independence, from incompetence to competence, and from simplicity to complexity. Finally, a *process* dimension helps to explain how people learn and modify their behavior. Some persons need to experience something first and then reflect on the learnings—experiential learning. Others need to understand it and see all the parts first and then do it—cognitive learning. Occasionally, some use a trial-and-error process and seem to stumble into answers to problems, or insights emerge unexpectedly—discovery learning. Each of us has a style that works best under a given set of learning requirements, and our basic task in learning how to help others is to discover their most effective learning style.

As you think about your own theory of helpfulness, the following questions should be considered:

1. *Values and goals.* What is my view of the "good life"? What is my model of an effective, well-functioning, mature person in our society at the present time? What do I want for my life? What is my responsibility to others? What does it mean to be helpful to another person?

2. *The nature of humanity.* How is the human personality structured? What motivates people to behave as they do? How do thinking processes take place? What are the relationships among thinking, feeling, and valuing? How does a person make choices? Does each person create his or her own life, or does each live out the history of the race or culture in a unique way?

3. *Behavior change.* How do we learn? Do we change the environment first, or our personality characteristics first, and then expect behavior to change? Do we act first, then learn, or do we obtain understanding first, then act? What factors prevent people from changing?

These questions contain profound philosophical issues over which people have been arguing for centuries. Some are religious and require a declaration of faith; some require awareness of personal myths; others are empirical and research provides some answers. In any case, they illustrate the complexity, depth of thought, and length of time required to develop a comprehensive working theory about people and the helping process.

If you are ready to think through your own ideas about helping in a more formal way than in Chapter 1, we suggest the following outline:

1. *Know yourself*—traits, values, beliefs about people from the questions listed above. These questions about values and beliefs lead to a statement of your personal myth.

These myths are a complex of often conflicting personal beliefs about the meaning of existence, the person's roles in the social order and how he or she progresses through life. These personal mythologies give meaning to the past, understanding of the present, and guidelines for the future. The task here is to describe your personal myth—your reality and the meaning of your existence.

There are two reasons for doing this task—as a foundation for your theory of helping and as an awareness of your reality and how it is different from others. This awareness is a good antidote to your deliberate or unaware tendency to force your belief system on helpees. On the other hand, your manifest myth may make you attractive to helpees who want to talk with someone like themselves. Writing your personal myth also makes you more aware of changes in the story and how those experiences shaped your life. To facilitate this task, we suggest that you read how one prominent helper, Carl Jung (1961), reported his personal myth. In addition, Keen and Fox (1973) produced a useful self-help book to encourage people to tell their personal stories.

2. *Read* about what others have said about helping.

3. *Write down the key ideas* from your self-study and attractive features of others' views. Use a systematic form, such as personal values and assumptions about people; main strategies and methods suggested by these assumptions; helping skills that are emphasized; and outcomes expected. Compare their myths to yours. How are they the same or different? A basic book about theories of helping might be beneficial to you for this structured exploration (e.g., Brammer, Abrego, & Shostrom, 1993; Corsini & Wedding, 1989).

4. Finally, *test your theory* in practice and change it with experience. One of the ways to test the usefulness of your theory of helping is to give your written statement to a friend or colleague who knows firsthand how you offer help. That person then can give feedback to you about how closely your statement of how you help corresponds to what you actually do in a helping relationship. Then, if you think the feedback is valid, you can change your theory or your helping style to bring them into closer correspondence. In training programs for helpers this process is refined to the extent of using videotape and multiple observers to get more reliable observations.

Our theory is also a guide to our practice, so that what we believe about the helping process influences the way we help others. Our theory should help us to answer key questions about helping:

What are the goals of helping—what am I trying to do as a helper?

What stages in the process of helping do I tend to follow?

What methods work best to achieve the helpee's goals?

How can the helpee be enlisted in the helping process?

How can helpees learn to apply these helping skills to their future problems?

How do I know that the helping process was truly helpful—how do I know as a helper whether or not I have succeeded?

Usefulness and Limitations of Helping Theory

A theory of helpfulness is useful when it enables one to describe and explain what one is doing in a helping relationship and why one is doing it. Theory is an intellectual tool to systematize and simplify the complex observations one makes continuously. It should help us fill in spaces in our perceptions that may be missing or vague, as we do when we put pieces in a puzzle. The process helps us in making choices of technique. If our theory focuses on rational problem solving, for example, we will utilize more rational methods, such as problem analysis, in our helping. If our theory stresses the significance of feelings, we will tend to focus on clarification of feeling states as a means to help.

If we have a theory with the elements described, we should be better able to explain helpee behavior. If a helpee, for example, is exhibiting unusual avoidance behavior while making a choice among alternative solutions to a personal problem, we can guess about the person's fear of commitment or of risking failure. Our theory may give us informed hunches on why people resist choice or change. These hunches also serve as research leads that can be verified with more precise and extended observations, and through systematic research. This research can take the form of an intensive case study of one helpee to answer the key questions about this person. In one sense, all helpees become research subjects since we begin the helping process with questions that are answered as the process unfolds. Helpers are thus both observers and participants in the helping process. Professional helpers call themselves scientists/practitioners because they are subjectively involved with their helpees and at the same time objectively observe themselves interacting with their helpees. Examples are: "Were the goals accomplished? If not, why not? How could I have improved my helping skills?" More complex research methods enable helpers to study categories of helpees so that more inclusive statements can be made about helpees in general.

The basic limitation of all theories, however, is that they are generalizations from observations of particular helping situations. When they are reapplied to an individual, one must be very careful not to oversimplify the situation or explain it away with a theoretical generalization. For example, our theory may indicate that generally the helper's self-revelation generates helpee self-revelation and that this is an essential condition to move the helping process forward. This generalization must be applied selectively to avoid destructive consequences of too much helpee or helper self-revelation.

The principal value of the thinking process we have labeled *theorizing* is that helpers can systematize their observations so the process makes sense to themselves and can be communicated to others. Theory is also useful when specific actions for the helpee must be outlined. For example, the helper explains to the helpee a rationale for a reward schedule. Since each of the following theory groups espouses a different idea of how to get helpees to act and solve their problems, a helper needs to be familiar with the available options.

As described previously, helpers tend to develop their own theories. For persons who operate rather intuitively, a simple statement of key assumptions may suffice. Others couch their theories in complex technical writings that at times seem mystical and even cultish.

A recent example of theory building is based on principles of psycholinguistics. Since accurate communication is so basic to the helping process, this theory focuses on helping people to clarify their sentences. This is done to make helpees more aware of their communication style. Another part of this theory states that helpers who match their language style, especially image words, to the helpee's style will achieve greater rapport. Helpers who are visually, aurally, or kinesthetically oriented will use descriptive language to conform to their personal styles and language preferences. Examples are "I *see* the problem more clearly now" or "What you say has a *ring* of truth" or "It is time to *kick* the habit."

Students and followers of past writers developed schools named after the person, such as Freudian, Sullivanian, or Rogerian. Descriptive titles, such as psychoanalytic or behavioral, are used more frequently now. The following section lists key features of the principal approaches currently in use. Such an outline has all the risks of oversimplification and culturally biased selection, but the illustrative summaries to follow are presented as an orienting overview to classification, contributions, and limitations of helping theories. Detailed information about specific theories may be obtained from the Suggestions for Further Study of Helping Theory. The following categories have broad labels to encompass over one hundred specific helping theories (Corsini & Wedding, 1989).

Professional helpers have been searching over five decades for the *common elements* in various theories of counseling and psychotherapy. Lively debates have been conducted over which elements are necessary and sufficient to make the helping process work. There is no consensus at present about what makes helping effective, but helpers have definite opinions on why they think their approach works best. Corsini and Wedding (1989) reported on Corsini's earlier survey of articles speaking to this question, "Why does the helping process work with individuals and groups?" The following is a summary of his analysis.

Change becomes possible when helpees:

1. Realize they are not facing problems alone—others have similar problems.
2. Perceive that human suffering is universal.
3. Understand themselves better and get a broader perspective on their lives when they realize that others believe in them.
4. Observe others working through their problems or see models.
5. Receive unconditional positive regard from the helper.
6. Recognize they are recipients of love and caring from the helper(s).
7. Identify a close emotional bond with the helper(s).
8. Experiment with new behaviors and receive support and feedback.

9. Express strong feelings in a permissive atmosphere.
10. Admit that there is something wrong with their behavior and are willing to explore changes.

This list expresses the wisdom of centuries: Know thyself, love thy neighbor, and do good works. *Persistence* was an additional factor that came out of a discussion with colleagues on the question of why people finally change their behavior. Persistence in working on the problem resulted either from urging by the helper or from internal drive in the helpee. We call this persistent effort the "TTA Rule" (try, try again). Helpees must realize that behavior change usually comes slowly and often after very hard work. Recall your own efforts to change annoying negative thinking or your attempts to lose weight consistently. Later in this chapter we will discuss the question, "What if I want to change, but I'm stuck?"

These tendencies of helpees to resist change and become "stuck" are very frustrating to helpers since they have such a heavy personal investment in the outcomes. If helpees do not move toward solutions of their problems, then helpers tend to feel like failures. Theorizing helps in that the helper has a cognitive framework for posing the critical questions about effectiveness. Sometimes it is necessary to accept the reality that the helper's responsibility for results is limited. Often we must settle for the satisfaction of having encountered the helpee for a time in the process. We must also realize that the helpee and the helper may have different views of positive outcomes. Hence we may be more, or less, helpful than we think we are. Perhaps both of us must settle for more modest improvements. Our theory should help us to define more clearly the tricky philosophical dimensions of improvement and a conception of the ideal helpee. What would you regard as characteristics of the ideal helpee?

General Theories of the Helping Process

Eclectic

Most helpers claim to have an eclectic, or integrative, orientation, taking a broad and flexible view on the critical questions about personality structure and behavior change. Although eclectic helpers synthesize concepts, techniques, and assumptions from many viewpoints, an eclectic view does not mean casual choosing from many different theories, a practice that has brought eclectic views into disrepute in some professional groups. It is a difficult theoretical stance to adopt because of the hard work required to integrate many complex ideas along a broad spectrum of helping functions; yet, many established leaders among helping professionals are moving toward this integrative view. After extensive study of this identity issue over the past quarter century, Kanfer and Goldstein (1992) observed that multiple-systems models have replaced single-factor theories of etiology and change. This trend has grown out of a need to treat helpees not as general problems but as persons with unique life settings, values, and biosocial characteristics.

Eclectic views must be consistent as well as comprehensive. There appears to be renewed interest in a sophisticated eclecticism that emphasizes development of one's own personal theory of helping. It is still stylish in professional helping circles, however, to identify with a particular psychoanalytic, behavioral, or phenomenological view. This integrative viewpoint emphasizes use of all skill clusters included in Figure 1-2, although each theory group emphasizes different skills at each stage in the helping process. An example of this creative synthesis type of theory is described in Brammer, Abrego, & Shostrom, (1993). The multimodal theory of Lazarus (1976), the Adaptive Counseling and Therapy (ACT) of Howard, Nance, and Myers (1986), and Ivey's (1986) *Developmental Therapy* are additional examples.

Psychoanalytic

The psychoanalytic view has a long history and perhaps the most complex set of assumptions and structures of all the helping theories. The essential idea is that understanding one's psychosexual life history and intrapsychic conflicts is crucial to working through personal problems and achieving normal development. Psychoanalytic writers following Freud emphasized social learning as opposed to genetic influences in development. This view postulates a life energy that is stored in a location of the personality called the unconscious. The intrapsychic conflict among the various forms of energy expression in the person are the sources of human problems. Psychoanalytic theories are known as depth views because of their emphasis on life history factors and the involvement of various levels of personality structure. The levels are ego (mastery), id (impulses), and superego (conscience). A key contribution of psychoanalytic theory to the helping professions is the idea of defense mechanisms whereby the personality seeks its internal stability by defending itself against disintegration within and attack from without. The principal means for helping people under this system is a process of working through their developmental problems into the present.

One of the main limitations of the psychoanalytic view is that, since their conflicts arise out of their past history, helpees consider their problems beyond their present control and responsibility. The methods of helping used in this approach are long, arduous, and unpredictable. Long and demanding training is required of helpers who wish to use psychoanalytic methods. The main skills emphasized by analytically oriented helpers are reflecting, confronting, interpreting, and informing.

Phenomenological

The phenomenological view of helping focuses on the uniqueness of each person's perception of reality. The helper is understanding to the extent that he or she can perceive the phenomenal world of helpees. The emphasis is on the present rather than the past or the future, and so how helpees feel about themselves and their worlds now is the crucial consideration. This view includes a cluster of theories, some of which emphasize a self as the main perceiving instrument. Sometimes these views are called *self-* or *person-centered* theories because they focus on persons and their perceptions of themselves. Key assumptions are a person's drive toward growth and integration and the interrelatedness of all phenomena in the natural and supernatural worlds.

A related helping theory is *gestalt,* which emphasizes confrontation with self in the present. This view stresses honesty and openness in encounters with other people as the basis for helping and personal integration. Broadened awareness is one of the principal goals of gestalt helpers. A key aspect of gestalt and similar theories is the importance of grounding one's reality, especially feelings, in the body. Thinking is regarded as ephemeral and undependable as a source of help. Bodily experience reflects a basic honesty and is the source of psychic energy and awareness. Therefore, the helping process focuses on body experience.

A cluster of phenomenological viewpoints known as *existentialism* is attractive to people-helpers because of its focus on humanness. Existentialism is a philosophical outlook speaking to issues of time, meaning, purpose, feelings, and the human potential. The main skill clusters emphasized by this group are listening, reflecting, summarizing, and confronting (for understanding), with some supportive and centering skill (for awareness and comfort).

The main limitation of phenomenological and gestalt theories is their high degree of subjectivity, which leads to vagueness and problems of determining effectiveness and validation through research.

Behavioral

Although most of the theories mentioned so far emphasize inferred subjective states such as feelings, behaviorally focused helpers concentrate on objective observation of behavior and the person's environment. They focus especially on learning as a form of behavior change. In this sense all helping in formal counseling is behavioral, since learning or changing behavior in some form is the basic process. The main differences appear in explanations of how behavior changes and in the degree of emphasis put on outcomes in helpee behavior rather than on process. For the behavioral counselor the function of reward is very important because much evidence suggests that rewarded behavior tends to be repeated. For example, if one wishes to increase the helpees' search for information to help them solve their planning problems, helpers must see that their information-seeking behavior is rewarded in appropriate ways.

Behavioral helpers stress specific and concise goals, such as developing an educational plan, eliminating an undesirable habit, or making a choice between two potential marriage partners. The main standard of success for such helpers is the degree to which their helpees reach their stated goals. This emphasis on precise goals and measurable outcomes is an attractive feature to helpers with a behavioral set. Because observable behaviors are the variables studied, the behavioral framework lends itself to research on counseling processes and outcomes. The principal skill clusters emphasized by this group are problem solving and behavior changing (for positive action).

The principal limitations of behavioral views are the difficulties in dealing with feelings through observable behavior. The emphasis on specificity, precision, and objectivity tends to lead the helper to focus on minute pieces of behavior and to ignore larger complex patterns. Some people view behavior management as "brainwashing." However, this skepticism or rejection is based on abusive applications of this powerful method for changing behavior.

Rational

Related to the behavioral approach is a cluster of viewpoints stressing *rationality*. Thinking processes are examined and corrected by pointing out faulty logic and beliefs to helpees on the assumption that altering their belief systems leads to changes in their behavior. Helpers using this approach would tell their helpees that their difficulties in making choices, for example, seemed to be due largely to their negative and even catastrophic expectations. Seeing clearly how their thinking was distorted would remove this obstacle to positive action. A teaching role on changing the helpee's thinking, therefore, is one of the principal helping functions.

A large group of helpee problems revolve around making plans and choices that require information about self or the world of work. Educational and career planning by students is an example. Here the emphasis is on rational *problem solving* and prediction of success in a given training event. Sometimes this viewpoint is known as the *trait and factor* theory because the focus is on assessment of personal traits (e.g., interests, attitudes) and intellectual factors (e.g., spatial visualization, verbal skills). This task of assessment is accomplished mainly through psychological tests that can predict success in study or work. Helpers stressing this viewpoint do not deny the significance of feelings in human events, but they tend mainly to focus on the more observable rational factors in the helping process. Computer technology is being tapped as an adjunct to the helping process where information and prediction are special needs.

The main skill clusters emphasized by this group are confronting, interpreting, informing, and problem solving. The chief limitation of rational approaches is a disproportionate emphasis on cognitive and observable behaviors to the neglect of the vast feeling realm of existence.

Transactional-Communicative-Reality

The group of transactional-communicative-reality theories focuses on *communication patterns,* such as those between parent and child or teacher and pupil. A study is made of the interaction patterns and the mechanisms people use to influence, manipulate, and reach other people. The assumption is made that all of us carry within ourselves remnants of child, parent, and adult communication patterns. The helping process consists of examining the effectiveness of these patterns, in particular, the distortions of these states of being between individuals (transactional analysis). One form of distortion, for example, is the "game" of deception helpees play with themselves and others.

Helping is facilitated by training in communication skills so that intentions are matched with behaviors. Feelings as well as thought patterns are considered. Much responsibility is placed on helpees for their own choices and actions. Helpees are taught that they are responsible for their own behavior, meaning that they must "own" their own problems rather than blame others (reality therapy). This theoretical framework is used extensively with groups of people where dysfunctional communication patterns are complex, rigid, and distorted. A whole family or business office may be helped as a group rather than singling out individuals for help. The main skill clusters emphasized are listening, reflecting, confronting, and interpreting (for increased awareness and understanding). The principal limitation of this cluster of communication approaches is its limited set of assumptions about behavior; a more comprehensive view usually is required to deal with the complexities of family problems or industrial group dynamics.

Life-Style

Although there is no general category among helping theories emphasizing body awareness, there is a strong emphasis in helping interviews and groups on body awareness, sensory awakening, wellness, pain control, healing acts, and brain wave functions. The basic idea is that many of our difficulties in living effectively result from our losing touch with the physical dimension of our existence. We deny our impulses, dilute our sensory awareness, and ignore messages from our bodies. In this framework, helping efforts are devoted to enriching life through reawakening the senses, following health rules, opening awareness to our bodies, enjoying physiological processes, and promoting relaxation and self-understanding. Examples of methods used are relaxation, mental imagery, behavioral management of the autonomic nerves, dietary education, exercise, massage, touch, and biofeedback. This training is conducted through numerous holistic and wellness centers, pain clinics, and life-style workshops. The main skill clusters emphasized by this group are informing, confronting, interpreting, and supporting.

Family Systems Theories

The preceding theories of personality and counseling have largely European/ North American roots. These theories focus on individualism, view the world from a linear cause and effect perspective, and emphasize autonomous decision making and independent action. Family systems theories look at working with helpees as integrated parts of a system, be it a family or larger institution. It seems especially unproductive to help young people apart from this system. Systems theory has its roots in biology, that living organisms undergo continuous change and reconstitution. They are open self-regulating systems. By analogy human systems are interactive systems within the person, and each person interacts within a social system. People are changing continuously with only moments of stability or homeostasis. People strive for a steady state where change and stability are in balance. Thus, families, neighborhoods, schools and businesses are systems, and each of these groups has subsystems (Thomas, 1992). The main implication of systems theory for the helping process is that the helper must take into account the place of the helpee in the family or neighborhood system. People do not live in isolation. Each system has its own set of rules that govern the expectations for how each individual should behave. It is important for helpers to observe or infer what those rules and expectations may be, since what affects one affects all members. It is also important to know who makes and enforces the rules and how conflicts are negotiated. It is these rules and customs in the nuclear family, extended family, and neighborhood that provide the person with a sense of identity and belonging and a meaningful view of the world.

Cross-Cultural Theories

Some of these preceding theories have grave limitations when one is working in helping relationships with helpees who do not have historical Caucasian and European cultural roots. As we discussed in earlier chapters, helpees may have such a different cultural upbringing from the helper that the help offered appears confusing and irrelevant to them. This section covers topics that may help to bridge these cultural gaps. The following theories are recommended to helpers who serve in a variety of settings with a wide range of helpee backgrounds.

The importance of having a cross-cultural perspective has been cited several times in this book. An effective helper must have a larger view than merely appreciating other cultural contributions, knowing his or her own culture biases, and adapting historical counseling theories and methods to other cultures. Adopting a culture-specific model of counseling as described by Nwachuku and Ivey (1991) is essential. This view emphasizes looking at the helpee's culture as an insider would view it, noting especially natural helping approaches. It is an attempt to see the cultural background of the helpee as he or she experienced it. This means, for example, looking at language patterns, nonverbal signs, proverbs, beliefs, rituals and reward systems. In addition, the prospective helper should note the child-rearing styles, self-referents, space and time consciousness, and individual-group relationships.

The helper also must ask the questions, "How does this culture view the helping relationship?" "What helping skills are utilized?" The answers to these questions complicate what is ordinarily a simple relationship when the two people come from the same cultural background. They also help to explain the probable difficulties of the helper when the helpee comes from a different background.

The same kind of culture-specific analysis could be applied to sub-subcultures within a country, such as the United States, where people may speak the same language and have a common national culture, but have vastly different views of helping. Examples are Jewish American, Native American, African American, Asian American, or Hispanic American subcultures.

We have made the case for helpers to be aware of and sensitive to people in other cultures, especially subcultural groups in the United States. If you work with cultural groups different from your own, it is important to review the competencies and standards for multicultural helping relationships cited in the Further Study section (Sue, Arredondo, & McDavis, 1992; *The Counseling Psychologist: Special Edition on Culture and Counseling,* 1995).

Gender differences in attitudes and beliefs often are as great a barrier in helping relationships as race or national origin. A helping approach called feminist counseling has arisen precisely because male helpers often do not take the culture-specific view described above where the helper tries hard to view issues from the "insider's" perspective. For example, feminist counseling emphasizes relationships and feelings. Counselors start with the experience of being a woman and awareness of their values and beliefs. Unless male helpers are sensitive to these differences from their own traditional male beliefs and attitudes, they will not be effective; and they will continue to elicit the common response, "Men just don't get it."

Social Issues Awareness

Values Issues

It is useful for helpers to remain up-to-date on social values and trends since almost all the actions the helpee and helper take have a values basis. Sexual behavior is a conspicuous example. People who have lived at least five decades can recall the dramatic shifts in values the culture has experienced. Some of these values, such as the meaning of life itself, have religious overtones. The debates about abortion and euthanasia are examples of conflicts many helpees face. The main implications of values theory for the helper is that it gives a foundation for ethical decisions in the helping relationship. It helps to be clear about the fundamental human values underlying an ethical judgment as well as the current community standards in regard to sexual behavior, substance use, or medical life support, for example.

Political Issues

Since helpers conduct their relationships in the real world of people, it helps to have a working knowledge of political theory. For example, the helper needs to have clear ideas about the use and limits of power, influence, control, and privilege. These issues come up continuously since the helping relationship involves large elements of power and control, especially when gender and authority issues intrude. There are also human rights and due process considerations whenever decisions about people are being made.

Since helping rarely takes place in a social vacuum the helper must be informed about issues related to people in a social context. For example, it is crucial for the helper to be informed on issues of child, spouse, and elder abuse, crime victimization, gay/lesbian relationships, minority rights and problems related to jobs, housing, and advancement, abortion, euthanasia, problems and rights of AIDS patients and the disabled, homelessness, rape and sexual harassment, and substance abuse. This list could go on and on but the main implication of this litany of social concerns is that helpers must be informed about current issues affecting special groups in the society to maintain their credibility and effectiveness.

Religious and Spiritual Issues

For many years there was a futile attempt to keep values out of the helping arena; so also has there been an avoidance of the religious or spiritual element of the helping relationship (Corey, Corey, & Callanan, 1993). It is clear, however, that helpees often have issues related to their faith belief system as a significant part of their problems. For example, in processing the death of a child, a helpee may doubt the existence of the God in whom they once believed.

Religious beliefs and practices are often connected to other beliefs, including political positions. When real-life dilemmas cause conflict between beliefs and practice, people become confused and need help sorting out these issues (Worthington, 1989). An example is when the fourteen-year-old daughter in a politically and religiously conservative family becomes pregnant and wants to consider abortion as an option. She and her family may seek out a helper who will not be judgmental, but who also will not ignore the spiritual dimension of the decision.

Tying Theory to the Practice of Helping Skills

Four theoretical threads run through the act of learning the skills described in this book: needs, learning, awareness, and communications.

Needs

The first theoretical thread is the *need approach* to motivation described in Chapter 1. Human beings are energized by basic psychological and physiological needs that push for satisfaction and stabilization of the personality, but occasionally they seek risky behavior to provide variety and meaning to their existence. That people act to satisfy their needs is the basic premise of this viewpoint. Helping skills are designed to assist helpees to fulfill their needs for understanding, support, and action.

Learning

A second thread tying the helping skills together is a behavior change, or learning, approach. A key concept useful for skill development is *modeling,* the use of examples of effective and ineffective helping skills. *Reinforcement,* or management of rewards, is another key learning concept. Rewarded behaviors tend to become fixed in the repertoire of the person; satisfying a need tends to be a reinforcing condition, for example. Conversely, behaviors that are not rewarded, such as those that are ignored or that may even be aversive or noxious, tend to disappear from the behavioral repertoire of the person.

The principle of *transfer* is important for skill learning also, since the skills learned in simulated settings are transferred to similar real-life helping situations. Listening skills practiced in a controlled laboratory setting, for example, can then be applied in comparable helping interviews. *Stimulus substitution,* or reconditioning, also takes place in some helping situations. We may wish to substitute a relaxation response, for example, for a tension response in a test situation. *Goal-setting* and *problem-solving* principles are important in learning helping skills also.

A common, well-researched approach to learning helping skills called *microskills training* emphasizes learning individual skills. This is done by observing good models of helping behavior and then trying it out under supervision, where the supervisor can reward by praise or modify the skills by correction. These component skills then are combined in the artful act of helping, being gradually transferred from a practice setting to more complex real-life helping situations. It is like learning to play golf where the individual skills of stance, grip, and swing are combined into the complex act of swinging the club such that the ball will travel to the desired place.

Awareness

A third theory covers the idea of *awareness of feelings* and their effects. As indicated earlier in this chapter, a dominant view of helpers is that our reality is what we perceive it to be. Therefore, when we talk about understanding, we mean perceiving the helpee's unique way of looking at the world. The helper responds to helpees in such a way that they perceive themselves as being understood both in thoughts and feelings. Helpees manifest this understanding by verbal behavior that describes their subjective feelings, such as "I feel confident," or "I feel angry toward you," or "I feel good about you and me." Awareness is the first step to behavior change.

Communications

A fourth thread that ties the whole theory/skill bundle together is *communications* theory. An underlying assumption in helping is that people do not understand one another because they cannot communicate with one another. Therefore, skills covered in earlier chapters are aimed at facilitating interpersonal communication by enabling one to listen and speak more clearly. The basic communication problem is to make one's intent as a speaker clear by matching intent with words. The result is directness, clarity of meaning, and awareness of communication style.

The usual state of affairs, however, is a communications gap where the effect on the hearer does not match the message the speaker intended, and so much time is spent in clearing up the resulting misunderstanding. Sometimes this condition is caused by a double message—one given by one's body, which says "I'm afraid," and another by one's words, which say "I'm calm and confident." The result is confusion in the hearer and projection of the hearer's personal meanings on the mixed message in order to make sense of it.

It seems almost absurdly simple to state that often the most helpful thing we can do is to make it possible for helpees to improve their communication. This approach includes attention to nonverbal, or body, language as well as to speech. Our actions, rather than our words, are more honest and direct forms of communication because we have learned that words can conceal, distort, and deny real feelings, but our bodies do not. As one helper, Perls (1969), expressed it clearly, "Our bodies do not lie." One means to make our messages more clear, then, is to get in touch with our bodies (our feelings) so we know what they are saying. By pointing out discrepancies between verbal messages and body messages in helpees, we help them to communicate more consistently and clearly with themselves and others.

The preceding discussion implies that communication problems in helping interviews result from unclear intent of, or confused messages from, helpees. We need to remind ourselves constantly that communication, a two-way process, requires that we look into the way we distort what we hear from helpees. Are my needs, of which I am unaware, acting as filters through which I hear the helpee's message my way? If I am only vaguely aware, or creating fantasies about this helpee—do I hear what I *want* to hear? Am I fearful that I will be attacked, seduced, or conned? Am I fearful that I might do the same to the helpee? The kinds of awareness and the conditions discussed in the earlier chapters under transference and countertransference and cultural bias help here. The main point is that unrecognized needs and feelings distort messages and compound problems.

When Helpees Do Not Change

One of the greatest frustrations for helpers is to use all the skills and personal resources described in this book and yet helpees will not change. This is especially unnerving when the helper has a heavy personal investment in the helpee's change, such as a teacher–pupil relationship. It is a sober warning to the helper that maybe he or she has placed too much emphasis on the outcome and that more attention is needed on the process of change. Perhaps your theory of helpfulness needs reexamination also. For example, what assumptions are you making about why people resist change?

What can be done about this common helpee tendency? There are many reasons why helpees do not change. For example, they may fear the change. They do not know why, but they just procrastinate. They may be trapped in their old attitudes or behaviors, but they are uncomfortable and may want to change. At the same time such helpees bring up numerous reasons not to change. Simon (1988) calls this process "getting stuck." Getting stuck is a common event for all of us and covers such things as putting off plans, not keeping promises, neglecting health, and ignoring signs of potential trouble. It is like being stuck in the mud with wheels spinning. It is being unable to escape an abusive situation, staying in a dead-end job, tolerating a chronic illness, or retreating into one's own little world and feeling sorry. Words that describe being stuck are trapped, helpless, hopeless, exasperated, annoyed, supersensitive, and self-critical.

Helpees who are stuck in their old ways appear to be blind to alternatives, unable to take any risks, complainers about being tired, and pessimistic about future actions. They start and stop improvement programs, such as exercise, dieting, or hobbies, frequently. They adopt extreme behaviors without careful planning or considering alternatives. This negative thinking is frustrating to all who care about the helpee's welfare, as well as to the helpees themselves. Stuck helpees worry a lot and spend much energy on impulsive and abortive solutions to their problems.

What can helpers do? Helpers need to resist the temptation to criticize, cajole, persuade, and moralize. Helpers need to be alert to the possibility that the helpee is severely depressed and should be referred to an appropriate specialist. Helpers would do well to reassert their basic belief in the capacity and will to change in people, which is sorely tested by people who are stuck. The basic helping strategy is to assist helpees to become aware of their stalemate, their motivational impasse (if they are not already painfully aware). The principal helping strategy is to assist helpees to remove barriers to changing old habits, unfulfilling relationships, limited goals, frustrating work, and debilitating health problems before a crisis develops.

Sometimes helpers need to accept the inevitability of a crisis, however, before the person is ready to consider a change. Examples are the emotional explosion, the heart attack, the panic, or the immobilizing frustration. Sometimes postponement of the change becomes more intolerable than the fear of change itself, like being on a child's teeter-totter. The helper needs to be available at these crisis points that ready the helpee for possible change.

Simon suggests that barriers can be reduced by working on the helpee's self-esteem—to change perceptions of failure and unrealistically high standards. Seeing increased options and reviewing problem-solving skills are important helping approaches. Clarifying goals and values, along with deciding what the helpee really wants out of life, sparks motivation and increases energy. Many of the helping skills described in earlier chapters, such as listening, restructuring thoughts, support, reinforcement, and contracting, are applicable to the tough task of helping the person to get unstuck. Thus, helpees are better able to realize their potential for more effective living.

In addition to the questions about resistance to change, the helper should ask about elements of *their* relationship that may be blocking change. For example, does the helper have goals for change that are different from the helpee's goals? Is the helper moving too fast in demanding instant change on the part of the helpee? Or, perhaps is the helpee–helper relationship mirroring an outside relationship? For example, does the helpee rebel against the helper just like she rebels against her mother? It can be useful for a helper who believes the helpee–helper relationship may be blocking change to get an outside opinion from someone who is less close to the situation.

After this description of stuckness and barriers to change, it appears desirable to summarize helpee characteristics that facilitate change. First is *involvement* in the process. If helpees give the helping process a reasonable opportunity to work, it will overcome half their resistance. They are also willing to take personal *responsibility* for their behavior—neither blaming others nor deprecating themselves. They do not make excuses. They realize that change is difficult and painful at times and that life itself is difficult and hazardous. A related quality is to be able to look at oneself *objectively*—to be honest with oneself. Effective helpees attempt to discuss and experience their *feelings* accurately. Finally, helpees must be willing to use their *rationality* to correct negative thinking, plan for the future, and then act on those plans.

Helping through Groups

Most of the focus in earlier chapters was on a one-to-one helping relationship, but the same principles and skills apply to helping groups. Because of the interactional complexities, however, group work involves additional helper skills. We are referring here to small personal growth groups of ten or fewer where all members are committed to helping each other to grow. Members give support, exhibit caring, and demonstrate accountability. This growth process follows predictable stages that are comparable to stages in helping individuals.

Helping groups come in many forms. Some self-help types offer primarily mutual support and are self-managed, such as groups for the recently widowed and divorced, retired, or physically handicapped. Other groups focus on learning skills such as parenting, job seeking, and weight or substance control. Special community groups focus on stress reduction from traumas and disasters. Group helping methods are used in spiritual retreats, women's support groups, men's awareness events, and managerial effectiveness training. Helping groups take the form of quality circles and work teams in industry. The special leadership skills required to facilitate the helping process in groups are learned most effectively by participating as a group member or cofacilitator with an experienced leader. The Suggestions for Further Study of Helping Theory contain references to the vast literature on facilitating helping groups.

Outcomes Self-Check

The major outcomes you should have achieved by studying this chapter are (1) you have thought through your own ideas about helping and have the beginnings of your own unique theory; (2) you have a basis for improved judgment about the use of theory and research flowing from theory to affect your helpee's behavior constructively; (3) you can cite four conceptual threads running through all applications of helping skills training; and (4) you can identify barriers to change and describe helping strategies to overcome them.

Personal Epilogue

This brief venture into the nature of the helping process and related skills has been like a conversation with you. At times we found ourselves persuading you to accept our points of view and at other times confronting you with a challenge to examine your beliefs about people and your style of helping. We did not intend to present an exhaustive formal treatise on the philosophical and scientific bases of helping. Rather, this book has been a distillation of our experiences with helpees, a composite of our dialogues with colleagues and students, and a summary of our readings through the vast literature on helping. It is our hope that these ideas will assist you in tapping your resources, provide a framework for thinking through your experiences, and offer methods for improving your helping skills.

Helping relationships and behavior technology present a monumental challenge and opportunity to all people to make this world a more humane place to live. We need to remind ourselves constantly that the main objective of all helping activity is self-help—teaching people the skills they need to work out their own problems and achieve their own growth goals. We are convinced from personal experience and observation that we must seek constantly for more effective helping modes and methods. We begin this process with rigorous self-renewal followed by a continuous program of personal and professional growth. Evidence is mounting that our helping skills have little impact unless we are open to change, willing to risk, and are concerned about human welfare. The fact that helpees move toward their helper's interpersonal functioning level places a heavy burden on all helpers to be the best possible models of effective human beings.

Suggestions for Further Study of Helping Theory

Brammer, L., Abrego, P., and Shostrom, E. *Therapeutic Counseling and Psychotherapy*. 6th ed. Englewood Cliffs, NJ: Prentice Hall, 1993. (Ch. 2 on overview of theories, their contributions and limitations; Ch. 3 on a creative synthesis; Ch. 8 is an overview of group facilitator skills and stages of group development.)

Corey, G., Corey, M., Callanan, P., and Russell, J. *Group-Techniques*. 2nd ed. Pacific Grove, CA: Brooks/Cole, 1992. (A manual of techniques for helping groups.)

Corey, M., and Corey, G. *Group Process and Practice*. 4th ed. Pacific Grove, CA: Brooks/Cole, 1992. (An overview of group process and methods of organizing and leading various kinds of groups.)

Corsini, R., and Wedding, D. *Current Psychotherapies*. 4th ed. Itasca, IL: Peacock, 1989. (Each chapter describes a specific group and individual theory in depth, written by the original theorist.)

The Counseling Psychologist: Special Edition on Culture and Counseling 23: 1995.

Gazda, G. *Group Counseling: A Developmental Approach.* 4th ed. Boston: Allyn & Bacon, 1989. (A comprehensive description of group process and required facilitator skills.)

Glasser, W. *Reality Therapy.* New York: Harper & Row, 1965. (How to take personal responsibility in the interview.)

Harris, T. *I'm OK; You're OK.* New York: Harper & Row, 1969. (Popular version of transactional analysis terms and methods.)

Hayashi, S., Kuno, T., Osawa, M., Shimizu, M., and Suetake, Y. The client-centered therapy and person-centered approach in Japan: Historical development, current status, and perspectives. *Journal of Humanistic Psychology* 32 (1992):115–136.

Ivey, A., Ivey, M., and Simek-Downing, L. *Counseling and Psychotherapy.* 3rd ed. Englewood Cliffs, NJ: Prentice Hall, 1993. (Ch. 14 provides an excellent coverage of integrating theory and practice.)

James, M., and Jongward, D. *Born to Win.* Reading, MA: Addison-Wesley, 1971. (Application of gestalt theory and method.)

Jung, C. *Memories, Dreams and Reflections.* New York: Random House, 1961. (Jung's autobiography and review of his personal myth.)

Keen, S., and Fox, A. *Telling Your Story: A Guide to Who You Are and Who You Can Be.* New York: Signet, 1973. (A self-help book with outlines for telling one's own story, or personal myth.)

Krippner, S., and Aanastoos, C., Eds. Personal mythology: Psychological perspectives. *The Humanistic Psychologist* 18:137–240. (A special issue on developing a personal mythology.)

Krumboltz, J. Behavioral counseling: Rationale and research. In *Behavior Change in Counseling: Readings and Cases,* edited by S. Osipow and B. Walsh. New York: Appleton-Century-Crofts, 1970. (Overview of behavioral approach to helping.)

Sue, D. W., Arredondo, P., and McDavis, R. J. Multicultural counseling competencies and standards: A call to the profession. *Journal of Counseling and Development* 70 (1992):477–486.

Bibliography

Aguilera, D., and Messick, J. (1994). *Crisis Intervention: Theory and Methodology*. 7th ed. St. Louis: Mosby.

Albee, G. (1982). Preventing psychopathology and promoting human potential. *American Psychologist* 37:1043–1050.

American Association of Counseling and Development. (1987). New group to coordinate peer counseling nationwide. *Guidepost,* February, 10.

American Psychological Association. (1992). Ethical principles of psychologist and code of conduct. *American Psychologist* 47:1597–1611.

Assagioli, R. (1973). *The Act of Will*. Baltimore: Penguin Books.

Atkinson, D., and Matsushita, Y. (1991). Japanese-American acculturation, counseling style, counselor ethnicity, and perceived counselor credibility. *Journal of Counseling Psychotherapy* 38:473–478.

Atkinson, D., Morten, G., and Sue, D. (1993). *Counseling American Minorities: A Cross Cultural Perspective,* 4th ed. Dubuque, IA: Wm C. Brown & Benchmark.

Authier, J., Gustafson, K., Guerney, B. and Kasdorf, J. (1975). The psychological practitioner as a teacher: A theoretical-historical and practical review. *The Counseling Psychologist* 5:31–50.

Bandler, R. and Grinder, J. (1975). *The Structure of Magic I.* Cupertino, CA: Meta Publications.

———, and Grinder, J. (1982). *Reframing*. Moab, Utah: Real People Press.

Bandura, A. (1969). *Principles of Behavior Modification*. New York: Holt, Rinehart & Winston.

———. (1986). *Social Foundations Of Thought And Action: A Social Cognitive Theory*. Englewood Cliffs, NJ: Prentice Hall.

———. (1989). Human agency in social cognitive theory. *American Psychologist* 44:1175–1184.

Baron, R., and Liebert, R. (1971). *Human Social Behavior*. Homewood, IL: Dorsey Press.

Barton, L. (1992). Crisis counseling can minimize employee trauma. *Journal of Compensation and Benefits* 8:15–19.

Becvar, D. S., and Becvar, R. (1988). *Family Therapy: A Systemic Integration*. Boston: Allyn & Bacon.

Bents, M., and Bents, R. (1986). Intuition in decision making. *Journal of Coun-*

seling and Human Service Professions 1:48–57.

Bloom, B. (1963). Definitional aspects of crisis. *Journal of Counsulting Psychology* 27:184–89.

Bogat, A. G., Jones, J. W., and Jason, L. A. (1980). School transitions: Preventive intervention following an elementary school closing. *Journal of Community Psychology* 8:343–352.

Bowman, R. P. (1986). Peer facilitator programs for middle graders: Students helping each other grow up. *The School Counselor* 33:221–229.

Brammer, L. (1990). Teaching personal problem solving to adults. *Journal of Cognitive Psychotherapy* 4:267–280.

———, and Abrego, P. (1981). Intervention strategies for coping with transitions. *The Counseling Psychologist* 9:31–48.

———, Abrego, P., and Shostrom, E. (1993). *Therapeutic Counseling and Psychotherapy.* 6th ed. Englewood Cliffs, NJ: Prentice Hall.

Bruner, J. (1972). Nature and uses of immaturity. *American Psychologist* 27:1–22.

Buscaglia, L. (1982). *Living, Loving, and Learning.* New York: Holt, Rinehart & Winston.

Byrne, R. C., and Overline, H. M. (1992). A study of divorce adjustment among paraprofessional group leaders and group participants. *Journal of Divorce & Remarriage* 17:171–192.

Caine, L. (1974). *Widow.* New York: William Morrow.

Caplan, G. (1964). *Principles of Preventive Psychiatry.* New York: Basic Books.

Carkhuff, R. (1968). Differential functioning of lay and professional helpers. *Journal of Counseling Psychology* 15:117–26.

———. (1969). *Helping and Human Relations* (2 vols.). New York: Holt, Rinehart and Winston.

———. (1993). *The Art of Helping,* 7th ed. Amherst, MA: Human Resources Development Press.

———, and Berenson, B. (1967). *Beyond Counseling and Psychotherapy.* New York: Holt, Rinehart and Winston.

Cautela, J., and Groden, J. (1986). *Relaxation: A Comprehensive Manual for Adults, Children, and Children with Special Needs.* Champaign, IL: Research Press.

Colgrove, M., Bloomfield, H., and McWilliams, P. (1976). *How to Survive the Loss of a Love.* New York: Bantam Books.

Combs, A. (1982). *A Personal Approach to Teaching: Beliefs That Make a Difference.* Boston: Allyn & Bacon.

——— et al. (1969). *Florida Studies in the Helping Professions.* Gainesville, FL: University Presses of Florida.

———, and Avila, D. (1985). *Helping Relationships: Basic Concepts for the Helping Professions.* Boston: Allyn & Bacon.

Cooper, C. L., Sadri, G., Allison, T., and Reynolds, P. (1990). Stress counselling in the post office. *Counselling Psychology Quarterly* 3:3–11.

Corey, G., Corey, M. S., and Callanan, P. (1993). *Issues And Ethics in the Helping Professions.* 3rd ed. Pacific Grove, CA: Brooks/Cole.

Corliss, R., and Rabe, P. (1969). *Psychotherapy from the Center: A Humanistic View of Change and Growth.* Scranton, PA: International Textbook.

Cornish, E., Ed. (1990). *The 1990's and Beyond.* Bethesda, MD: World Futures Society.

Correll, J., and Keel, L. (1986). A field study of helping relationships in a cross-age tutoring program. *Elementary School Guidance and Counseling* 20.

Corrigan, J., Dell, D., Lewis, K., and Schmidt, L. (1980). Counseling as a social influence process: A review. *Journal of Counseling Psychology Monograph* 27:395–441.

Corsini, R., and Wedding, D., Eds. (1989). *Current Psychotherapies.* 4th ed. Itasca, IL: F. Peacock.

The Counseling Psychologist: Special Edition on Culture and Counseling, 23:1995.

Cunningham, C., Davis, J. R., Bremner, R., Dunn, K. W., and Rzasa, T. (1993). Coping modeling problem solving versus mastery modeling: Effects on adherence, in-session process, and skill acquisition in a residential parent-training program. *Journal of Consulting and Clinical Psychology.*

Dean, C. (1988). *Nam Vet: Making Peace with Your Past.* Portland: Multnomah Press.

Diener, E. (1984). Subjective well-being. *Psychological Bulletin* 95:542–575.

Dilley, J., Lee, J., and Verrill, E. (1971). Is empathy ear-to-ear or face-to-face? *Personnel and Guidance Journal* 50:188–191.

Dixon, D., and Glover, J. (1984). *Counseling: A Problem-Solving Approach.* New York: Wiley.

Dodge, M. K. (1984). Learning to care: Developing prosocial behavior among one- and two-year olds in group settings. *Journal of Research and Development in Education* 17:26–30.

Dougherty, A. M., and Dyal, M. A. (1976). Community involvement: Training parents as tutors in a junior high school. *The School Counselor* 23:353–356.

Dougherty, A. M., and Taylor, B. L. B. (1983). Evaluation of peer helper programs. *Elementary School Guidance and Counseling* 17:130–136.

Downe, A. G., Altmann, H. A., and Nysetvold, I. (1986). Peer counseling: More on an emerging strategy. *The School Counselor* 33:355–364.

Duckworth, D. (1991). Facilitating recovery from disaster-work experiences. *British Journal of Guidance and Counselling* 19:13–22.

Egan, G. (1994). *The Skilled Helper.* 5th ed. Pacific Grove, CA: Brooks/Cole.

Eisenberg, N. (1982). *The Development of Prosocial Behavior.* New York: Academic Press.

———. (1986). *Altruistic Emotion, Cognition, and Behavior.* Hillsdale, NJ: Erlbaum.

Ellis, A. (1962). *Reason and Emotion in Psychotherapy.* New York: Lyle Stuart.

———, and Dryden, W. (1990). *The Practice of RET.* New York: Institute for Rational-Emotive Therapy.

Epperson, D., Bushway, D., and Warmna, R. (1983). Client self-terminations after one counseling session. *Journal of Counseling Psychology* 30:307–315.

Epperson, M. (1977). Families in sudden crisis: Process and intervention in a critical care center. *Social Work in Health Care* 2:265–73.

Erfurt, J. C., Foote, A., and Heirich, M. A. (1991). Worksite wellness programs: Incremental comparison of screening and referral alone, health education, follow-up counseling, and plant organization. *American Journal of Health Promotion* 5:438–448.

Farber, B. A., and Heifetz. L. J. (1982). The process and dimensions of burnout in psychotherapists. *Professional Psychology* 19:293–301.

Farver, J. M., and Branstetter, W. H. (1994). Preschoolers' prosocial responses to their peers' distress. *Developmental Psychology* 30:334–341.

Frankl, V. (1965). *The Doctor and the Soul, from Psychotherapy to Logotherapy.* 2nd ed. New York: Knopf.

Freiberg, P. (1991). The guru of prevention calls for social change. *APA Monitor,* Jan., 28–29.

Garfield, C. (1986). *Peak Performance.* New York: William Morrow.

Gartner, A., and Reissman, F. (1980). *Help: A Working Guide to Self-Help Groups.* New York: New Viewpoint/Vision Books.

Gazda, G., Childers, J., and Brooks, B. (1987). *Foundations of Counseling and Human Services.* New York: McGraw-Hill.

Gelatt, H., and Brew, S. (1980). *Teaching Personalized Decision Making.* San Jose, CA: Santa Clara County Schools.

Gelso, C., and Carter, J. (1985). The relationship in counseling and psychotherapy. *The Counseling Psychologist* 13:155–243.

Gelso, C. J., and Carter, J. A. (1994). Components of the psychotherapy relationship: Their interaction and unfolding. *Journal of Counseling Psychology* 41:296–309.

Gendlin, E. (1978). *Focusing.* New York: Everett House.

Gillis, J. S. (1974). Social influence therapy: The therapist as manipulator. *Psychology Today* 7:91–95.

Goodman, G., and Dooley, D. (1976). A framework for help-intended communication. *Psychotherapy: Theory, Research, and Practice.* 13:106–117.

Gottlieb, B. (1983). Social support and risk reduction. *Journal of Primary Prevention* 3:71–76.

Gray, H. D., and Tindall, J. (1987) Communications training study: A model of training junior high school peer counselors. *The School Counselor* 2:107–112.

Guerney, B. (1969). *Psychotherapeutic Agents.* New York: Holt, Rinehart & Winston.

Gutheil, T. G. (1989, Nov./Dec.). Patient-therapist sexual relations. *The California Therapist,* pp. 29–31.

Hadley, J., and Strupp, H. (1976). Contemporary views of negative effects in psychotherapy. *Archives of General Psychiatry* 33:1291–1294.

Hattie, J., Sharpley, C., and Rogers, H. (1984). The comparative effectiveness of professional and paraprofessional helpers. *Psychological Bulletin* 49:223–231.

Hedin, D. (1987, Winter). Students as teachers: A tool for improving school. *Social Policy.*

Hemfelt, R., and Fowler, R. (1990). *Serenity: A Companion for Twelve-Step Recovery.* Nashville: Thomas Nelson.

Heppner, P., Ed. (1990). Special issue: Problem solving and cognitive therapy. *Journal of Cognitive Psychotherapy* 4:243–317.

———, and Krauskopf, C. (1987). An information processing approach to personal problem solving. *The Counseling Psychologist* 15:371–447.

Holmes, T., and Rahe, R. (1967). The social readjustment rating scale. *Journal of Psychosomatic Research* 2:216–218.

Homme, L. (1971). *How to Use Contingency Contracting in the Classroom.* Rev. ed. Champaign, IL: Research Press.

Hosford, R., and Sorenson, D. (1969). Participating in classroom discussions. Ch. 24 in Krumboltz, J., and Thoreson, C. (1976). *Counseling.* New York: Holt, Rinehart & Winston.

Howard, G., Nance, D., and Myers, P. (1986). Adaptive counseling and therapy: An integrative eclectic model. *The Counseling Psychologist* 14:363–442.

Hurvitz, N. (1970). Peer self-help psychotherapy groups and their implications for psychotherapy. *Psychotherapy: Theory and Research* 7:4–49.

Ibrahim, F. (1991). Contributions of cultural worldview to generic counseling and development. *Journal of Counseling and Development* 70:13–19.

Ivey, A. E. (1986). *Developmental Therapy.* San Francisco: Jossey-Bass.

———. (1991). *Developmental Strategies for Helpers: Individual, Family and Network Interventions.* Boston, MA: Microtraining.

———. (1994). *Intentional Interviewing and Counseling.* 3rd ed. Pacific Grove, CA: Brooks/Cole.

———, and Weinstein, G. (1970). The counselor as a specialist in psychological education. *Personnel and Guidance Journal* 49:98–107.

———, Ivey, M., and Simek-Downing, L. (1994). *Counseling and Psychotherapy: Integrating Skills, Theory, and Practice.* 3rd ed. Englewood Cliffs, NJ: Prentice Hall.

Jacobson, E. (1938). *Progressive Relaxation.* 2nd ed. Chicago: The University of Chicago Press.

Janosik, E. (1994). *Crisis Counseling: A Contemporary Approach.* 2nd ed. Boston: Jones/Bartlett.

Jourard, S. (1968). *Disclosing Man to Himself.* Princeton, NJ: Van Nostrand.

———, and Landsman, T. (1980). *Healthy Personality.* New York: Macmillan.

Jung, C. (1961). *Memories, Dreams, and Reflectiveness.* New York: Random House.

Kanfer, F., and Goldstein, A. (1992). *Helping People Change.* 4th ed. Boston: Allyn & Bacon.

Kaul, T., and Schmidt, L. (1971). *Dimensions of interviewer trustworthiness. Journal of Counseling Psychology* 18:542–548.

Keen, S., and Fox, A. (1973). *Telling Your Story: A Guide to Who You Are and Who You Can Be.* New York: Signet.

Kellerman, S. T., Felts, W. M., and Chenier, T. C. (1992). The impact on factory workers of health risk appraisal and counseling in health promotion. *American Journal of Preventative Medicine* 8:37–42.

Kobassa, S. (1979). Stressful life events, personality, and health: An inquiry into hardiness. *Journal of Personality and Social Psychology* 37:1–11.

Korner, I. (1970). Hope as a method of coping. *Journal of Consulting and Clinical Psychology* 34:132–139.

Krumboltz, J., and Sheppard, L. (1976). Vocational problem-solving experiences. Ch. 32 in Krumboltz, J., and Thoreson, C. (1976). *Counseling.* New York: Holt, Rinehart & Winston.

———, and Thoreson, C. (1976). *Counseling.* New York: Holt, Rinehart & Winston.

LaFramboise, T. D., and Dixon., D. N. (1981). American Indian perception of trustworthiness in a counseling interview. *Journal of Counseling Psychology* 28:135–139.

Lawrence, J. (1983). From an unpublished course presentation, January 17, 1983.

Lazarus, A. (1966). Behavior rehearsal vs. non-directive therapy vs. advice in effecting behavior change. *Behavior Research and Therapy* 4:209–212.

———. (1976). *Multimodal Behavior Therapy.* New York: Springer.

Lazarus, R. S. (1984). Puzzles in the study of daily hassles. *Journal of Behavioral Medicine* 7:375–389.

Lenihan, G., and Kirk, W. (1990). Using student paraprofessionals in the treatment of eating disorders. *Journal of Counseling and Development* 68:332–335.

Levasseur, R. E. (1991). People skills: Effective communication—A critical skill for MS/OR professionals. *Interfaces* 21:22–24.

Lewin, K. (1969). Quasi-stationary social equilibria and the problem of permanent change. In W. G. Bennis, K. D. Benne, and R. Chin (Eds.) *The Planning of Change.* New York: Holt, Rinehart & Winston.

Lewis, J., and Lewis, M. (1989). *Community Counseling.* New York: Wiley.

Lewis, M., Hayes, R., and Lewis, J. (1986). *An Introduction to the Counseling Profession.* Itasca, IL: Peacock.

Libow, J., and Doty, D. W. (1976). An evaluation of empathic listening in telephone counseling. *Journal of Counseling Psychology* 23:532–537.

Lindemann, E. (1944). Symptomatology and management of acute grief. *American Journal of Psychiatry* 101:7–21. Reprinted in Parad, H. (1965). *Crisis Intervention: Selected Readings.* New York: Family Service Association of America.

Locke, D. C., and Zimmerman, N.A. (1987). Effects of peer-counseling training on psychological maturity of Black students. *Journal of College Student Personnel* 28:525–532.

Loewenberg, F., and Dolgoff, R. (1988). *Ethical Decisions for Social Work Practice.* 3rd ed. Itasca, IL: Peacock.

Lopez, R., Lopez, A., and Fong, K. (1991). Mexican Americans' initial preferences for counselors: The role of ethnic factors. *Journal of Counseling Psychology* 38:487–496.

Luks, A., and Payne, P. (1991). *The Healing Powers of Doing Good: The Health Benefits of Helping Others.* New York: Ballentine Books.

Marlatt, G., and Gordon, J. (1985). *Relapse Prevention: Maintenance Strategies in the Treatment of Addictive Behaviors.* New York: Guilford.

Marx, R. (1984). Self-control strategies in management training. Paper given at the annual meeting of the American Psychological Association in Toronto, Canada, August.

Maslow, A. (1962). *Toward a Psychology of Being.* New York: Van Nostrand.

McCormack, N. (1981). *Mutual Help Groups.* NIMH pamphlet, DHHS Pub. (ADM 81-1138). Washington, DC: Superintendent of Documents.

Meer, J. (1985). Me and My Compeer. *Psychology Today* 19:73.

Meichenbaum, D. (1977). *Cognitive Behavior Modification: An Integrative Approach.* New York: Plenum.

———. (1985). *Stress Inoculation Training.* Boston: Allyn & Bacon.

Meyer J., Strowig, W., and Hosford, R. (1970). Behavior reinforcement with rural high school youth. *Journal of Counseling Psychology* 17:127–132.

Mickelson, D., and Stevic, R. (1971). Differential effects of facilitative and nonfacilitative behavioral counsels. *Journal of Counseling Psychology* 18:314–319.

Mitchell, J., and Resnik, H. (1981). *Emergency Response to Crisis.* Baltimore, MD: Robert J. Brady.

Monat, A., and Lazarus, R., eds. (1991). *Stress and Coping: An Anthology.* 3rd ed. New York: Columbia University Press.

Murgatroyd, S., and Woolfe, R. (1982). *Coping with Crisis: Understanding and Helping People in Need.* Milton Keynes, England: Open University Press.

Myers, J., Finnerty-Fried, P., and Graves, C., Eds. (1981). *Counseling Older Persons.* Vols. I, II, and III. Washington, DC: American Personnel and Guidance Association.

Naisbitt, J., and Aburdene, P. (1990). *Megatrends 2000: Ten New Directions for the 1990's.* New York: Avon.

National Wellness Institute. (1989). *Lifestyle Assessment Questionnaire.* 5.5th ed. Stevens Point, WI: National Wellness Institute.

Nezu, A. M., Nezu, C. M., and Perri, M. G. (1990). Psychotherapy for adults within a problem-solving framework: Focus on depression. *Journal of Cognitive Psychotherapy* 4:247–257.

Nwachuku, U., and Ivey, H. (1991). Culture-specific counseling: An alternative training model. *Journal of Counseling and Development* 70:106–111.

O'Leary, K., Poulos, R., and Devine, B. (1972). Tangible reinforcers: Bonuses or bribes? *Journal of Consulting and Clinical Psychology* 38:1–8.

Parad, H. (1965). *Crisis Intervention: Selected Readings.* New York: Family Service Association of America.

Pedersen, P., Ed. (1994). *Handbook of Cross-Cultural Counseling and Therapy.* Westport, CT: Greenwood Publishing Group.

Perls, F. (1969). *Gestalt Therapy Verbatim.* Lafayette, CA: Real People's Press.

Pirsig, R. (1974). *Zen and the Art of Motorcycle Maintenance.* New York: William Morrow.

Pyle, R., and Snyder, F. (1971). Students as paraprofessional counselors at community colleges. *Journal of College Student Personnel* 12:259–262.

Reik, T. (1948). *Listening with the Third Ear.* New York: Grove Press.

Reissman, F. (1965). The helper therapy principle. *Social Work* 10:27–32.

Rioch, M. (1966). Changing concepts in the training of therapists. *Journal of Consulting Psychology* 30:290–292.

Rogers, C. (1957). The necessary and sufficient conditions of therapeutic personality change. *Journal of Consulting Psychology* 21:95–103.

———. (1961). *On Becoming a Person.* Boston: Houghton Mifflin.

———. (1980). *A Way of Being.* Boston: Houghton Mifflin.

Ryan, T., and Krumboltz, J. (1964). Effect of planned reinforcement counseling on client decision-making behavior. *Journal of Counseling Psychology* 11:315–323.

Saccuzo, D. (1975). What patients want from counseling and psychotherapy. *Journal of Clinical Psychology* 31:471–475.

Sarason, I. (1968). Verbal learning, modeling and juvenile delinquency. *American Psychologist* 23:254–266.

———. (1985). *Caring and Compassion in Clinical Practice.* San Francisco: Jossey-Bass.

Schmidt, L., and Strong, S. (1970). Expert and inexpert counselors. *Journal of Counseling Psychology* 17:115–118.

Schunk, D. H. (1991). *Learning Theories: An Educational Perspective.* New York: Merrill.

Sell, J. M., Gottlieb, M. C., and Schoenfeld, L. (1986). Ethical considerations of social/romantic relationships with present and former clients. *Professional Psychology: Research and Practice* 17:504–508.

Sexton, T. L., and Whiston, S. C. (1994). The status of a counseling relationship: An empirical review. *The Counseling Psychologist* 22:6–78.

Simmons, J. (1990). *Future Lives: A Fearless Guide to Our Transition Times.* New York: Bear.

Simon, S. (1988). *Getting Unstuck: Breaking Through Your Barriers to Change.* New York: Warner.

Slaiken, K. (1990). *Crisis Intervention: A Handbook for Practice and Research.* Boston: Allyn & Bacon.

Steenland, R. (1973). Paraprofessionals in counseling centers. *Personnel and Guidance Journal* 51:417–418.

Stewart, N. (1969). Exploring and processing information about educational and vocational opportunities in groups. Ch. 26 in Krumboltz, J., and Thoreson, C. (1976). *Counseling.* New York: Holt, Rinehart & Winston.

Strong, S. (1968). Counseling: An interpersonal influence process. *Journal of Counseling Psychology* 15:215–224.

Sue, D. W., Arredondo, P., and McDavis, R. J. (1992). Multicultural counseling competencies and standards: A call to the profession. *Journal of Counseling and Development* 70:477–486.

Sweeney, M., Cottle, W., and Kobayashi, M. (1980). Nonverbal communication: A cross-cultural companion of American and Japanese counseling students. *Journal of Counseling Psychology* 27:150–156.

Thomas, M. (1992). *An Introduction to Marital and Family Therapy.* New York: Macmillan.

Truax, C., and Carkhuff, R. (1967). *Toward Effective Counseling and Psychotherapy: Training and Practice.* Chicago: Aldine.

Varenhorst, B. (1972). Progress report and current status of the Palo Alto peer counseling program. Palo Alto, CA: Palo Alto Unified School District. Mimeographed.

———. (1976). Learning the consequences of life's decisions. Ch. 33 in Krumboltz, J., and Thoreson, C. (1976). *Counseling.* New York: Holt, Rinehart & Winston.

———, and Hamburg, B. (1971). Peer counselor program and curriculum. Palo Alto, CA: Palo Alto Unified School District. Mimeographed.

———, and Sparks, L. (1988). Training teenagers for peer ministry. Loveland, Colo.: Group Books.

Walsh, R. (1983). Meditation practice and research. *Journal of Humanistic Psychology* 28:18–50.

Weissberg, M. (1977). The curative factor in counseling and psychotherapy. *Personnel and Guidance Journal* 56:439–441.

Wolpe, J. (1952). Objective psychotherapy of the neuroses. *South African Medical Journal* 26:825–829.

Worthington, E. L., Jr. (1989). Religious faith across the life-span: Implications for counseling and research. *The Counseling Psychologist* 17:555–612.

Index

Aanastoos, C., 200
Abrego, P., 22, 42, 49, 74, 106, 115, 136, 147, 168, 181, 183, 187, 199
Aburdene, P., 17
Adaptive Counseling and Therapy (ACT), 187
advice giving, 102
affective mode, 52
Aguilera, D., 108, 133
Albee, G., 16
Allison, T., 113
Altmann, H., 19
altruism, 36
American Association for Marriage and Family Therapy (AAMFT), 178
American Association of Retired Persons (AARP), 48
American Counseling Association (ACA), 49, 178
American Psychological Association (APA), 49, 174, 178
American School Counseling Association (ASCA), 49, 178
Andrus, P., 48

anticipatory grief, 118
Arredondo, P., 192, 200
Assagioli, R., 130
Atkinson, D., 30, 33, 49
attending skills, 78
    eye contact, 47, 78
    gesture, 79
    posture, 78
    verbal behavior, 79
Authier, J., 7
aversive techniques, 164–165
Avila, D., 25, 31, 44
awareness, 195

Bandler, R., 47, 100, 159
Bandura, A., 48, 152, 156, 168
Baron, L., 37
Barton, L., 114
Becvar, D., 112
Becvar, R., 112
behavior change approach, 152–167. See also positive action approach
behavior changing methods, 140–167
    assumptions, 152
    strategies, 153
behavior-changing skills, 152–167. See also helping skills

decision-making techniques, 145–148
problem-solving techniques, 148–152
intuitive process, 150–152
rational process, 148–150
behavioral engineer model, 40
behavioral theory, 188
behavior modification. See behavior change approach
Benjamin, A., 106
Benson, A., 136
Bents, M., 145
Bents, R., 145
Berenson, B., 28
Bogat, A., 19
Borman, L., 26
Bowman, R. P., 20
Bloom, B., 115
Bloomfield, H., 127
Brammer, L., 22, 42, 49, 74, 106, 115, 136, 145, 147, 168, 181, 183, 187, 199
Branstetter, W., 37
Bremmer, R., 48
Brew, S., 148
Bridges, W., 136
Brooks, B., 11

Bruner, J., 20
Buckley, N., 168
burnout, 171
Buscaglia, L., 128
Bushway, D., 65
business community, stress,
    113
Byrne, R., 18

Caine, L., 127
Callanan, P., 49, 169, 170,
    178, 193, 199
Caplan, G., 25, 114, 136
caring, 43
Carkhuff, R., 6, 15, 25, 28,
    29, 31, 41, 168
Carlton, J., 106
Carter, J., 52
Cautela, J., 130, 136
centering skills, 131
change, first and second
    order, 112
Chenier, T., 113
Childers, J., 11
clarifying skills, 82
client-centered theories, 188
cognitive ecology, 95
Cohen, A., 137
Colgrove, M., 127
Combs, A., 25, 27, 31, 36,
    41, 44
communications theory, 195
community helping, 18–20
Compeer Program, 18
concreteness, 46
confidentiality, 176
    limits of, 176
confronting skills, 90–98
    changing thoughts, 95
    feedback, 93
    meditation, 96
    recognizing helpee's
        feelings, 91
    sharing feelings, 91
        cautions, 92
        helper as model, 91
        self, 93, 96
congruence, 41, 45
contingency, 158
contracting techniques, 7,
    67, 161–164
contract, sample, 163

Cooper, C., 113
coping, 22–23, 111
Corey, G., 49, 169, 170, 178,
    193, 199
Corey, M., 49, 169, 170, 178,
    193, 199
Corliss, R., 74, 131
Cornish, E., 17
Correll, J., 20
Corrigan, J., 71
Corsini, R., 183, 185, 199
Cottle, W., 42
Cox, B., 74
countertransference, 35,
    70–71
crisis, 108–137
    daily hassles, definition,
        112
    definition, 113
    despair, definition, 117
    hope, definition, 117
    intervention strategies,
        119–127. See also
        crisis intervention
        strategies
    life transitions as, 110
    phases of, 114
    response, ethics in,
        177–178
    skills, 127–135. See also
        crisis skills
    stress, definition, 112
    support definition, 115
crisis intervention strategies,
    119–127
    consoling, 126
    counseling, 126
    crisis centers, 125
    growth centers, 124
    halfway houses, 125
    hope rebuilding, 121–122
    multiple impact support,
        120
    renewal and growth, 124
    treatment centers, 125
crisis skills, 127–135
    action alternatives skills,
        133
    centering skills, 131
    physical contacting skills,
        128
    reassuring skills, 128

referring skills, 133
relaxing skills, 128
support system rebuilding
    skills, 134–135
critical incident stress
    debriefing, 121
cross-age helping, 18–20
cross-cultural theories, 191
cultural values, 32–33
Cunningham, C., 48

daily hassles, 112
Davis, J., 48
Dean, C., 127
decision-making techniques,
    145–148
Dell, D., 71
desensitization, 165–167
Devine, B., 158
Diener, E., 11
Dilley, J., 42
Dixon, D., 55, 145
Dodge, M., 37
Dolgoff, R., 169
Dooley, D., 23
Doty, D., 123
Dougherty, A., 19, 20
Downe, A., 19
Dryden, W., 122, 136
dual relationships, 172
Duckworth, D., 171
Dunn, K., 48
Dyal, M., 19

eclecticism, 186
Egan, G., 36, 49, 106
Eisenberg, N., 37
Ellis, A., 122, 136
empathy, 41
Epperson, D., 133, 165
Erfurt, J., 113
ethics, 38, 169–178
existentialism, 188
exploration, 68
extinguishing techniques,
    160–161
eye contact, 47

family crisis, 111–112
family systems theory, 191
Farber, M., 136, 171
Farver, J., 37

feedback, 93–94
Feife, H., 136
Felts, W., 113
Ferguson, L., 17
Field, P., 127
Figley, C., 136
Finnerty-Fried, P., 7
Fong, K., 30
Fong, M., 74
Foot, A., 113
force field analysis, 148
Fowler, R., 127
Fox, A., 183, 200
Frankl, V., 8, 126
Freiberg, P., 16
Freud, S., 43, 187
friendships, differences, 53

Galton, L., 11
Gardner, J., 136
Garfield, C., 11
Gartner, A., 21–22, 25
Gazda, G., 11, 200
Gelatt, H., 148
Gelso, C., 52
gender, 192
Gendlin, E., 168
genuineness, 44
Gestalt theory, 188
Gillis, J., 36
Glaser, B., 136
Glasser, W., 199
Glover, J., 145
goal formation, 141
    difficulties, 142
    follow-up action, 144
Goldstein, A., 26, 74, 187
Goodman, G., 23
Gordon, D., 106
Gordon., J., 155
Gottlieb, B., 108, 136,
    174
Graves, C., 7
Gray, H., 20
grief, 110–111, 118, 119
Grinder, J., 47, 100, 159
Groden, B., 130–136
Grossberg, J., 168
groups, 198
growth centers, 124
growth facilitator model, 41
Guerney, B., 7, 16

Gustafson, K., 7
Gutheil, T., 174

Hadley, J., 43
Hamachek, D., 49
Hamburg, B., 19
Harris, T., 200
Hattie, J., 16, 26
Hayashi, S., 200
Hayes, R., 16
Hedin, D., 20
Heifetz, L., 171
Heirich, M., 113
helpee
    growth of, 4–12
    needs of, 8–10
    perceptions of helper, 30
    responsibilities of, 4, 6–7,
        39, 56–57
helper
    agency relationship, 6, 32
    competence, 175
    crisis intervention, steps
        of, 113–120
    ethics, 169
    examination of motives,
        1–2, 5
    facilitative traits, 40–47
        caring, 43
        communication compe-
            tence, 46
        concreteness, 46
        congruence, 45
        empathy, 41
        genuineness, 44
        intentionality, 47
        openness, 44
        positive regard, 41, 45
        warmth, 43
    formal
        paraprofessional, 14–18
        professional, 7–8, 14–18
    goals, 3, 7
    informal
        cross-age, 18–20
        peer, 18–20
        self-help groups, 21
    levels of functioning, 28
    life-style, 30
    limitations, 175
    needs, 12–13
    peer-helpers, 18–20

personal characteristics,
    27–39
    altruism, 36–37
    cultural experience, 32
    feelings, 33
    personal power, 34
    responsibility, 38–39
    as scholar-researcher,
        39–40
    self-awareness, 31–35
personal theory of
    helping, 180
    construction, 181
    dimensions, 181
    limitations, 183
    process goals, 57
    professionalization of,
        15–18
    renewal experiences, 30
    as role model, 35
    self-care, 170–172
    self-help, 21
    values, 31, 34
helping process
    aim, 6–10, 51–61
    as art, 14
    definition of, 2–5, 51
    elements of, 3
    growth facilitation, 4–7,
        40
    need theory, 8–10
    relationship building,
        67–68. *See also*
        helping relationships
    as science, 14
    stages, 69. *See also*
        helping process
        stages
    structured, 14
    unstructured, 15
helping process stages, 23,
    56
    building relationship,
        57–58
    clarification, 62
        ownership of problems,
            64
        questions, use of, 62
    consolidation, 72
    exploration, 68
        countertransference,
            70–71

helping process stages
(cont'd)
helper goals, 64
transference, 70–71
facilitating positive action,
57, 59
interview opening, 62
readiness, 57
resistance, 59–60
setting, 61
planning, 64–72
relationship, 57–58
structuring, 65–67
contracts, 67, 161–163
helpee behavior, 67
relationship, 66
helping relationships
contracts, in, 67, 161–163
dimensions, 53
ambiguity-clarity, 54
intellectual emotional
content, 53
trust-distrust, 54
uniqueness common-
ality, 53
formal, 14–18
for growth, 4–7
helper-helpee matching,
30
informal, 14–18
termination, 72
helping skills, 23–25,
76–107, 138
application of theory, 183,
194
awareness approach,
195
behavior change
approach, 194
communication theory,
195
constructing a theory,
184
needs approach, 194
behavior-changing, 140
aversive control, 164
contracting, 161–164
desensitizing, 165
extinguishing, 160
modeling, 156
rewarding, 157–160
confronting, 90–91

crisis, 108
informing, 102
advice giving, 102
indigenous counselor,
103
limitations, 104
interpreting, 98
fantasy and metaphor,
99
levels of, 100
questions, use of, 99
leading, 83–84
direct leading, 86
focusing, 86
indirect leading, 85
listening, 77
reflecting, 87–90
common errors, 89
content, 89
experience, 88
feelings, 87
summarizing, 105–106
helping skills training, 183
helping stage, 23
helping theories, 179
behavioral, 188
eclectic, 186
phenomenological, 188
psychoanalytic, 187
rational, 189
transactional-
communicative-
reality, 190
Hemfelt, R., 127
Heppner, P., 145, 150
hierarchy of human needs
(Maslow), 9
Holmes, T., 112
Homme, L., 164
hope
definition, 117, 121
rebuilding of, 121–124
Hosford, R., 157, 159
Howard, G., 187
Hurvitz, N., 21

informed consent, 175–177
informing skills, 100, 104
advice-giving, 102
indigenous counselors,
103
limitations, 104

intentionality, 47
interpreting skills, 98
fantasy and metaphor, 99
levels of, 100
questions, use of, 99
intervention, 69
intervention strategies,
119–127
interview opening, 57, 62
Ivey, A., 7, 17, 19, 26, 30, 36,
47, 50, 74, 77, 78,
192, 200
Ivey, M., 7, 74, 200

Jacobson, E., 130
James, M., 200
Janosik, E., 112–113, 136
Jason, J., 19
Johnson, K., 107
Jones, L., 19
Jongward, D., 200
Jourard, S., 28, 44
Jung, C., 183, 200

Kanfer, F., 26, 74, 187
Kasdorf, J., 7
Kaul, T., 55
Keel, L., 20
Keen, S., 183, 200
Kellerman, S., 113
Killilea, M., 25, 136
Kirk, W., 18
Kirschenbaum, H., 136
Kobassa, S., 111
Kobayashi, M., 42
Korner, I., 103, 117, 122
Krauskopf, C., 145
Krippner, S., 200
Krumboltz, H., 168
Krumboltz, J., 74, 142,
147, 156, 158,
168, 200
Kübler-Ross, E., 136
Kuno, T., 200

LaFramboise, T., 55
Landsman, T., 28
Lane, D., 136
law and ethics, 170
Lawrence, J., 150
Lazarus, A., 136, 161, 187
Lazarus, R., 112

leading skills, 83–84
  direct leading, 86
  focusing, 86
  indirect leading, 85
  questioning, 84
learning, 194
Lee, J., 42
Lenihan, G.,18
Lester, D., 137
Lester, G., 137
Levasseur, 77
Lewis, J., 16, 125, 137
Lewis, K., 71
Lewis, M., 16, 125, 137
Libow, J., 123
Lieberman, M., 26
Liebert, R., 37
life-style change theories, 190
Lindemann, E., 118, 137
listening skills, 77
  attending, 80
    eye contact, 47, 78
    gesture, 79
    posture, 78
    verbal behavior, 79
  clarifying, 82
  paraphrasing, 80–81
  perception checking, 82–83
Locke, D., 20
Loewenberg, F., 169
logotherapy, 126
Long, L., 74, 107
Long, T., 74, 107
Lopez, A., 30
Lopez, R., 30
loss, severe, 109
Luks, A., 22

Marin, P., 137
Marlatt, G., 155
Martin, D., 74
Marx, R., 155
Maslow, A., 8, 131
Matsushita, Y., 30
McDavis, R., 192, 200
medical model, 40
meditation, 96
Meichenbaum, D., 35, 95, 137, 142, 145, 152, 156, 168

men's movement, 21
Messick, J., 108, 133
Meyer, J., 159
Mickelson, D., 141
microskills methods, 195
Mitchell, J., 121
modeling, 35, 156
Monat, A., 112
Morten, G., 30, 33, 49
multicultural, 191
Multimodal theory, 187
Murgatroyd, S., 127
Myers, J., 7, 187

Naisbitt, J., 17
Nance, D., 187
National Association of
  Social Workers,
  ethics, 178
National Peer Helpers
  Association, 26
National Referral Network
  for Kids in Crisis, 137
National Self-Help Clearing
  House, 21
National Wellness Institute, 10
need theory, 9–10, 194
Nezu, A., 148
Nezu, C., 148
Nwachuku, U., 192
Nysetvold., I., 19

O'Leary, K., 158
Osawa, M., 200
Osipow, S., 168
Overline, H., 18
ownership of problems, 64

Parad, H., 114, 137
Paradise, L., 74, 107
paraphrasing skills, 80–81
paraprofessionals, 14–18
Paraprofessionals as
  Companion Therapist
  (PACT), 18
Payne, P., 22
Pederson, P., 33, 50
peer helpers, 18–20
Perls, F., 196
Perri, M., 148
personal myth, 180

person-centered therapy, 188
phenomenology, 188
physical contact, 173
Pirsig, R., 138
political issues, 193
positive action approach, 140–167. *See also* behavior change approach
  goal formulation, 141–142
  overview, 141
  problem-solving techniques, 140–144
  process, 64, 146
  skills, 148
posttraumatic stress disorder, 121
Poulos, R., 158
power difference, 172
prevention, 17
priest model, 40
problem-solving techniques, 145. *See also* positive action approach
  intuitive, 150
psychoanalysis, 186
psycholinguistics, 185
Pyle, R., 20

Questions, use of, 62, 65, 84

Rabe, P., 74
Rahe, R., 112
rational-emotive approach, 123
rational problem-solving process, 146
rationality, 189
readiness, 57
reassuring skills, 128
reciprocity principle, 37
referral, 73
reflecting skills, 87–90
  common errors, 89
  content, 89
  experience, 88
  feelings, 87
Reik, T., 78
reinforcing techniques, 158
relapse, 155

relationships, 67. *See also*
    helping relationships
relaxing skills, 130
religious issues, 193
resistance, 59, 196–198
Resnick, H., 121
respect, 45
responsibility, 38–39
rewarding techniques, 157,
    160
Reynolds, P., 113
Rhodes, W., 168
Riessman, F., 21–22, 25
Rioch, M., 15
Rogers, C., 26, 28, 29, 31, 44,
    50
Rogers, H., 16, 26
role limits, 173
Ryan, T., 158
Rzasa, T., 48

Saccuzo, D., 59
Sadri, G., 113
Salo, M., 178
Sarason, I., 44, 50, 156
Scholossberg, N., 137
Schmidt, L., 36, 54, 55, 71
Schrunk, D., 10, 26
Schoenfeld, L., 174
self-actualization, 8–9
self-awareness of helper,
    31–39
self-help, 6, 21
Seligman, L., 64, 74
Sell, J., 174
Sexton, L., 52
sexual harassment, 174
sexual relationships, 173
Sharpley, C., 16, 26

Sheppard, L., 147
Shimuzu, M., 200
Shostrum, E., 42, 49, 74,
    106, 136, 147, 168,
    181, 183, 187, 199
Shumate, S., 178
silence, use of, 68
Simek-Downing, L., 7, 74,
    200
Simmons, J., 17
Simon, S., 196
simulation, 145
Slaiken, S., 108, 113
Snyder, F., 20
social issues awareness, 193
Sorenson, D., 157
Sparks, L., 26
Steenland, R., 16
Stevic, R., 141
Stewart, N., 157
strength analysis, 132
stress, 112. *See also* crisis
Strong, S., 36, 55, 71
Strowig, W., 159
Strupp, H., 43
Sue, D., 30, 33, 49, 50, 192,
    200
Suetake, Y., 200
summarizing skills, 105
support, 115
Sweeny, M., 42

Taylor, B., 19, 20
Terrell, F., 75
theory, elements of, 181
Thomas, M., 191
Thoreson, C., 74, 142, 156,
    168
Tindall, H., 20

trait and factor theory, 189
transactional-
    communicative-
    reality theories, 190
transference, 70–71
transitions, 111
treatment planning, 64
Truax, C., 41
trust, 54, 91
Tyler, L., 168

unconditional positive
    regard, 41

values and ethics, 169
values issues, 193
Varenhorst, B., 19, 26, 145
Verrill, E., 42

Walker, H., 168
Walsh, B., 168
Walsh, R., 97
warmth, 43
Watkins, C., 75
Wedding, D., 183, 185, 199
Weinstein, G., 17
Weissberg, M., 33
wellness, 10
Whiston, S., 52
Williamson, T., 107
Wolfe, R., 127
Wolpe, J., 166, 168
Woody, R., 168
working alliance, 53
Worthington, E., 194

Zaro, J., 75
Zifferblatt, S., 168
Zimmerman, D., 20